Return

A Traveler's Companion

Jonathan Foster, O.F.M.

Copyright © 2015 Jonathan Foster, O.F.M.

All rights reserved.

ISBN:1518857256
ISBN-13:978-1518857256

Cover Photo
Tree Swallows
Greene Valley Forest Preserve, Naperville, IL
Brian Tang
www.hardrain.me

Dedication

To all those migratory souls whose spiritual lives have been enriched at the St. Francis Retreat House, and later at Mayslake Ministries.

INTRODUCTION

It's formal name was **St. Francis Retreat House**, but most people knew it by its more historic designation, **Mayslake**. That's what coal magnate Francis Stuyvesant Peabody called his country estate to honor his daughter May. The Franciscans of the Sacred Heart Province acquired this residence in 1924 and quickly made it available for a fledgling retreat ministry that was just beginning to develop in the Chicago area at that time. St. Francis Retreat House took seriously the spiritual needs of at least 250,000 people from its opening in 1925 until it closed in 1991. Retreats at Mayslake were a regular feature of Catholic life not only in the parishes of the region, but in a number of labor unions and other organizations. An efficient and effective structure of Team Captains encouraged annual retreats in their communities, and people responded. Mr. Peabody's son Jack, made four retreats at Mayslake himself. By the time St. Francis Retreat House concluded its ministry in 1991, there were retreatants who would proudly proclaim that they had made eight times that many retreats.

Jonathan Foster, O.F.M. served as Director of St. Francis Retreat House from 1976 until 1991. It is hard to imagine a ministry more perfectly suited to Father Jonathan than this particular one which his Franciscan Brothers entrusted to him. Petoskey, Michigan, located on the shores of Lake Michigan and surrounded by some of Michigan's most wonderful forests, was his childhood home. The beauty of nature was an essential dimension of the experience of Mayslake Retreat House, and Father Jonathan was right at home in that environment.

Father Jonathan's early ministries were focused on religious education. He taught at St. Francis Catholic High School and Seminary for several years (1962-1970) and served as Religious Education Coordinator in Hinsdale, Illinois at St.

Isaac Jogues Catholic Church from 1970 to 1974. Those experiences encouraged him to pursue additional professional development in order to better serve the people who came to him in their desire to deepen their spiritual lives. A doctoral degree from the University of Chicago was a result of that decision.

Father Jonathan not only ably guided St. Francis Retreat House for fifteen years, he was its staunchest advocate, especially with his Franciscan Brothers. When the decision was made to discontinue the retreat ministry at Mayslake and sell the property, there was no doubt in anyone's mind that Father Jonathan thought a mistake was being made. Yet, in what has to be one of the best measures of his integrity and character, he found a way to deeply disagree with the decision, but remain a brother to those who made the decision. What he did ask of his Franciscan Brothers was understanding and appreciation for a fundamental truth, "If we don't bleed when we leave somewhere, were we ever really there?"

Jonathan Foster, O.F.M. certainly "bled", and then, just as certainly, he turned his crisis into an opportunity to do something new and, perhaps, even more wonderful for God and for God's people. The retreat house may not have been there any longer, but the need it served still was.

What Father Jonathan realized in his years of retreat ministry was that walls weren't what was needed, relationships were what really mattered. Mayslake Ministries was founded in response to that insight; and since 1991, its various services have ministered to the determination of God's beloved and diverse community of people to live happy, healthy, holy and whole spiritual lives.

There's much that can be said about Jonathan Foster, O.F.M. His reverence for nature gave good example long before a lot of the rest of us realized that we have a similar responsibility and privilege. His dedication to an adult spiritual life reassured many of us that we could hope to have the same. He has been willing to work hard and risk new ventures. His own hurt and healing have offered encouragement to anyone who has ever wondered when, where and whether our own pain will end.

Our Bible asks, "How we can say that we love the God we don't see, if we don't love the people we do see?" (1 John 4:20) Jonathan Foster, O.F.M. has spent a lifetime treasuring the people who have become a part of his life. The homily that is his life leaves no doubt about how much Father Jonathan loves God and also challenges all of us to welcome people into our own lives with similar reverence.

Many more things could, and probably should, be said about Jonathan Foster, O.F.M.; but the two truths that have to be acknowledged, in conclusion, are that Father Jonathan has always had something to say and he's always found a way to gracefully and eloquently share his wisdom and insights. It's an understatement to say that he has a "way with words". These essays will leave no doubt about that. I hope that you will find them as enriching as I have.

William Spencer, O.F.M.
Provincial Minister
Franciscan Friars of the Sacred Heart Province

CONTENTS

A Seasonal Column of Commentary 11

Of Cardinals, Winter's Light, and Justice 16

The Goose and the Phoenix 20

The Bishops' Pastoral and the Red Fox 24

Meadowing 29

Crying Over Broken Eggs 34

Short Days, Dark Days 39

The Gift of a Chilly April 44

A Bald Eagle Flies Over Mayslake 50

The Good Soil at Mayslake 56

The Weed Perspective 61

Get the Hell Off My Property! 66

Are Those Cardinals Singing? 72

The Wind Comes Through Open Windows 78

From Cornfield to Prairie 85

A Fox in the Swale 91

Life in the Slow Lane 95

Lawns and Weeds: Who's Really in Charge Here? 99

The Gatehouse Goes Down and Trees Go Up 103

The Pope is - So to Speak - For the Birds. 107

Rain - Grace 112

A Bloom of Asters 118

Jerusalem 123

The Goose as Neighbor 127

"There is Not Enough Silence" - T.S. Eliot	132
Homesick	136
The Meaning of Squirrels	140
Dispatch from Guelph - Woodchucks	145
Clare and the Red Fox: A Cautionary Tale	150
Bridges, Not Piers	155
Soil for the Ministry	159
Time for Christmas, But Not for Christ?	164
"Stupid Galatians" and a Walk in the Snow	169
Nighthawks: A Personal Observation	172
Christmas and the Electronic Sun	176
Trust: A Cardinal's Song, or A Walk on the Lake?	180
The Illusive Iris	184
Ripening	188
When Work Is Toil	192
Learning What Trust in God Means	197
The Church as Chatty Cathy	201
Spirituality for Males	206
Sandpipers	211
Visiting a Visitor	215
The Prayer of the Mourning Dove	219
A People Without Rest	223
"Them're Geese"	228
God, Let Me Swallow My Spit	233
The Standing Sabbath of the Sea	238

Francis of Assisi - 1999	243
The Spiritual Life	247
Esau and Email	251
God as 'Old Faithful'	256
All the World's an Audience	260
In the Realm of Grace	265
The Little Brother	268
Spirituality and Politics	273
Are You Bowling with Me Jesus?	278
A Million Signs	283
Does Prayer Work?	288
The Dark Side of Christmas	293
Upon Which Rock?	297
We Are All Like Matthew	302
Culture Christians	305
Reflections of a Bird-Watching Spiritual Director	309
Catholic Pride...An Oxymoron?	313
You Gave Me Wonder	316
The Great Handshake	319
Christmas Column: Why I Like the Magi	323
The God of Tsunamis	327
The Shepherd and the Rock: A Letter to Pope Benedict XVI	330
A Big Year for Apples	334
All I Want for Christmas is a Few More Priests	337

In the Playground of the Lord 341
Good Words for an Old Bishop, Retiring 345
"What Was it Like?" - A Pilgrimage to Russia 349
Sunset in Key West 353
The Death of Sacred Space 357
The Spider's Web 362
About the Author 363

A Seasonal Column of Commentary
Nov/Dec 1982

Yesterday, it turned to November here at Mayslake. Unseasonably warm over the weekend, temperatures had risen as high as 70 degrees. Some torrential thunderstorms had accompanied this warmth, and blessedly recharged our drained and rip-rapped lakes, so that they now look less like abandoned gravel pits, and more like the lovely water our promotional brochures have invited people to come to. But behind that Spring-like mass, real Fall weather snapped in, temperatures sank below freezing, a flurry of snow swirled down briefly as we ate breakfast, and the comforting sounds of steam radiators was heard throughout the building.

I went out for a walk a little after sunrise, but despite the November-y chill, it was bright and sunny.

All that is left of the autumnal color are brilliant islands of gold where the poplars and sugar maples stand, as usual, holding their leaves to the very last warmth of the year. Now, however, even their leaves come shaking down before a brisk northwesterly breeze. Under the same breeze, a gingko tree vigorously sends down a shower of small yellowed leaves, but the maples and poplars are less responsive, and their larger leaves come sailing down, it seems, in ones and twos. Soon these and the rest of the hardwoods will be completely stripped. Already, all the apples in our orchard have been picked. Already the blackbirds have plucked our sunflowers clean of their millions of seeds. We will be able to see unaccustomed distances through the bare grey branches of the trees. You can see and feel winter coming - just a few weeks away.

There is an irony here. For just at this time of year when we come to the end of earth's lushness and begin to experience its depletion, we Americans settle into a great season of consuming. Perhaps it is an atavistic memory of harvest celebrations. Or perhaps we are not unlike squirrels who spend the winter months doing nothing but consuming the riches of summer. Whatever the reason, the gaudy season already comes upon us with the celebration of Halloween - once a slightly macabre but still faintly religious celebration of ancestral saints, but now a greedy and demanding collection of enormous amounts of very unhealthy foods. Thanksgiving follows but a few weeks later. In its time, this was one of the most beautiful celebrations of the year, certainly the national holiday that Americans can be most proud of creating. But now Thanksgiving has become a day when most churches stand empty, and when the prayers, if they are said at all, are reduced to a brief gesture that melts away before the irresistible waves of savory smells. It has become a day when Americans probably eat more and drink more than they do any other day of the year - and with greater abandon. Thanksgiving, however, only opens the floodgates to Christmas, the greatest of all consumer feasts. The day after Thanksgiving the Christmas parades hit the streets, and here in Chicago that means the heaviest shopping day of the year.

For the next thirty days all other values are swallowed up in the rising crescendo of buying and selling, and the numbing countdown that leads with increasing degrees of panic right down to the final hours before the sacred day begins.

The real tragedy of this season, however, is not that we consume a lot and celebrate a lot. The real problem is that we have forgotten why we do both. The Puritans realized why they celebrated Thanksgiving. For them it expressed their dependence not only upon the bounty of the earth, but upon God who gifted them with that bounty. Such an awareness was surely occasion for joy and a big celebration, and the Puritans, for all their severity and frugality, realized this.

It is for similar reasons that we celebrate this season that stretches from Thanksgiving through Advent to Christmas. We celebrate because we realize two things: that not only has God given us the gifts of this earth for our happiness, but that he has himself in his Son come to live upon that earth as his home. At least this is what our Christmas cards say. But in reality we have forgotten most of this. We have thrown out this joyous sense of fragility before nature and God, and kept only the party. And because we have forgotten why we celebrate, we have settled for celebrating something else. That something else may not always be conscious to us, but it is nonetheless real. For we have ceased to acknowledge that the earth is God's creation. We have indeed taken the earth away from Him. We have ceased to believe in any functional way that He is present in it, and so we have made the object of our Christmas celebration our own mastery and possession of the earth. We have, therefore, no one left to thank for the gift of earth, and so we thank ourselves. We congratulate ourselves, in a rising drumbeat of consumption, on our own ownership of the earth, mindlessly gouging from it whatever we desire. Christmas has become a celebration of our power over God's creation.

To protect us against this kind of arrogance, the Church has established the season of Advent. But, like a windbreak of trees that has been torn apart by a hurricane, Advent stands, no longer ahead of the storm, but behind it, providing us only with tattered remembrances of why we set out to celebrate Christmas in the first place. A few Christians wander about through this liturgical wreckage, but even in these visitations there is more nostalgia than refreshment. How sadly we recall those hopeful campaigns of the 'forties and 'fifties to "Put Christ Back into Christmas." How dismally they have failed.

What is needed to restore 'Christ' to Christmas, indeed to restore 'Thanks' to Thanksgiving (and for that matter to restore the 'saints' to Halloween) is not a better liturgical celebration of Advent and Christmas (though I welcome that too). What is needed is a reconsideration of our values. We need, above all, to reject out of hand any idea that the way we celebrate Thanksgiving and Christmas now, apart from our ritual attendance at Mass, has anything at all to do with the Gospel. The accumulation of loot, the obsessive manipulation of one another that goes into much of the gift-giving and card-sending - the gluttony, the drunkenness, the punishment of our bodies through the intake of excessive amounts of food, often unhealthy, the wastefulness of food and goods - whatever plausible reason we may conjure up for doing these things, let us at least be forthright and acknowledge that they have nothing to do with the meaning of these days.

If we can do this, we have a chance of really celebrating God's ownership of this earth and His presence in it. That is, after all, the meaning of this season of the year.

Let me end with a cautionary tale. Last spring we planted 1500 mammoth sunflowers, mostly to provide seeds for wintering birds. We assumed that we were doing this as a favor, and it was after all our patch of ground. But the birds had no sense of this. Long before it was even getting chilly at night, they possessively took over the sunflower patch from us, and mindlessly stripped away all the seeds. Winter is near now, and those birds that are left have no more seeds. We celebrate Thanksgiving and Christmas in the same possessive and mindless way. This year, if we do nothing else spiritual about Christmas, let us remember whose sunflower patch this earth really is. Then perhaps we will celebrate a little more respectfully.

Jonathan Foster, O.F.M.

Of Cardinals, Winter's Light, and Justice
Winter 1983

A cardinal is a brilliant bird any time of the year. But in the dead of winter, he can be startlingly so. He can stop you in your tracks, drop your mouth open to snatch murmurs of delight from your lips. It's not that he gets more brilliant in the winter - birds usually save their peak colors for the Spring breeding - but, it's the snow. That's one reason there are a lot of cardinals on Christmas cards.

Richard the Third (Shakespeare's version) may have made winter the gloomy symbol for his 'discontent', but in truth, winter can be a very lightsome time. You can see a lot in the winter that you don't notice in the summer. For starters, all the foliage has been stripped away, and you can see right into the woods to what they hide within themselves, and right through to their other sides. Vistas loom up in the winter, and carry our eyes away in ways they never do when we are surrounded by the lush enclosures of summer. And for most of the winter, a shining blanket of snow provides powerful backlight for such as cardinals, skiers, and other brightly clad life.

Even the darkest nights are luminescent with snow in the winter. It is the phenomenon of 'winter's light.'

There is a kind of 'winter's light' going on right now in the world and in the Church. We certainly seem to live in dark and wintry times. The hot breath of nuclear holocaust, for example, grows closer and warmer on our necks. A materialistic consumerism threatens not only our spirit but our resources as well. An obsession with self, identified more and more with the label, 'me-ism,' preoccupies our energies. And, closest to home, our economy tilts dangerously, and many have already slipped off its inclined plane. But just as 'winter's light' can bring a clarity summer never knows, so also, it is quite predictable that in the midst of severe crisis, we sometimes see more clearly what is to be done.

Such a thing is happening now. The Church and society are beginning to understand that what has to be done is justice - justice, that ancient virtue first described by Aristotle 2300 years ago. Justice is the virtue that preeminently has to do with getting along with people. Before we can ever begin to practice charity, we need to practice justice. For justice is the value that recognizes and respects the other person's dignity and rights - whether we like him or not, whether we want him around or not, whether indeed he agrees with our values or not. Justice precedes affection, precedes love, and precedes compassion, precedes taking care of people. Justice is the first relationship we must have with anybody and any group.

In previous centuries, humanity could dispense with justice or give it a lower priority, because there was a widespread belief among people that some were better than others, and hence could mistreat them, or, if they were Christians, could take care of them, feed them, teach them new ways of living, even run their lives and their countries for them. Moreover, the human race never had the problems we have today. I should say rather that they never had them quite the way we have them today. The problems aren't new: war, materialism, selfishness, exploitation. What is new is that there are billions more of us on the earth. We jostle and push against each other's space. We bring our differing values and customs closer and closer together. We clamor and struggle for our share of the world's goods and lands, resources that continue to shrink in size and availability. So, all our ancient problems become critically dangerous, and begin to threaten our very survival as a people. The problem then today is how to get along in this overcrowded, over-heated world; indeed, how to survive. Hence, justice.

So, the Church's recent expressions of concern for justice isn't just faddish, trendy or 'liberal'. It is a response to the needs of our times. And, we would add, it is a recognition that the Church, too, has been amiss in practicing this great virtue.

If the Church considers justice important, then justice, whether popular or not, has to be a major concern here at Mayslake. We do this, not by promoting this or that movement or issue, certainly not by taking public political stands. We are not headquarters for activists. Our business is the spirit, and that's the vantage point from which we approach the virtue of justice. Those of you who make the weekend retreats have noticed the stress we have been placing on values. Justice is one of the highest of those values. You have also noted the attention we pay to consumerism and materialism - values that undercut justice. You perhaps have attended one of the lively Saturday night forums on 'social issues,' or read some of the literature we put out on abortion, the peace movement, and other issues of justice. There will be more of this coming, as the friars here continue to educate themselves. Father Evan has just completed a unit on social justice in his studies for the doctorate in ministry. Jonathan attended a workshop for retreat house personnel on justice. And we have begun negotiating with a team of friars representing all the Franciscan provinces in North America to undertake an analysis of the ministry we do here at Mayslake in terms of justice.

The world may appear darksome. But there are always flashes of winter-light. In these flashes, we are seeing more clearly the shape of the great virtue of justice. It is showing up better in these hard times - like cardinals on a cold snowy landscape.

The Goose and the Phoenix
Lent/Easter 1983

It is a dull day in February as I look out my office window. Typical of this incredibly mild winter, it is overcast and warmish. Wet snow, more like rain, is dropping straight down as though run through a strainer. And we are surrounded by geese - the great Canada geese that you see so often here. They ring us around like a besieging army. They stalk about the property, skate on our still-frozen ponds, nibble at crumbs fallen from the bird feeders, pluck the first of the resurgent grasses, peer in at us through our glass doors, and wait expectantly near the kitchen door for old pancakes and such. Yesterday I counted nearly two hundred and fifty of them hanging about the back lawn. Most of these are 'welfare geese', which means that because they are well-fed in this area, they don't feel the need to migrate. For some reason though, they leave our grounds during the winter, preferring other watering holes throughout DuPage County. They always come back, however, in February, restless for open water and anxious to begin the mating process. Those that finally settle here (eight to ten pair) will remain, with their young, till the Fall.

They can get to be a nuisance. Their imperious honking is very romantic when they are flying V-shaped to the North. But when it goes on all night outside your bedroom window as they quarrel over nesting sites, it is a very different sound. And they are - well - untidy. There are times in the summer, right now for that matter, when our lawns are so bestrewn with carelessly cast goose droppings as to resemble a barnyard, and you have to step smartly to escape with unsmeared shoes. For these and other reasons, there are guests who ask us, sometimes indignantly, "Why don't you get rid of those damn geese?"

We have no intentions of doing so, of course. We are followers of Francis here, and all the world knows how close to his heart all God's creatures were - including, I am sure, geese with unsanitary habits. Francis' affection for wildlife, however, like ours, was not purely romantic. Francis knew that the family of God's creation extended beyond the human, to include everything that lived and came from the hand of God. 'Family' was the key word for him. It was for no light reason then that Francis called the sun 'Brother' and the water 'Sister', and preached to birds, fish, and even cornfields. We try here at Mayslake to preserve some of that sensitivity to the family of life, and hope that our guests pick up some of the same - despite whatever else they might pick up on their shoes.

But, I have another reason for welcoming the geese back. I know why they are here - they are urgent to continue life by making it anew. Lent is their starting season. It is no accident that the Church celebrates resurrection at the same time as the geese begin to nest. It is the season of new life everywhere when new and living things push up through the dry but nurturing wrappings of death. So, the experience of the geese and of all new life in Springtime may be said to be Easter-y. As it does in nature, life returned to Jesus at Easter. As we watch then, there comes an increased sense of hope about our own lives. Most of us are not spiritually dead, but we barely live enough spiritually - "living and partly living" as the women of Canterbury say of themselves in T. S. Eliot's *Murder in the Cathedral.* What Easter says to us is not that we must begin to live where we did not live before, but that to continue the effort to live spiritually is worthwhile. Easter is not an either/or thing, either death or life. It is a commitment to "Again", to beginning "again" to carry out the struggle for a deeper life, to try "again" to pray, to try "again" to work at that marriage, to try "again" to be free of bigotry, or to stop drinking.

Nature makes this matter of resurrection look much more dramatic than it is. Every Spring life bursts out of dormancy with excitement, promise, color, music, warmth and beauty. Every Spring stands out like the first year of creation. But it's only temporary. The life of Spring begins to slow down and dry out in summer's heat. Only some of it produces full fruit, much produces only a part, and some none at all. Some life simply ends, its promise never fulfilled - an eggshell breaks, a honey bee dies, some corn dries up, a car crushes a baby raccoon. All of it eventually succumbs to the cold fingers of Fall, and is pushed back into the earth while the long death of winter slides across the land. So it is with humans. We make promises, commitments, start actions, set hearts on fire; but, invariably, we stumble in the reality, fall far short of goals, sometimes never succeed at all, and sometimes we even quit. Lent is the ritual time in which we face all this failure, ask God's forgiveness and receive a kind of amnesty - and once more make the commitment to "again," to "again" keep at it.

There is another bird that has an Easter message - the mythical Phoenix. The Phoenix was reputed to look more like an eagle than a goose, and it didn't migrate, or even nest every Spring. What it did do, however, was not carry on the species in the normal way. Instead, periodically, it would undertake a strange ritual. After, we may assume, it had gotten fat, its feathers faded and its eye lost its lustre, it would build itself a nest of spices, and, fanning its great wings over the nest, set it afire. Then, settling down into the burning nest, it would allow itself to be consumed by flames till nothing remained but a pile of cold ashes. But, from within the ashes, would then emerge a new version of the Phoenix, fully alive, all its feathers brilliant and in place, sharp of beak and keen of eye, and more beautiful than it had been before. It is not surprising that the Phoenix bird became one of the Christian symbols of Easter.

What is important to remember about both the Phoenix and the goose is that they didn't do this only once, but over and over again. What is important for us to remember *as* we celebrate Easter all decked out in stiff new clothes and brisk new spirit, is that we most likely will look shabby again come next Lent. But that's all right. What resurrection means is that, like the goose and the Phoenix, we keep at it.

Jonathan Foster, O.F.M.

The Bishops' Pastoral and the Red Fox
Spring 1983

A couple of years ago, I returned home one night very late. It was a Spring night, soft, pleasant, and the air stood still as though waiting for someone. Except for the random murmur of insects, it was quiet. Suddenly, as I rounded the building, from down near the shore of the lake, a loud, agonizing shriek shredded the quiet drape of the night. I stopped, startled. The cry continued, rising like a human scream in pain. Forming a hideous base to its trembling falsetto was a snarling, growling rumble. My first instinct was to stop whatever horror was taking place down there. But then, I remembered, and simply stood there listening as the snarling and screaming slowly subsided to a methodical, gnashing growl. Daylight the next morning confirmed my suspicion. One of the few red fox that still den at Mayslake had pounced upon a dozing mallard duck and turned it quickly, albeit noisily into its supper.

I am quite content to stand by and watch these bloody little exploitations of the weak and unwary by the strong and the clever. I even resent the motherly efforts of people who want to get rid of the fox to protect "those cute little ducklings". This is, after all, the predator/prey relationship, an indispensable component of the balance of nature, something God intended to be. We see it every day here at Mayslake. Swallows swoop and dart over our lakes devouring insects. Sharp-eyed sparrow hawks bend eagerly from our telephone wires, waiting for a hapless field mouse to show its head. And light-footed fox quietly stalk the lines of ducklings that trail out behind their mother. I say to them all, "Go for it!"

But, what I am not content to stand by and tolerate, much less encourage, is another kind of predator/prey relationship, the highly sophisticated one that goes on between nations as they hunt each other, slung with an awesome assemblage of rocketry, nuclear bombs, poisonous gases, flaming gasoline, and laser beams. There are those who see little difference, other than one of degree, between a team of pilots wiping out hundreds of thousands of lives with a single bomb, and a fox satisfying his appetite on a sleepy duck. For them too it is a simple matter of balancing nature, is indeed manly, even good for the soul. It was Mussolini, I believe, who used to say that the only thing that would make the Italian people grow up was war, constant warfare. Some even call upon God to justify all this savagery, smugly calling to our memory the God who burned down Sodom and Gomorrah, drowned the Egyptian army in the Red Sea, and smashed the walls of Jericho, ordered the massacre of its population, and who regularly promised that he would fight alongside his chosen people, armed as much with a sword as he was with justice. I oppose this kind of thinking, because, much as we may admire the skill of the fox and respect his instincts, we ought rather to be thought of as human beings, not as some kind of highly sophisticated predators.

The recent Bishops' pastoral on the nuclear arms race clearly wishes Catholics to see themselves not as predators upon other nations or races but as peacemakers. Much has been made of the pastoral's position on specific aspects of the nuclear arms debate, such as 'Deterrence', 'No First Strike', and the 'Nuclear Freeze'. Twenty-five years from now, it is to be fondly hoped, these issues will no longer be with us. But the nuclear arms race will hardly be the last chapter in our mad pursuit of power over others. We will still be human beings with our atavistic memories of survival through force and might. We will still envy other predators who, with sharp tooth and claw - and untroubled consciences - overpower their weaker prey. We will still, after the nuclear arms race, continue to wish to take bloody vengeance upon our enemies. The Bishops, however, are reminding us that, as Catholics and Christians, we are to be mainly on the side of the angels who announced the good news, not those apocalyptic ones who carry sickles and go screaming triumphantly through the skies trailing the red of sinners' blood. The Bishops are reminding us that the symbols for Christians, indeed their Memory, is not King David who "killed his ten thousands" but Jesus, hanging on the cross, shedding not the blood of others but only his own.

There is in the tradition of Franciscans a furthering of this call from Christ to be peacemakers, one that has startling relevance to the conditions of the modern world. Medieval Italy, where Francis of Assisi lived, was a patchwork of city-states, each of which was independent of the other. Each of them also had their own armies, which, like Indian raiding parties or college football teams, they sent out regularly to skirmish with their neighbors. They would also, from time to time, tie themselves into alliances with the Italian superpowers of the day: the Holy Roman Empire and the Papal States. This was very hard on the peasants, because they had to bear the brunt of these nasty and continuous little wars. Many died; many saw their crops confiscated, their property burned. It is not surprising then that, except for some of the merchants and nobility who got to be iron-encased knights, there was little enthusiasm for military duty among the Italian citizenry. Francis, after an early and disillusioning experience with the military (he was immediately taken prisoner-of-war and spent the duration ingloriously and uncomfortably locked up), became an ardent peacemaker. And when he wrote his rule for lay Franciscans (Third Order members as we came to call them later, and Secular Franciscans as we call them now), Francis summoned his brothers and sisters to peacemaking. He first forbade them to make any oaths to other persons. Their sole fidelity was to be to God. This action cancelled the feudal oath which their lords called upon to press them into military service. Second, Francis forbade any member of the order to bear arms. It was one of the earliest acts of gun control or arms control in history! The peasants immediately caught on. The early chroniclers tell us that "half of Italy" flocked into the lay order, and for decades thereafter northern Italy was free of war.

The Franciscans no longer have these kinds of regulations in their Rules. But, if they did, they would be much closer to the Gospel than those who put their confidence in guns and weapons as a means of bringing peace into the world. To admire a fox killing a duck is one thing. But to admire a human being who finds the meaning of his life, or a nation which finds the definition of its identity in force and power ("Peace Through Strength"), is to allow the whole Gospel and its central symbol of the cross to pass us right by.

Meadowing
Summer 1983

The north and east sections of the retreat house property form a meadow now, and have for the past two years. But for many years before that, when the Brothers used to run the farm, it was cropland - one year, corn; another year, soybeans. Though it may be more apparent to a farmer - not to mention the ducks, geese and pigeons that scavenge the field after harvest - corn and soybean fields have their own beauty. They never surprise you, however. You know that a cornfield is going to look the same this year as last year. The only surprise we had when our fields were cropland was the very mild one of which would it be this year: 'beans or corn'. Because farmers are always organizing its agenda, a field dedicated to crops never gets to reveal its full potential, to show what it can really do.

This is not the case with our meadow. When the farming was finished here at Mayslake, Russ simply disced under the last of the corn, and we let the land go. It turned into a meadow. Now, when we look north and east of the building, we no longer see draughtsman's rows of identical shoots, but a soft green rug of land parted only by a windbreak of silver maples and buckeyes. In the corner of this meadow nearest the building sits a pretty vernal pond that collects rainwater seeping down from the higher land on which the retreat house sits, and whose size, depending on the amount of rain and snow we get, ranges from a large mud puddle to a brimming acre. The rest of the meadow is drained by a sluggish cut ditch that we hope someday, when the developer is all finished around here, will become a real creek.

What I like most about the meadow, however, is not just its gentle beauty, but the fact that it always surprises me. When you let a piece of land go, you never know what it will come up with next. For example, when there was just corn and soybeans, we never had meadowlarks and bobolinks. This year we had them both. But you don't have to wait till next year for surprises in a meadow. Every few weeks, sometimes days, there is something new as wildflowers come in waves, like pulses of passion. Right now - mid-June - we have in our meadow red clover, yellow clover and clusters of daisies forming white caps on the deep green of the hay-like grass. Later this summer, there will be pale blue chicory, white fleabane, morning glory, purple blazing star; in the Fall there will be asters and the soft white explosion of milkweed. And this is the way it will go on, month after month, year after year. Surprise will succeed surprise as the meadow reaches for its maturity. For this is nature's way. Plants scattered randomly over any given piece of land interact continually with each other, the soil, the air and the life of the surrounding environment. Sometimes they come up with something new. Sometimes they push out something old, till a climax is reached in which the community of life on that plot of land becomes stable, even relatively predictable. And then it will be the best it can produce.

You would never get this with cornfields.

There is, of course, a parable here. Take human beings. If you load them down with lots of merely human expectations, such as success, wealth, and power, then, like a farmer planting corn and beans, that's all you get from them year after year. They will not grow. They will not surprise anyone, including themselves.

This is why praying is so important for human beings. For when we pray, we are squarely in the path of the most daring adventure we are capable of - the journey towards God, a journey full of surprises and mystery that never really ends. There is nothing else you can do - taking a personality inventory, starting your own business, taking a wife or husband, having a mid-life crisis, or getting your portrait painted - that so surely reveals who you are and establishes the outlines of your own individuality than praying before God. Psalm 139 details how intimately God knows you. He knows you standing and sitting; he reads your thoughts; he knows what you are going to say before you say it. He knows right where you are, even if you run away from him, climb the bowl of heaven or fly off to the sunset. He stitched together the intricacy of you in your mother's womb, and so he watched your very bones grow. Before no other person, including yourself, do you stand in such individuality. And so it is that the Psalmist can say, "I thank you for the wonder of myself." The "wonder of myself" - the mystery, the marvel, the irreplaceableness of who I am, the awe of me. But there is only one way I can really know this - when I pray. With the vision and power that comes from prayer, like a meadow that is left alone, I can really become the best I can be.

It is for this reason that prayer is such an important part of the ministry here at Saint Francis. What is uppermost in our minds when we conduct retreats here, including directed retreats, and when we provide spiritual direction is helping people to pray. We have committed public prayer - the Eucharist, the Sacrament of Reconciliation and other services of all kinds - into the capable hands of our staff liturgist, Father Ted Haag. This year, moreover, we begin in Advent the celebration of Solemn Evening Prayer (Vespers) for the people of the area.

The subject of prayer arose again as we sat down early this past Spring to begin planning the program for the weekend retreats. We were undecided about whether to build a retreat around helping people make moral judgments today, or helping people to pray. It was our unanimous decision that before we could honestly deal with morality, it was imperative that we deal with the most basic reason why we are moral - because we are sons and daughters of God. We need to know first who we are and where we belong. For that we need prayer.

So the theme of this year's series of weekend retreats - starting in late September - will be prayer. We will attempt to help people pray in the context of our times. We will reflect on how Jesus himself prayed, and try to learn from him. We will lead people to pray out of their own experience and feelings ("thank you for the wonder of my being"). We will deal with the difficulties of praying. And we shall explore how to best pray publicly with the revised rites of the Eucharist and the Sacrament of Reconciliation.

Jesus invited us to consider the lilies of the field. May I suggest meadows as well? If you leave the land alone with the rain, it will never stop till it reaches its fullest potential. If you leave a man or a woman alone with God, if you do not sow too heavily with corn and soybeans, they too will "meadow". And, glory be to God! - they will never stop surprising you.

Crying Over Broken Eggs
Thanksgiving/Christmas 1983

We have had a nice autumn so far this year at Mayslake - warmish for the most part, dry and sunny. The Fall colors, following the dynamic of cool nights and warm days, are, like milkweed pods, exploding quietly to old gold climax. But it has not been a pleasant Fall to walk around in. At least, not around what we call Third Lake. This is the lower pond that lies between the retreat house and Saint Paschal Friary. Ten acres in size, it is the only natural one of the three May's lakes. For several years now, the developer who bought land from the Franciscans is converting it into what he calls Trinity Lakes and has been draining and dredging Third Lake. Because of various meteorological and economic conditions, however, the dredging has been a hit-and-miss affair so that we have had, for three or four years, something that resembles a pit more than a lake. This unsightliness has been reaching its climax just recently, however. Because the summer was very hot and dry, the lake bed dried out sufficiently so that the earth-movers have been able to get into it on a consistent basis.

I should explain why they are doing this. The

developer owns about a quarter of the shoreline of Third Lake, and will be putting expensive homes up on the ridge overlooking the lake from the Southwest. It is a very shallow lake - typically one to two feet in depth. Because it is shallow, the sun's rays were able to penetrate to the underlying mud and stimulate plant growth. As a result, great stands of cattails and other tall grasses sprang up in the shallower sections of the lake. This has been marvelous for waterfowl and other wildlife. I can remember just five years ago standing on the banks of the lake during October sunsets watching anywhere from three hundred to seven hundred migrating ducks dropping into the rich shallow waters for the night. One winter I counted fifteen large muskrat lodges perched above the frozen waters. But, to most people the lake was ugly, "just a swamp". The village manager of Oak Brook, whose policy it is that requires the dredging, put it to me quite succinctly when I asked him why the lake had to be cleaned out: "Who wants to live next to a swamp?" Apparently no one who is going to put up several hundred thousand dollars for a house wants to, so the lake has been drained, and is, finally this Fall, being dredged. When it fills again from the rains, the lake will be sufficiently deep as to fend off the subversive, life-giving rays of the sun.

 Because of all this, the air has been filled these lambent days with noise: the whine of compressor-run pumps sucking the water from the lake; the clank and rattle of draglines and backhoes; the thunderous pounding of huge dump-trucks hauling away cattail-studded muck; the bouncing and banging of pickup trucks; the bullish snorting of bulldozers. Autumn is usually one of the quietest times of the year. The winds blow less, and you can hear the still fall of the acorn, the faint song of the migrating warbler, and the soft brush of a leaf as it slips onto the dry grass floor. But not this year.

The land begins to look even worse than the sounds. The meadows and grassy patches near the lake have been rolled down into a cement-y hardpan sealed with dry mud-slick. Saplings have been smashed down, branches ripped from the willow trees on the shore, and the underbrush randomly crushed. Food and work-litter of the working man is kicked back into the bushes, and piles of rubble are dumped into the woods. The thick, carelessly sprawling greenery that formed the shoreline has all been sheared away and the banks smoothed down to prepare for the inevitable belt of riprap that will give the lakes the appearance of a clean bathtub.

Many folk stand on the ridge overlooking all this and nod their approval. No one likes the noise, of course, and the smashing, and the litter. But, as they say, "It's the price of progress." Or, more quaintly, "You can't have omelettes without breaking a few eggs."

I thought about broken eggs and omelettes as I walked along the edge of our wrecked pond yesterday. I had just come from a session with a well-to-do woman from the area. She lives in a home like the ones for which this lake is being drained and gutted. In two of them, in fact, for a second one stands in Florida. At age 60, she is bitterly unhappy, idle, with a husband who ignores her, and an only son who is thousands of miles away and who has already failed in life. In the midst of the ruin of their lives, her husband wants to build an even bigger house - as though this might solve something - and she cries out in pain to me, "Why? What we have hasn't made us happy. What makes him think a bigger house is going to make us less miserable?" And then she said over and over again, "Why can't we just thank God for what we have, and be satisfied with that?"

That's what I remembered as I gazed out on our lake that looks like a gravel pit. How little gratitude there is in our lives. How ready we are to destroy what we have for what often merely appears to be something better. And how little we regret the loss of what we have destroyed. Because their entire culture and way of life depended on them, the Plains Indians destroyed a lot of buffalo. But, it is said, the Indian always apologized to the buffalo for killing him. Small consolation for the buffalo, but what a comment about the Indian! Some part of life had to be destroyed, but he knew it was for a necessary cause; he rarely over-killed; and he always stood in awe of the buffalo. It was indeed for him the sign of wisdom. Can you imagine some resident of an overbuilt house in Oak Brook, staring down proudly at his country club lake, and recognizing wisdom in the muskrat that used to live there? Feeling sad that he had to drive out three hundred ducks so he could have his dream house? Indeed, can you imagine yourself being grateful to the same Indian, whose land you now live in because your forefathers drove him out? If it is true that we sometimes have to crush willows, evict ducks, even sometimes make others miserable, it is just as true that at the very least we must do something like apologize. We need to cry over broken eggs.

Ingratitude runs deep in our culture. We feel things are ours by right. With our Bill of Rights, with our long tradition of pioneering and frontier individualism, with our legal system of entitlements which intensifies our sense of rightful ownership of life, we have become a proud people convinced that it all belongs to us, and, that if part of it doesn't, we can go right out and take it. We are forgetting how to be grateful.

The season of Thanksgiving and Christmas ought to drive us to our knees in humble rejection of such nonsense. It is a time for us to remember that we are the sons and daughters of the people who wiped out the buffalo herds and the cultures dependent on them. It is time for us to remember that we are the people whose lifestyle, even the modest affluence of most of us, requires that we destroy marshes, wipe out species of wildlife, and exploit other people. If we don't do it any other time of the year, Christmas, because the Word Himself became Gift, is the time for us to realize that all is gift. With this kind of gratitude, we may find ourselves less grasping and possessive about things, less destructive of the world's resources. And, even if we can't quite manage that, perhaps at least we will notice the wreckage we cause the earth and other people and say: "I'm sorry."

Short Days, Dark Days
January Reflections on Whether
Christianity Will Ever Succeed

Winter 1984

T.S. Eliot, Anglo-American poet, called April the 'cruelest' month of the year. I'll take January in Chicago anytime for that distinction. The snow is the worst - remember the great storms of 1967 and 1979? The cold is the worst - remember January, 1982, when the earth almost cracked open under records of minus 23 and 24 degrees? The midweek of January is statistically the coldest week of the year in these parts. The days, it is true, are getting longer, but it isn't obvious, and the sun still rises and sets during rush hour. The weak, south-hanging sun provides little warmth and produces only honey-colored sunsets. Here at Mayslake, the geese abandon our frozen ponds, the knifelike north winds cause us to bundle up in our north-facing offices, and Russ regularly wakes us up at 6:00 A.M. with a plow scraping still more snow off the parking lot. Skiers and other outdoor aficionados of course glory in all this and scoff at those of us who huddle together waiting for

Spring. But cold is cold and snow is snow. And this is the time of year when the poor and the elderly regularly burn themselves to death in their cold apartments, seeking heat from open gas ovens and rickety kerosene burners. In the pits of January, you are as far from July as you can get.

One of the least attractive things about this time of year is the sixteen hours of darkness we have to endure every day. When the sun isn't shining, it's a brief and gloomy day. I don't dislike the full-dark so much. It is the half-gloom of too early dusks and too-late sunrises. All this half-light tends to make me gloomy and pessimistic. I am writing these lines on a January-like day in December, and I fully expect this January to be one of the gloomiest months I have ever known. For like the growing darkness and coldness of winter, events of the past few months have drawn themselves heavily around my soul.

We have seen the brutal and pointless shooting down of a commercial airliner in Russia. We have seen hundreds of Americans blown up in Lebanon, and the loss of their lives has brought no victories. Like a Dallas Cowboy spiking a football in the end zone of Podunk High School, we have seen a powerful nation revel in the glory of overpowering a tiny country the size of Peoria. We have watched relationships between the superpowers sink to their lowest and most dangerous levels in twenty years. We have vicariously lived through the apocalyptic denouement of all this militarist posturing in the TV production of "The Day After". And in another TV film, "Choices of the Heart", we have witnessed the story of a pretty and dedicated young American missionary, raped and murdered along with three of her companions in bloody El Salvador. And as we watched we remembered that this happened three years ago, that nothing has been done about it, that the overall situation has not improved because of their witness - have they died in vain? - and that our government continues to support the government that did it. And if this were not enough, they tell us there are over forty wars going on throughout the world these days.

I am normally a very optimistic person about the situation in the world. I have always had confidence that things would get better, especially as the Church has begun to bring her not inconsiderable forces to bear in bringing the social message of the Gospel to this shattered earth. Now, as I sit here reaching for warmth on a cold day, I am not so sure.

You see, I have always felt that sooner or later Christianity would be successful. I know it was not to come quickly, but I have always felt that someday we would have a Christian 'Pax Romana', a Christian International Order, or a peaceable kingdom in which swords would be beaten into plowshares and infants would play safely over the adder's lair. I felt I could look back over the two thousand years of Christianity and chalk up measurable gains from 1 A.D. till now. I would find more and more schools. Social problems, like violence, oppression, exploitation, racial hatred, would, I was sure, steadily wear away under the persistent warmth and light of the Gospel. Slow, to be sure. Though we were not yet ready to lie down with them, I have always been quite sure that the Christians were gaining on the lions. Now, in January, 1984, for the first time in my life, I find myself questioning whether Christianity will ever succeed.

What has happened? Have things really gotten worse, or have I just gotten older, and, in a cynical sort of way, wiser? Am I losing perspective because this happens to be an administration that I didn't vote for? Is all this just a temporary phenomenon, a period of biting the bullet till a painful surgery is over with? Will Christianity continue to succeed as I have always been confident that it would?

Now, I say, "Perhaps!" And every time I do, I wonder if I am losing my faith in the Providence of God, a doctrine which bulks rather largely in the history of Christian thought. Read the Psalms, for example, and you will be broadly assured that Good will triumph over the present Evil, probably in our lifetime. But recently I heard a story about Dorothy Day, the saintly American Catholic radical, that has helped me get some perspective on Providence. Dorothy was extremely active in a lot of very unpopular movements, such as pacifism, simple life style, advocacy of the poor, and so forth. She spent most of her life passionately involved in campaigns that displayed very little, if any, success, as we normally measure success. Towards the end of her life, she was asked by a reporter if she felt her life had been, well, successful. She looked him straight in the eye, and responded, "I have read the Gospels many times, but I have never seen the word 'success' in them."

Apparently, Dorothy Day was not impressed by the spiritual and moral statistics that most of us depend upon to sustain our notion of Divine Providence. I am sure she welcomes the fact that more people turned up at one meeting than at another, that she raised more money for the poor of the Catholic Worker Center one year than in the year previous. But apparently she did not consider her work more successful in one instance than another. For her, to be successful meant not to feed this many, convert a certain number, raise so much money, stop this war, but purely and simply to be faithful to the Gospel as God had given her to understand it. She realized, as Job did, that "The Lord gives, the Lord takes away." She understood, as Paul did, that while one plants and another waters, "God gives the increase." She never looked at bottom lines. She only kept her eye on the Gospel.

This of course is not a prescription for incompetence, a justification for not understanding how to do things like feeding the hungry, stopping wars, controlling abortions, combatting exploitation and injustice. It is not a license to 'stick to the pulpit' and patriotically endorse everything our government and economic establishment decrees. Least of all is it an excuse to withdraw from the social scene altogether, like so many, indeed devout Christians do, piously leaving it all in the hands of God, and never, ever, have an opinion on, say, the cruise missile, one way or the other. It is simply a recognition that the Kingdom of God does not operate like AT&T. Surely God's word will not be in vain, as Isaiah tells us. It comes down on the earth and waters the crops, and they bear fruit. But the harvest will be in his time not ours, in his way, not ours. We will work steadily for him, but he will write the bottom line, and what we need to recognize is that we may not even be able to read it.

This is a helpful perspective in these days, especially in this January. Our faith is proven not by its success, but simply by its persistence. And so it is possible on a brief, dark and cold January day to still feel and see the Warmth.

Jonathan Foster, O.F.M.

The Gift of a Chilly April
March/April 1984

The weather for last year's Easter was miserable - chilly, rain-drenched, and overcast. But we were forgiving. Easter was a little early last year, April 3. There was no such excuse this year. Easter was very late, April 22, and should have been the kind that shows up on greeting cards - full of sun, green grass, lilies, and pastel Easter clothes that do not have to be hidden under winter coats. But this year's Easter was as ill-tempered as last year's.

Each year on Easter Sunday I go for a hike about our land. I did it again this year, but had to do it somewhat more quickly, because we were being hammered by rain and gusty, northeasterly winds. Ponds had accumulated everywhere, and water possessed the land like a squishy incubus. As I tramped about in the light but chilly rain, my shoes quickly got soaked and felt like hunks of soaking turf strapped to my feet. Cheeks red from the pelting East wind and feet icy cold, I was grateful for the steam heat still running through the building when I came in. While out that morning, however, I saw the first wildflowers of the year just beginning to unfurl their tight little heads. Checking my journal, I noted that the same bed of flowers had been in full bloom two weeks earlier last year.

It is indeed a late Spring. As of this writing, April 24, we still have not had a day when the temperature has reached 60 degrees. The mother goose who annually broods a clutch of eggs on the little point that juts out into our lake knows it. She still hasn't come to nest yet, and last year she was settled by the end of March. Someone corrected me about that sixty-degree day, and pointed out that we did have one back in February. Remember February? It was a 'fool's gold' month. It only looked like Spring, and let March and April show us what February is really like.

It's not the sort of Spring you would call a bargain. Nor would you appreciate getting it for your birthday. A nice, warm, sunny April, with just enough rain to green the grass and start the wildflowers - that we appreciate. That's the way things should be. We might even go so far as to say, "That's the kind of Spring we deserve."

The truth of course is that we don't deserve either a pleasant Spring or a rotten one. Weather comes on God's terms, never mindful of whether we have been good or bad. He does not keep score on Chicago's morals, and then, depending on the results, send us a mild winter or a mean one. And so it is that any nice weather we get should not be greeted with an indignant, "It's about time!" but should be looked upon as a gift from God, and honored with simple praise.

The experience of a warm, sunny day as gift is only part of a larger experience Christians are committed to - and that is to see everything as Gift. God made it all, and

God gave it away. There is little claim we can make to responsibility for any of it.

We seem to have lost this sense of gift. We tend rather to think in terms of having a right to things, of having earned them, of "having it coming to me". There is some reason for this. We are a highly educated people. Education and knowledge impart a great deal of control and power over nature and even over other people. We also have a highly sophisticated set of tools in our ever-advancing technology. Such exquisitely honed tools make it possible for us to achieve undreamed of, and centuries ago, undreamable goals. And we have been successful. In many respects, America is the most successful society in history - in terms of health, opportunity, affluence, power, and good government. The experience of success deepens the sense of self-achievement. Moreover, deeply imbedded in our culture is a theological vision that tells us that the great bounties of this land are not ours as gift, but as right. The 19th century doctrine of "manifest destiny" (which guided the westward expansion of this country at the expense of the Mexicans and Native Americans) taught us that all this land was ours by right. We nodded to the fact that the "allotment" was by Divine Providence, but what the doctrine in fact passed on to us was a sense of possessiveness and right, not only about the land, but about everything in our experience. As a consequence, we tend to take credit for all our success, progress, wealth and achievement. On the other hand, we tend to be pretty harsh on those who fail, who are low achievers, who are poor, and especially the unambitious. They could do better if they wanted to. We have forgotten that all our success, as a nation and as individuals, is due more to the bounty bestowed upon us than it is to our own hard work.

I will never forget an experience I had some years ago at a workshop in Oakland, California. The participants were invited to play one of the strategy games then popular. This one was called 'Starpower'. Each participant was given a stack of poker chips of three different values. We were then instructed to negotiate with each other to try to increase our hoard. To this end we had to use sharp negotiating skills, take aggressive positions, swing creative deals, form imaginative coalitions - in other words, engage in all the skills normally associated with success and getting ahead. Somewhat to my surprise, for I had never envisioned myself as good at this sort of thing, I began to move out ahead of everyone else. As the game progressed, the most successful traders were formed into a separate group and given more power than the face value of their chips indicated. I was one of these select few. I felt vaguely uneasy about all this success, because I saw people with what I thought were superior skills doing far more poorly than I was. Despite this however I became the leader of the power group, and in the swirl of success, finally became convinced I really was good at all this. The game ended after a couple of hours because those who were not successful ceased to trust those who were and refused further trade. Our small group of four or five - including one very shy young nun - did everything but 'high fives' to celebrate our victory. You can only imagine what a letdown it was then to discover in the debriefing session that our win was fraudulent. We had won, yes, but not because we were better at the game than others, but because from the very beginning, though this was not communicated to anyone, all of us who had ended up winners had been given substantially more chips than everyone else. We had been blessed with gifts we were not aware of. And, assuming that everyone else had been blessed the same as we, it was no surprise that we began to think ourselves better than they because we won.

The problem of misplaced credit is widespread and historic. The Jews suffered from it. It was God who had delivered them out of slavery, brought them through the desert, and presented them with the Promised Land. But, lest they forget, there on the borders of that new land, God, through Moses, had to remind them not to take credit for all their success: "When you have built your fine houses to live in," he said, "when you have seen your flocks and herds increase, your silver and gold abound, and all your possessions grow great - beware of saying in your hearts, "My own strength and the might of my own hand won this power for me." (Deuteronomy 8). The Jews, of course, like us, promptly forgot all this good advice, and began to act like landlords instead of tenants. It was their undoing, as it is ours.

This same possessiveness extends even to our spiritual life. We feel we have to earn heaven, and by God, we'll do it. If we have been good, we feel God owes us. And he ought to punish those who are not. And when we find out after many years of life, that despite our good efforts, we are still sinners, we begin to cringe, and fear the wrath of God because we haven't measured up. This fear is the price we pay for our own arrogance in thinking that it is "my own strength and the might of my own hand" that will gain for me the friendship of God. We have forgotten that it is all Gift - our world, our life, our salvation - and no matter what we do or don't do, whether we deserve it or not, it will be there for us. The most descriptive word for the spiritual life is 'Grace'. It comes from a Latin word, 'gratia', which means free and unearned.

It is this theme of a heaven that can't be earned, of salvation as gift that will form the heart of the retreat program for the weekend retreats next year at Mayslake (beginning the first weekend of October). The talks, the prayer-sessions, the penance service, etc., will all help us achieve a greater understanding of our spiritual lives, not as an exam to be passed or a promotion to be earned, but as Gift.

In the meantime, keep your eye on the weather. Depending on what meteorologist you read, the world's climate is either getting colder (due to the inability of the sun's rays to get through all our pollution), or getting warmer (because the same pollution is trapping the earth's heat like a greenhouse). There is evidence to support both viewpoints, but both portend catastrophe in a few thousand years. And there are people out there who are going to look upon the coming coastal floods or returning glaciers as some kind of judgment of God upon our sins. Don't be taken in by all of this. Take it all, miserable and mild, as gift, and remember that, despite Mark Twain, there is something you can do about the weather besides talk about it. You can praise God in his gifts.

Jonathan Foster, O.F.M.

A Bald Eagle Flies Over Mayslake
Some Reflections on Losing a Priest
Summer 1984

On the last day of May this year, we celebrated here at Mayslake the Silver Jubilee of twelve Franciscan priests of the Sacred Heart Province. There was a fine, midmorning liturgy, with trumpets, and a real choir, backed up by our wheezy, out-of-tune organ. Twelve priests, identically clad in crisp white vestments (including totally blind Father Sigismund accompanied by his seeing-eye dog) formed a half-circle of elders about the altar. And elders they looked: their balding, greying heads sharp reminders to those of us who went to school with them that we are all getting a bit older. The weather was just right - sunny, windless, temperatures in the 70's, and so the hundred-plus guests were able to enjoy refreshments on off-white covered tables. Finally, there followed a jovial banquet on tables set with wine and bedecked with the last of this year's lilacs, a dinner not the least of whose many distinctions was that it featured no speeches. Afterwards, folks lingered on the neatly trimmed lawns, took pictures, and just sort of basked in the day.

That evening, about 7:15, I sat meditating on the small stone bench that sits along the east wall of the Portiuncula Chapel, allowing the day to run through me like a breeze through tall grass. I looked up for a moment and caught sight of a large bird flying overhead. I am a birdwatcher, and routinely judged it, by its size, to be a vulture - they occasionally fly over Mayslake. But they are unusual, so I reached for my binoculars to get a better look. The better look revealed not the ugly, featherless head of the vulture, but a head swathed in white, and a tail filled with white feathers as well. It was, without doubt, a bald eagle. Rare enough in the lower forty-eight states, it is extremely rare in the Chicago area, (they are occasionally sighted in the forest preserves of south Cook County), and I had never seen one near Mayslake. Excited, I stood and followed his wing-flapping flight across the Portiuncula Chapel. I watched him steer vaguely northwestward, calmly ignore the protective sallies of lesser birds, mingle with the great planes going in and out of O'Hare, and finally disappear into the evening haze.

The bald eagle is our national symbol. But at that moment I thought instead of the symbolism the Dakota (Sioux) Indians attach to the bald eagle. To them he is a symbol of the holy man, the one who flies between heaven and earth, bringing heaven to earth and earth to heaven. When the white man came with his Christian faith and black-robed holy men, they extended this symbolism to include the Catholic priest. Hanging on the wall of my office is a gift from a Dakota woman that expresses this. I had visited South Dakota on business in 1980. She learned of my business, and although she never met me, insisted on presenting me with this gift. It is a simple piece of red cloth, with a ring of mink fur in the middle symbolizing the earth and the unity of all things. From the middle of the ring of fur hangs a genuine tail feather from a bald eagle. It is the sign of the priest.

I thought of this as I watched in the wake of the now disappeared bird. Then I thought, "What a coincidence that the first time I see a bald eagle at Mayslake is a day on which we signally honor priesthood." Or, was it a sign?

This memory comes to me now as we experience a shift in our staff here at Mayslake. As many of you already know, Father Evan Eckhoff, O.F.M., leaves the staff of the retreat house in July. He is being replaced, not with another Franciscan priest, but with Franciscan Brother Clarence Klingert, O.F.M. We are grateful for the six years of ministry and hard work that Father Evan gave to the retreat house. As Business Manager, he was in great part responsible for professionalizing our operation. He created the first budget we ever had, computerized much of the operation, and was almost totally responsible for the enormous task of smoothly integrating Father Oliver's 45 years of experience into our front office. But I am sure what was most satisfying to him was the work he did as a priest - his leadership in designing the weekend program from year to year, his incisive talks widely appreciated by the men, his challenging spiritual direction, and his devoted work with Marriage Encounter, both in the Diocese of Joliet and around the country.

This priest will be replaced by a Brother, who will function both as Business Manager, and as member of the retreat staff. He is the first non-priest to occupy such a position at Mayslake. Brother Clarence comes well-equipped for both tasks. He has just finished six years as business manager for Hales Franciscan High School in Chicago. He served a term as assistant novice-master for our Franciscan Province. He was one of the first brothers in our Province to be appointed Superior of a Franciscan community (of both priests and brothers). He is well-grounded in theology and the human sciences, and has considerable experience in the art of spiritual direction.

But he isn't a priest. He is "just a Brother". And so we ask, gazing into the evening haze, "Has an eagle ceased to fly over Mayslake, and is he being replaced with, say, a common red-tailed hawk? Is Brother Clarence being brought on board just because there aren't enough priests to go around? Is Mayslake being shortchanged?" The whole Church is struggling with such questions these days as we witness more and more roles carried out by brothers, nuns, laypersons. The answer lies at two levels.

First, there is the simple fact that a large number of things priests have traditionally done do not require fourteen years of training and ordination. All of us priests have had this experience over and over again. We have trained servers, lead boy scout troops, taught catechism, headed up CYO, conducted fund drives, planned and built churches and schools, gotten degrees in Math and English, counseled the distraught and so on. I spent five years of my priesthood teaching speech and drama and putting on plays. Whenever we stepped back to look at what we actually ended up doing after we finished seminary, each of us asked himself, often doubtfully, "For this I was ordained?" Not everything a priest does, perhaps not even most of what he does is "priestly". So the first answer to these questions about whether a non-ordained person should be doing things priests customarily have done, is, "Why not?"

The second level of response lies deeper. It has to do not with how priests have traditionally practiced their ministry, but with how - and I assume with some humility that He does this - the Holy Spirit looks at the Church. Never has the Church taught that the work of the Spirit is restricted to those who are ordained. These have a unique ministry in the communication of the Spirit, but the Spirit is not bound to them. A classic example of this is that the Order to which Franciscans belong (and when you add up all its branches, it is the largest Order) was founded by someone who wasn't ordained. Francis of Assisi, later in his life, became a deacon, but it never made much difference to him, and it certainly wasn't because of this clerical status halfway to the priesthood that he was enabled to found the Order which bears his name. Most of the literally hundreds of communities of religious sisters and brothers which have had such a profound effect on the life of the Church were not founded by priests. Most of what theology and religion the average Catholic knows was not taught to him or her by priests but by religious sisters or brothers. Over half the several hundred retreat houses in the U.S.A. are run, not by priests, but by sisters, brothers, and an increasingly large number of lay people. The Spirit has clerical ways. It is clear also that He has non-clerical ways.

Willy-nilly, the Church is learning this lesson in our times. Many of the developments we are reading about these days - women religious and lay people who are not only parish ministers, but in some places even administrators of parishes - have indeed been prompted by the priest shortage. But there is a widely felt suspicion in respected circles that the priest shortage itself is in part the Holy Spirit's idea. Just, we may suppose, to remind us that He is not bound.

What of the eagle that flew over Mayslake the day of the jubilee? This year we shall carry on our ministry with a lay brother on our staff. And, at its end I shall be celebrating the silver jubilee of my own ordination. And I shall be sitting out on that stone bench again next May awaiting, nay fully expecting to see the eagle's return.

Jonathan Foster, O.F.M.

The Good Soil at Mayslake
Meadows of Ecumenism
Autumn 1984

Outside our front door there is a plastic bucket filled with sand, a depository for cigarette butts. The bucket has developed a rent along its side, and is slowly leaking sand. But the opening has also caught the fancy of a passing seed and now a bright green plant is growing up saucily from the side of the torn bucket. It is a parable of sorts.

The air is filled with far more seeds than we are usually aware of, a phenomenon that becomes particularly noticeable in the late Summer and Fall when most plants release pollen. The haze we associate with October and "Indian Summer" is simply a mist of seeds drifting aimlessly through the air looking for a place to take root. Most of them of course never find the right soil, but many do and manage to spring to life. Mayslake is filled with little clumps of life where seeds have found the particular soil they prefer. There is an old pile of spoiled fruit rinds - a compost of sorts - out in the middle of the Northeast Field, and a rich green outcropping of plants, including one majestic twelve foot sunflower, has prospered there, forming a thick island in the midst of the thinner grasses of the meadow. Tall, spiky and lovely purple loosestrife - a pilgrim from Europe - is rooting down in all the damp spots (and uprooting a lot of native grasses as it does so). A thickly studded pink-and-white wild rose bush blooms near the orchard quite unattended and quite unconceived by humans. Back in the thickets north of Third Lake we have suddenly seen flowering crab trees. Like the roses, no one knows where they came from. Volunteer sunflowers mass heavily in one part of the Northeast Field, but not in another. Dozens of cottonwoods are springing up in a marshy area near the Frontage Road, but only there, not elsewhere. Blue-flowering bull thistles make their prickly appearance wherever the soil has been disturbed. Cattails form a river of green and brown along the bottom of the summer-dried creek that drains Third Lake. Emerald green and soft grasses provide a luxuriant contrast to the cakey mud of the dried out Vernal Pond below the Portiuncula Chapel, obviously nursed to life when the pond was full. And the lawn, despite its regular manicuring, reluctantly hosts an increasing number of tough squatters - dandelions, sweet clover, heal-all, queen anne's lace, and chicory in party-blue dress.

These plants, in all their ecumenical variety, have one thing in common. They have grown to life where they found the earth and air to be hospitable. It reminds you of Jesus' parable about seed falling on good ground. Jesus may have been the son of a carpenter, but he was never very far from the countryside.

Another kind of life, more properly called ecumenical, also takes root at Mayslake. Theological and spiritual flora of many different shapes and hues dot the landscape of the Mayslake calendar. Just look at this calendar for the current year. We are, or will be hosting the following groups here to do their own programs: Northern Baptists, American Baptists; Lutherans from the Missouri Synod, from the Lutheran Church in America, and from the Evangelical Lutheran Church; fundamentalist Protestants, Episcopalians, Unitarian-Universalists, Presbyterians; Dignity (an organization of Catholic gays), Alcoholics Anonymous, women promoting breast-feeding (LaLeche League), the Midwest Organization for Religion and the Social Sciences; school staffs, Protestant and Catholic, black and white, city and suburban; Secular and First Order Franciscans, Brothers of the Holy Cross, Servites, White Fathers (African missionaries), and religious sisters from a variety of orders; charismatics, Hispanic parish groups, Catholic vocation directors, Protestant ministerial career planners, Catholic and Protestant seminarians, trustees of a Catholic seminary, hospital chaplains and therapists, and Presidents and Deans of every seminary in the Chicago area, Catholic and Protestant.

Why do we welcome all these groups? We are, after all, a retreat house not a conference center. The obvious reason, which everyone seems to understand, is that it helps to pay the bills. Indeed, it does, and I would be less than candid were I to suggest that this is not a motive for accepting such visitors. But as important as it is for us to sit with our retreatants like Mary and listen quietly to the Lord - and this is our primary mission - we believe it is also important for us to put on Martha's apron and help others do the same thing in their own way. There is an old Benedictine proverb, "Hospes, Christus" - the guest is Christ Himself - and I do not think the Benedictines mind if we appropriate to our own activity this wonderful statement of Christian charity.

There are some who, admitting this, raise an eyebrow at the fact that we allow groups, whose theological and moral beliefs are not always in agreement with ours, to use our facilities, our Catholic facilities. First, it must be understood that to host a group is not to sponsor it, that is, does not constitute an approval of their beliefs and practices. Second, it must be remembered that we are Catholic, and that to be Catholic is more than just wearing a religious name tag. "Catholic" means Universal, inclusive, reaching out to all peoples. Hence in the ecumenical spirit of Christian fellowship, we rarely require a theological or moral means test from groups that seek bed and board with us. If our soil will help them to grow in their love of God and their fellow-human beings, then they are welcome to sink their roots into it.

Illinois is called the "Prairie State". A prairie is not just any field or meadow, much less what Chicagoans have always called it, a mere empty lot full of weeds. A prairie is a distinctive and rich complex of a variety of grasses and flowers and trees. There isn't much original prairie left in Illinois, less than one percent of the original, they tell us. But I have walked original prairie, both in undisturbed lands out West, and in restored prairies such as the 1,700 acres in the Morton Arboretum. Their variety and colors are surprising, beautiful. Our grounds, while not original prairie, provide the right kind of soils to support an amazing variety of life. Mayslake Retreat House is like that prairie, providing the good soil for a stimulating and endlessly exciting meadow of ecumenism. Our Lord, who called our attention to the lilies of the field, is, I am sure, very pleased.

The Weed Perspective
Thanksgiving/Christmas 1984

The Village of Oak Brook may be issuing us a citation any day now. We didn't mow our fields this year, and an ordinance requires us to do it at least once, preferably around the first of August, before everything goes to seed. We didn't get around to it this year, mostly because we were shorthanded; but partly because some of us, at least the director of the retreat house, are a little curious as to what happens when you just let things grow up. We are not insensitive to the sufferings of those with hay fever, since two of the friars on the staff sink into this sneezing, weepy - eyed and heavily medicated phase every August. But we are not entirely convinced either that a meadow can just be written off by referring to it, as the village ordinance does, as "noxious weeds".

There are certain wild plants that do indeed provide a nuisance for humankind, and so have come to merit the unflattering name of "weeds". Crop damage from such plants is estimated annually to cost five billion dollars, and that is a very conservative figure. Consequently, the making of herbicides is a major industry. Millions of people suffer every year from allergies stirred up by the aggressive procreative tactics of weeds, and another major industry has grown up servicing these unfortunate bodies. And then there are those that hate weeds because of what they do to lawns. This of course is a matter of taste - and who is to judge about taste? But many millions of Americans are committed to the aesthetic perspective that a vast stretch of uniform grass is one of the ultimate scenic views. And there is another major industry that supports this endless struggle for the perfect lawn.

Despite all this, there is something to be said for "weeds". Biologists praise them because their sturdiness and resourcefulness make them the first plants to grip and hold the soil after floods, fire, or other natural disasters. They are called "pioneers" and without them, our weak - sister cultivated plants would have little to grow in. Weeds also, in a rough kind of poetic justice, make recompense for the misery they inflict by providing certain drugs and medicines for human beings. Moreover, many of these plants provide both food for humans (dandelion greens, ironically, being one of the most desirable of such "weeds") and especially forage for birds and wild animals. Our uncut fields this Fall sported the best looking asters I have ever seen around here. Little cottonwood (poplar) saplings are springing up all over the place. I saw some red berries that I have never seen before. And the fields were thick and deep with crumpled old queen anne's lace and goldenrod that provided cover, the last time I was out there, for a large band of migrating yellow rump warblers.

So, whether a plant is a weed or not depends on your perspective. If your perspective is entirely utilitarian and commercial, then anything that doesn't contribute to the economy or is in any way dysfunctional to human comfort is a weed and may be dealt with summarily. The same "weed perspective" extends to other forms of life as well. I am constantly amused by a large encyclopedia I own describing all the birds of North America. It was first published, long before the environmental movement, in 1917, when the relatively few lovers of wildlife for its own sake were forced constantly to apologize for their passion by demonstrating its usefulness to society, especially economic usefulness. And so, this book carefully documents the economic value of every bird, often by describing the contents of a bird's sliced open stomach to count what pestiferous insect or seed it had consumed.

This somewhat crass and human-centered view of the world around us is bad enough. But the 'weed perspective', tragically, extends to human beings as well. If a given group of people is not useful to the well-being of whatever group is in charge of things, or is a nuisance of any kind - economic, racial, philosophical, or theological, then it is helpful if we can consider them as "weeds" and dispose of them accordingly. The largest crop of people-become-weeds of course is that lost to the terrible human herbicide of abortion-on-demand. More than a million lives annually are cut down to smooth the way of those for whom the existence of these infants would be inconvenient clutter. Something similar may be said of the desperately poor. We reduce them to weeds when we simply write them off as lazy, irresponsible leeches expecting the government to take care of them. I encountered a phrase recently that I find profoundly unsettling. Economists are beginning to speak of a portion of our population as 'naturally unemployable'. These are those people, given the economic structure of the country, that may never expect to have meaningful and responsible work. I suppose the phrase itself isn't all that bad, since there are people physically or emotionally incapable of work who are 'naturally unemployable'. What is disturbing is that the figure assigned to this group is in the range of 6-7% of the total workforce! That is close to the current levels of unemployment in this country, and just about double what just a few years ago used to be considered the highest level of "acceptable" unemployment. It is convenient to reduce human beings to weeds by describing them as "naturally unemployable" - that is, useless to society. And if this is true here in the prosperous U.S.A., how much greater is the indignity in those fourth-world countries of teeming populations where actual, let alone "natural", unemployment runs as high as 25-30%. The weed fields of the world are growing.

Christians of course cannot take the 'weed' perspective on anything. Oh, I suppose we can tolerate it when it comes to dandelions, but it is absolutely intolerable when someone who professes to be a friend of Jesus reduces anyone or any group to weeds. We are celebrating Christmas soon. We have so gussied up the feast that we tend to forget what kind of people they were to whom the birth of Jesus was first announced. They were shepherds; rough, crude, coarse folk, occupying the lowest rung of the social ladder, possessing about the same degree of social acceptance as illegal migrants from Mexico. Economically useful (if exploitable) but socially weeds. But these were the first to see the Incarnate God, and the rest of the world's acceptable people had, for once, to stand in line and wait their turn. This selectivity means a lot of things, but one of its meanings is that God does not have a "weed perspective". Everyone out there counts, not in terms of their usefulness to another part of society, but strictly by their own lights.

In October, I went out and waded in our uncut fields. I shouldn't have been wearing a good pair of slacks and shoes because I came in with my socks and the lower lengths of my pants festooned with wild seeds. I tried to brush them off with my hand, and they resisted. I got a clothes brush, but that didn't work either. I pulled one of the seeds off and looked at it. It had three little hook-shaped tines that had fastened themselves firmly in the fabric. Nothing would do but that I had to pull each of more than a hundred seeds off my clothing one by one. A good lesson about the weed perspective. Like each of those determined little seeds, every human being has to be taken on individually. You can't take a clothes brush to them and dispose of them in large numbers. That's the weed perspective. The perspective of Jesus Christ is to take each of them individually. Jesus taught that, to his Father, each of us is like a common sparrow, not one of which falls to the ground without his knowledge. If sparrows are that important to God, surely no one can ever be considered a weed.

Jonathan Foster, O.F.M.

Get the Hell Off My Property!
Some Reflections on the Bishops' Pastoral on the Economy
Winter 1985

For sixteen of the past eighteen years, I have lived at one or another of the three Franciscan friaries on the Mayslake campus. For well over half those years, I have been jogging around its grounds, gradually establishing my own preferred trail. One of the favored parts of that trail is a foot-and-weather-worn strip of asphalt that runs under a long canopy of maples, oaks and poplars lining the south bank of what we have always called First Lake, the part of the retreat house lake south of the bridge. The Franciscans sold off that part of my trail a number of years ago. But, since there was no construction going up there, and because nobody had put up any "No Trespassing" signs, I continued to run there. Early this past Fall, however, an imposing looking house began to rise on the low ridge above the trail. I kept on running. One day - the house was near completion, but no one had moved in - I was doing my regular late afternoon run. Suddenly, from up on the ridge, from deep within the new house, came a loud, growly, deeply masculine voice: "Get the hell off my property." I stopped, startled. I looked around for a face, waited for a repeat of the warning, or for an angry figure to come charging out of the building. Nothing. I walked around to the side of the building for another look. Nothing. Silence. It was as though the voice had come from a tape recording whose switch I had tripped as I ran by, and which now had lapsed into sullen mechanical silence.

I was immediately aware of two very strong feelings. First, I was angry at the man's rudeness. He could have been more pleasant. When I kick innocent trespassers off the retreat house grounds, I am always polite. He also might have had the courage to present to me more than his voice.

The second feeling boiled to the surface out of a long resentment I have had over the sale of this property. I suddenly had an intense desire to tell him who I was, that I had walked or run this trail times beyond counting, long before, I was sure, he had even heard of it; that I knew all the birds that nested there, and that it was right in front of his house that I would regularly spot the first migrating warbler in the cool spring; that I knew where the woodchucks denned in the slope below his house; that I loved how the poplars throw down a soft skin of cotton on the water each Spring and a splendid gold carpet each Fall; that, in a sense, this was my land, and that I resented him being there. I wanted to tell him that, yes, I would stop jogging on his property, but that this would be a painful separation for me.

I never saw or met the man. I ran that trail a few more times, but then as his house rounded into completion, and the family began showing up, I reluctantly chose another route. But I have come to one conclusion since then - both he and I were wrong. The Franciscans owned that land for a long time, and I had lived on it for a long time and loved it very much, even developed a proprietary interest in it. But, I don't own it, and had no right to react to my growly friend the way I did. But he doesn't own it either. He bought it from the developer, who in turn bought it from the Franciscans. His claims will clearly hold up in court, and he can kick trespassers like me off any time he wishes. But, it still isn't his. Not, at least, the way Catholics understand ownership.

Catholic social thought, contrary to what radical socialists and communists teach, has always taught that human beings have a right to private property. But she has also taught, contrary to what radical capitalists think, that this right is not absolute, and that it is subject to the requirements of the common good. And so, like the American constitution, the Church has always supported taxation, the right of eminent domain, etc.

But, if the private citizen doesn't hold the land outright, who does? The Indians used to say, "Nobody." Others say, "The State." The Church says, "God." He gives us the land, but never outright. We hold it only in stewardship. Which means that we have to be careful with it, and even share it with others. Someday we shall have to give it back to God, and, like the stewards in the Gospel, He will want to know what we did with it. One of the things He will want to know is how we shared it.

It is in this spirit that we have to read and study the current message of the American Bishops on the American economy. A lot of people (including most Catholics, it appears) have already written it off. The favored write-off is that it is simply a rehash of a "New

Deal/Great Society/Welfare Liberalism" that besides being quite out of keeping with the euphoria experienced in America today, hasn't really worked anyway. Some have even more unfairly labelled it as socialism in disguise. The Pastoral fits none of these descriptions of course. It is rather an appeal to the whole of society - business, labor and government - to collaborate in guaranteeing to all elements of society the economic rights that are theirs. The way the Bishops put it is that one of the principal elements of any economic policy is that there must be a "preferential option for the poor". To be specific, the bishops assert that no economic policy is justifiable which tolerates high levels of unemployment (currently twice as high as our legislated national policy requires), and which leaves almost one American in six living in poverty. That's a lot of people (35-40,000,000 in fact) being kicked out of the American dream.

Now of course even those who disagree with the Bishops do not view this sad situation with apathy. They too want unemployment relieved and poverty reduced. But they think it can be done if you just leave folks free to exercise their creative and entrepreneurial energies. This applies particularly to the marketplace. Don't regulate it, don't add new taxes, don't create burdensome governmental programs, don't be so generous with welfare. Let the "free market" do it all. The "free market" will make bigger pies so everybody will get bigger pieces. The tide will lift all boats, the little ones as well as the big ones. And so through the magic of the free market, everyone will have jobs and poverty will disappear. And if it doesn't, well, the goodwill of the private sector will pick up the pieces. Any other economic view, including that of the Bishops, smells just a little too much like communism.

The trouble with this viewpoint is that it is not realistic about the human race. What it assumes is a fairness and decency about human beings that simply doesn't exist. Given that kind of decency, I'm sure a free market economy would enlarge all pies and lift all boats. But the Catholic Church knows better, and has from the very beginning, that this is not the case with human beings. With her knowledge of the sons and daughters of God, she has steadfastly proclaimed the doctrine of original sin. This teaching reflects the shadow side of humanity, its inclination to greed and selfishness, its inability by itself to redeem itself. The doctrine of original sin teaches that humankind needs help to save itself from itself, and that this help is available from God, who in Christ Jesus offers humanity salvation.

It is out of this doctrine of human weakness overcome by divine grace that the Bishops teach. They suggest, first, that they, as teachers of Christian faith, have both a right and an obligation to speak out on the moral issues of the economy. They suggest, second, that we are simply going to have to allow considerable intervention by the state in the running of the economy. There are those who instinctively react to this with cries of "Socialism", or "Welfare State". But such criticisms are simply out of place. Nowhere does the bishops' pastoral call for the state to run the economy. They only call for collaboration between state, industry, and labor in working out the inequities of the economic system. Though it may sound so to many after the recent presidential election, this is not such a radical statement after all. For it simply continues the realism that every successful nation in the world, including ours, has followed in recent decades, a realism that recognizes that no simple answer, neither that of communism nor that of the free market economy, is going to solve the enormously complex economic problems of the world. But, more to the point, it is a realism which recognizes that, in our permanent state of original sin, justice is not one of the outstanding virtues of the human race, and that we all need a little stick-waving from both church and state to make sure we do with God's property what we are supposed to do.

I guess what I fear most of all is that if we let this theological faith - for that is what it is - in the free market economy follow its own lead (or "invisible hand"), what we shall have is not more justice, but just a lot more guys, like the one who lives on 'my' jogging trail, gruffly ordering the poor to "get the hell off my property."

Jonathan Foster, O.F.M.

Are Those Cardinals Singing?
The Bishops' Synod and the Abuses of Vatican II
Lent/Easter 1985

By the time you read this, most of you can open your window, stick your head out at almost any time of the day and hear cardinals flinging their chant to the sky. But I am writing this piece in the middle of February, when the land is drifted deep with snow, and great dunes circle gracefully about the trees and buildings, driven by northerly winds that make most of our north-facing offices a little too chilly for comfort. Cardinals, oblivious to the cold, and reacting instead to the steadily lengthening of daylight, usually start singing about this time of the year. But right now at Mayslake there is a difference of opinion on this. Fr. Kieran swears he has heard them already on his side of the building. He lives on the side of the building facing south and east where all the sun is, and I live on the cold, shadowy north side. But I also get out and run several times a week, and I haven't heard any cardinals. All I've heard is the whistling of starlings. Now starlings are pretty good mimics and can do a fair imitation of cardinals. So, I insist that what Fr. Kieran is hearing is starlings, but he persists with his cardinals. So far the argument hasn't been settled. And part of the reason is that the two of us have not made the effort to listen to the same bird at the same time.

I thought of this standoff as I reflected on reactions to the recent announcement by Pope John Paul that there will be a special gathering of bishops (a synod) this Fall to review the work of Vatican II. It isn't clear why he is doing this. It is of course an appropriate time, since December 8, 1985, marks the 20th anniversary of the closing of Vatican II. A lot of people, however, are greeting this announcement with some relief, since they view the Pope's action as an attempt to stop all the craziness that has gone on in the Church in the past two decades, a move to bring to an end all the "abuses" of Vatican II, and get us back to sanity.

Although nobody appears to really know what the Pope is up to on this one, I would like to suggest that it may very well be time to correct the "abuses" of Vatican II. We can't treat all of these abuses here, but we can at least indicate some general directions. They fall roughly into two categories.

The first category of abuses includes those excesses that clearly go beyond the intent and power of the Council. In the area of liturgy they include: clandestine celebrations of Mass by women angry at the Church's refusal to ordain both sexes; rash assertions that there is no longer an obligation for Catholics to worship on Sunday; the denial of the need to partake of the Sacrament of Reconciliation ("go to confession") and the unauthorized use of general absolution; indiscriminate intercommunion with non-Catholics; and so forth. In the area of doctrine, these abuses include outright rejections of clearly defined teachings of the Church, such as the possibility of eternal separation from God ("Hell"), the reality of original sin, and the teaching authority of the Church. In areas of social and moral behavior there are such abuses as the advocacy - indeed practice - of violence for other than self-defense in the achievement of social purposes; making light of sexual promiscuity and marital infidelity, even, in some instances, the advocacy and practice of abortion. All of these and other abuses have at various times been put forth in the name of Vatican II.

Many Catholics object to these abuses - and rightly so - on the grounds that they attack the roots and traditions of Catholicism. They have moreover noted with some satisfaction a number of recent developments in the Church that seem to be aimed at correcting these abuses - stripping theologian, Hans Küng, of the title "Catholic Theologian"; the withdrawal of official approval from Fr. Wilhelm's popular catechism; the ultimata delivered to the American nuns supporting free choice on abortion, and the Nicaraguan priests political activity in their country; the abrupt and almost total withdrawal of dispensations for Catholic priests requesting laicization; the Pope's attacks on "liberation theology" and the recent restoration of the Tridentine (Latin) Mass. It looks like a trend and many see the upcoming Synod as a welcome climax and formalization of that trend. The abuses, they hope, will come to an end.

But all of this represents only one category of the abuses of Vatican II. The second is probably even more widespread than the first, for it encompasses the widespread refusal of many Catholics to accept large parts, even the whole, of Vatican II. As with the abuses of the first kind, these are far too numerous to list comprehensively. I'll mention just four areas.

First, the social teachings of the Church. A lot of Catholics have dismissed the recent pastorals by the American bishops on the nuclear arms race and the economy. They have objected both to the content of these documents and to the bishops' right to speak out on the issues. What these same Catholics probably do not realize is that both this right and this content - though in lesser detail - are clearly outlined in the Constitution on the Church in the World (*Gaudium et Spes*), one of the key documents of Vatican II. Many Catholics, too, persist in denying to women, both within and outside the Church, the full equality guaranteed them by Vatican II.

Perhaps the most vigorous objections to Vatican II have come in the area of worship. What parish does not have its horror story about attempts to block the implementation of Vatican II in its worship? Such opposition has come unfortunately, not only from the laity, but from many clergy as well. To this day, there continues widespread, sullen opposition to Vatican II over liturgy, opposition that sometimes becomes very active, both overt and guerrilla-style.

Another area of non-acceptance has been that of lay leadership. Clearly called for by the Council, many clergy have rejected it because it is a threat to their power, and many lay people have refused it, and, where they have found it, fought against it, yearning instead, it seems, for the familiar clericalism of the past. An interesting aspect of this area of abuse is the objection of many Catholics to the Bishops using their "pulpit" to speak out against the evils of nuclear arms and an economy that neglects the poor. Many of these same lay persons, appealing to worn out old cliches such as "business is business", "war is hell", or, worst of all, "let's keep religion out of politics", completely disassociate themselves from the responsibility for reshaping the social order, a responsibility, which the Council makes clear, is primarily theirs, not the clergy.

Finally, the documents of Vatican II are rooted in the Scriptures - as all Church renewal must be - and lay down an eloquent mandate to Catholics to become steeped in the Scriptures: "In this way, therefore, through the reading and study of the sacred books, let the 'word of the Lord run and be glorified.' Just as the life of the Church grows through persistent participation in the Eucharistic mystery, so we may hope for a new surge of spiritual vitality from intensified veneration for God's word, which lasts forever." (Dogmatic Constitution on Divine Revelation, n. 26). If this simple, uncontroversial mandate to use the Bible is any indicator of the enthusiasm with which Catholics have accepted Vatican II, then it appears we are indeed in need of correcting abuses. In a series of studies in 1981, 1982 and 1983, by the Princeton Research Center, it was discovered that only 7% of American Catholics read the Bible every day, only 9% are involved in some kind of Bible study program, and only 24% read it at all. It comes as no surprise, then, to learn that only one American teenager in three could even name the four gospels, the four evangelists, and identify Easter! So much for the excesses of Vatican II!

What then is my hope for the Bishops' synod this Fall? It has something to do with hearing the cardinal sing. Fr. Kieran and I disagreed over what bird we heard, because we listened only from our respective sides of the building. Had we gone out together, stood under the same tree, and listened to the same bird, we might have both agreed on what we heard. The synod should be like that. Everybody has some feelings about the Council, and whether the Church has been faithful to it. But it's quite possible to be so preoccupied with the north side of the building that you fail to hear what's happening on the south side. There have been abuses of Vatican II, some by excess, some by neglect and rejection. We need people hearing both songs to stand together under the same tree. The song is Vatican II - all of it! That's my hope for the Bishops' synod.

The Wind Comes Through Open Windows
Reflections of a Silver Jubilarian
Spring 1985

It is a week after Easter as I write, and we have not opened our windows since November. We have steam heat here at Mayslake, so the air inside my office during the cold months is often close and heavy. I sweat gently from sitting too close to the radiator, and the air seizes and holds captive the remains of smoke from the few cigarettes I still consume as I struggle to quit. The windows of course get dirty. We long for open windows and even though it is 70 degrees today, we still have our storm windows up. April weather is dicey in Chicago.

I think of open windows as I reflect back on the twenty-five years of priesthood that I will celebrate this June. In 1959, with the felicitous phrase that he was "throwing open the windows", Pope John XXIII announced the convocation of the Second Vatican Council. That breeze was tugging at the windows as we received the Church's commission to ministry in the priesthood from exiled Chinese missionary, Bishop Ambrose Pinger, O.F.M., on June 24, 1960.

But the Catholic church that I was raised in, the Catholic church in which I prepared for religious life and priesthood, and, because the Council did not finally open till 1962, the Church in which I was actually ordained, resembled much more a storm-windowed office of winter than it did a breeze-filled office of Springtime. It was a comfortable church, but clubby. I loved it, and accepted everything it taught me, did what it told me, even what it merely suggested I do. I was taught to believe, and firmly did so, that the Catholic Church was the one true Church. That of course made us better than anyone else, and gave me an unhealthy tendency to be judgmental in an unkind way about anything and anybody that wasn't Catholic, and uncritical about anything and anyone that was. Consequently, I was suspicious of Protestants because they had "left" the one true Church. If that was not a blind and ignorant act, it was at least graceless. I was condescending towards religions that were not part of my culture - Muslims, Jews, oriental religions, even the Orthodox Catholics, whose complex and mystifying rites I snickered through on the few occasions I was exposed to them. Everyone else I lumped together as pagans - our generic name for non-Christians. I granted their sincerity, but to me they were simply childish and benighted.

But, most of all I counted Catholics. Though assured by my catechisms that the Catholic Church was the one true Church, I needed more proof. I sought that proof in numbers. Surely, if Catholics formed the largest religion in the world and claimed an increasing share of the world's population, then, though not everyone was

Catholic yet, we were getting there, and that was proof to me of the truth of the Church and its universality. And so I urged the missionaries and the convert-makers on. I rejoiced in famous people who became Catholics, like Clare Booth Luce and the whole flock of celebrities brought in by Fulton J. Sheen. They functioned for my Catholicism much the way endorsements by famous athletes function for automobiles. I took a special delight in counting as Catholics artists, writers and political figures, as though the literary successes of Catholics like Evelyn Waugh and Graham Greene were a special proof of the truth of the Church. This effort took some rather bizarre turns. I recall a college text we used called "The Catholic Literary Revival," which very straight-facedly included the works of Oscar Wilde. Now Mr. Wilde spent most of his life in sybaritic pursuits, was jailed for sexual perversion, died in despair, and wrote almost nothing that reflected the traditions of the Church. But, he was a Catholic, and so he got counted. As a college student, I defended Senator Joe McCarthy, in part because we were all fervid anti-Communists in those days, but in part just because Joe was a Catholic. The climax of all this affirmation of the one true faith was for me, as it was for many Catholics, the election of Catholic John Kennedy to the presidency in 1960. It was the year of my ordination. The Church had arrived.

My church was Catholic, mainly because it was big. But that kind of bigness does not constitute "universal", which is the real meaning of "Catholic". It just made the Church a big club, carefully measuring the "ins" and the "outs" and looking down on all the latter.

It was into this clubby Catholic world that Pope John opened the windows to let in the fresh air. When I finally open my windows in the springtime, the air immediately becomes fresh, and the sweat from sitting too close to the radiator dries off. The sounds of the out-of-doors are no longer muffled, distant, apart from my world, but the shrills of the redwing, the honking and barking of the geese, the chirping of insects, the sway and rustle of leaves and branches become a real and intimate part of my life. The world suddenly gets much larger. So it was for me with Vatican II.

Vatican II accompanied my entry into the priesthood. When it was announced by Pope John in 1959, I was studying theology. When I was ordained in 1960, preparations were going speedily forward. And the year I began my first assignment at St. Francis Academy in Joliet, 1962, the Council officially opened. I found myself, despite my closed Catholic upbringing, to be eminently prepared and eager for its unfolding. I was, it turned out, like the parched earth of the Bible, ready for its welcome rains and breezes. And so I followed its developments with the same daily compulsion with which I pursued the fortunes of my beloved Detroit Tigers. For many years I kept in my files - I can't find it now - the first page of an edition of the old Denver Register announcing the promulgation of the first conciliar document, the one on liturgy. On that page, in bold headlines of the kind you only see when a war starts or ends, was the thrilling announcement: "LATIN YIELDS." Almost everything the Council did pleased me, or, if it didn't, displeased me only because it didn't go far enough. I found emerging from these documents a Church that was truly universal because it could embrace all cultures and respect all beliefs. It was a Church that could continue to be confident of the Lord's presence in its midst, yet be humble enough to admit its mistakes and shortcomings. I found it to be incarnate, as Jesus was, not closing windows on this world, but deeply involved, especially in its commitments to justice, and renewing the social order. It was a Church in which I did not need to waste time counting members, adding up dignitaries, proving we were better than everyone else in every respect, and not having to awkwardly justify its every action, even those that did not deserve it. It had ceased being a club and had become a Church.

Vatican II has however been a mixed blessing for me. It brought a lot of the craziness of the kind that accompanies any radical change, much of which I found offensive and un-Christian. I found, for example, a lot of insensitivity to the traditions of the past, and especially to people who lived by these traditions. I found people who had rebelled against the rigidities of the old binding themselves up in the rigidities of the new. I found it ironic that a new spirit of openness to the world should breed such a closed mind to the past. I also experienced the pain of seeing so many of those I was ordained with leave the priesthood, a temptation that pulled at me as well. Of a class of nineteen ordained in 1960, only eight remain to celebrate our silver jubilee. My best friends were among those that left. But those pains and anxieties have healed, and I count them the coin one must pay to grow as the Church grows. When you open the windows, you get besides the song of birds a lot of dust and traffic noises.

The shape of the Church that has been emerging since Vatican II is "Catholic" in the sense that St. Paul understood the Church. He didn't use the word, Catholic, but he knew what Jesus was talking about. Paul vigorously withstood elements of the Church - including Peter himself - that would have tied it tightly to its Jewish past and made it little more than an interesting new cult of Judaism centered around Jesus - a clubby little affair. Paul bullied the early Church into its universal mission. He told the Galatians, in the same letter in which he reports how he told Peter off for his narrow-mindedness, that there can be no smallness in the Church of Christ. "There are no more distinctions," he wrote, "between Jew and Greek, slave and free, male and female, but all of you are one in Christ" (Galatians 3:28). The Church that is Catholic, therefore, is to include all cultures, "Jew and Greek", "slave and free"; it should include, indeed, ignore all economic classes; "male and female;" it is not to discriminate on the basis of sex.

This is the Church as it matures through the experience of Vatican II. It is a Church that has the universal, Catholic might of the pentecostal experience, when the Holy Spirit broke into the fear-locked Upper Room, burned away the disciples' mustiness and, through them, gathered into the Church people from every nation under the sun. It is a Church that keeps itself standing in Pentecostal winds.

Jesus tells us that the worst sins are those against the Holy Spirit (Mark 3:29). So it is that any attempts to make the Church small, culture-bound or time-bound, to make it exclusive rather than inclusive, discriminatory rather than humble and respectful, are in my mind sins against the Holy Spirit. For such sins close the windows, turn up the heat, and cause us to huddle close to the radiator. Cozy and safe such a Church may appear, but the air inside is still and close. The great winds of Pentecost are not allowed in.

Although raised and trained in a Church that was reluctant to leave the window open, I am proud to serve a Church 25 years later that has in the end allowed the Holy Spirit in. That is the Church I am priest for. I want, I need the Holy Wind inside the Church, not out there where I can't feel it.

From Cornfield to Prairie
A Brief Look at the Future of Mayslake
Autumn 1986

Ten years ago when you looked out at the fields north and east of the retreat house buildings, you saw a much different scene than what you see now. Then you would have seen corn. Just corn. Or, depending on the year, soybeans. Agricultural economists have a name for it -- monoculture, growing just one crop. It is widely practiced by farmers today, and it is economically sound. But, it is hell-to-pay for the soil. Excessive planting of one crop quickly exhausts the soil, and the only way it can be restored is to douse the earth with a lot of artificial fertilizers. Monoculture also runs the risk of not being flexible enough to meet the changing needs and demands of the market.

The same fields today present a far different, indeed far more complex picture. A seasonal pond swells and shrinks with the run-off from the rains and at its edge there stands, like a sentinel, a lone black willow, its rooted feet often covered with water. A creek, also seasonal, drains Third Lake out across 31st Street into

Ginger Creek, thence into Salt Creek and the Des Plaines River. The pond flooring is decked with a rich emerald tangle of moisture-loving plants, and even a few saplings have taken root. The creek is clogged with cattails and weeping willow saplings that almost obscure its brownish flow. Off on the ridge that bisects the northeast field stands a small grove of young poplars promising a new woods at Mayslake. Heather, fortuitously escaped from some expressway planting, has crept along the entire length of the creek from 31st Street nearly to Third Lake. Three years ago, Brother Otto planted yellow clover to provide browse for his bees at St. Paschal, and their volunteer descendants scatter brightly throughout the field. Milkweed, golden rod, and aster have seized their portion of the land, and there is even a cluster of shy wild iris hiding in a damp spot closer to the woods. Most dramatically, where corn once stood now a stand of restored Illinois prairie plants - turkey-foot, tickseed, compass, spiderwort, lead-plant, dropseed - begin to take firm root under the nurturing hand of volunteer Conrad Fialkowski.

It is a lot different from corn or soybeans. I think it's a lot more interesting. It invites a walk, and so this past summer we ran a woodchip path out into this field, and we have plans to extend it even further. As I walk this spongy path, this field suggests to me other developments taking place here at Mayslake.

As most of you know, the attendance at the weekend program for men has been declining steadily. This has been going on for over 20 years to be precise, but in recent years it has declined rather sharply. There are a lot of reasons for this. Some have to do with loyalty and tradition; some have to do with the way the retreat house is run; some have to do with conflicting ideas about religion; some have to do with cost; some have to do with the simple fact of illness, death, and retirement of veteran retreatants; and some are due to increased competition from other retreat programs and retreat houses. But at the bottom of this stack of reasons remains the steady decline. And when you consider that for much of its history this was the only program Mayslake did - a kind of ministerial monoculture -- you will realize how much damage such a decline does to an institution's morale.

Consequently, this past year we undertook the rather ambitious task of trying to find out if there will continue to be enough Catholics out there interested in attending these kinds of retreats to justify the great amount of effort that we put into them. We hired an expert and spent a lot of money and time on a study to see if we could get a grasp on the problem. The study is now complete, the reports written (and being snapped up by other retreat houses at $15 a copy). I'd like to share some of the findings of this study with you. You will find that the Mayslake of the future will look more like our current fields than the cornfields of the past.

The most important question that concerned us was what kind of future the weekend retreat for men seemed to have. What we discovered is that the kind of retreat we offer does indeed have a future, but that it shares that future almost equally with the other emerging styles of retreats such as Marriage Encounter, Cursillo, Christ Renews His Parish, and other experiences that focus on a lot of group dynamics. We were heartened at this response, but sobered to realize that the days when the weekend retreat for men monopolized Mayslake appear to be gone.

There were some issues everyone agreed on whether they favored the traditional style of retreat or not. Thus, what almost everybody wants most out of a retreat is to spend time alone with God, to strengthen their faith, and to deepen their own understanding of themselves. To achieve this, what everyone wants most of all is good presentations by the retreat directors and good worship - especially the Eucharist and the Sacrament of Reconciliation.

Even among those who want the kind of retreat we give, many evidence a strong preference for some significant changes in that model, i.e., having both men and women present; for having not only priests give the retreat, but lay persons and sisters as well; and the elimination of the rule of absolute silence (e.g., allowing conversation at some meals). The overwhelming majority of those in the study who make retreats at Mayslake now, however, don't favor these changes.

There is a lot more information in the study, and those interested are welcome to review the findings. The question now is what we are to do about what we've learned. First, we're getting reactions to them. The staff here at the retreat house, the Board of Directors, the governing council of the Franciscan Province of the Sacred Heart which owns Mayslake, and a group of weekend sponsors have all been consulted for their reaction. (Needless to say, I would be glad to hear from any of you concerning any of the findings cited above.)

Second, out of all this consultation will come some long-range planning. This will be done over the next months, and I hope to have something ready by mid-January. At the core of this planning will, of course, be the weekend program for men, reduced somewhat, but nonetheless central.

In the meantime, some new programs which suggest part of what Mayslake will look like in the future are already coming into view. These new retreats develop an understanding that Fr. Oliver had about how to make retreat houses work - collaboration. Fr. Oliver worked closely with other groups in bringing various groups of men (and later women) to Mayslake: the labor unions, the Knights of Columbus, Holy Name Societies, various businesses, the Secular Franciscans and others. What we are adding to his insight is to bring the collaborators into the actual planning and presentation of the retreat. Following this formula, we have already been working with Alcoholics Anonymous in collaborating on two retreats annually for recovering alcoholics. Last year we began working with the Office of Young Adult Ministry in Chicago to provide retreats for 20 to 35-year-olds (that effort alone brought 114 young adults to one weekend in March, and it will be repeated this year). This year we have been working with the Office of Family Ministry of the Joliet Diocese in designing our retreats for married couples. We are currently in the early stages of planning with the National Center for the Laity in presenting a retreat; in April on themes of lay spirituality, especially as it affects their work and professional life; and with the administration of Queen of Peace High School planning an overnight retreat for their administrators and faculty. We are also talking to the Chicago Federation of the Christian Family Movement and the Deacons of the Joliet Diocese about possible collaborative retreat programs. These are all people who would not be likely to attend the regular weekend program.

Consequently, Mayslake is already beginning to look like its fields, a lot of variety, not just corn, and will probably look a lot more like them in the future.

I referred to the new path we put in last summer to entice people out into our changing fields. The path first encircles the ridge east of the main building (a ridge I've always called Cardinal Ridge because so many of these birds make it their home), and this provides a natural, prayerful space for the relocated stations of the cross. A larger loop leads from there out into the open fields where the iris nod and the milkweed blow. Not many of our guests walk it as yet. One of our very urban retreatants who recently did, described it as a "wilderness", and said, "You could get lost out there." Well, it isn't and you couldn't. I know because I run it four or five times a week. But I'd like to see more of you take that trek out into those unfamiliar fields. As you do, keep in mind that what I have outlined above about the future of Mayslake are the beginnings of a new trail for the retreat movement, one that will continue to visit and celebrate all that is familiar and traditional about Mayslake, but which will be decorated with a lot of new plants and flowers as well. Come, take a walk with us!

A Fox in the Swale
Winter 1987

Last November, as winter struggled to supplant fall, a light fog drifted over the land. Taking a break from my office, I went and stood by the glass door that looks out onto Second Lake. Towards the far side of the lake there hung at water's edge a large white shape. Indistinct in the mist, reflecting whitely in the water, it seemed as large as, say, a swan. Motionless in still water, it seemed ghostly. I fetched binoculars and looked more intently. The white shape turned out to be neither swan nor ghost, but a common ring-billed gull, the kind that regularly swing by here for a bite of our carp. But the mix of mist obscuring his background and still water catching his reflection made him for a moment seem larger than he really was. For a moment, I was on a moor in a Scott novel or a quiet harbor in a Winslow painting; I was anywhere but Mayslake in the midst of suburbia.

The gull in the fog recalled for me other times when events in the cycle of nature have helped me forget where I am, or, perhaps better, to remember where I really am.

Often heavy rain and overcast does it. It blots out the lights and muffles the noises of Oak Brook, and brings me deeply to the center of the land, gives me, if just for a moment, a drink of the "tonic of wildness" that Thoreau wrote of. I remember Easter Sunday in 1983. It had rained for days, streams rushed wildly, lakes swelled, brimmed, overflowed, ponds sat everywhere on the grounds. The sky, drawn and exhausted from spilling rain that night, still hung a low overcast over the land and pulled in all around me like a gray tent. No one was up as yet - it was before nine on a Sunday - so even the highway offered only the occasional hum of a passing car.

I plunged out into all this, soaking my feet in cold spring rain in five minutes, and soon walking about felt like moving with slabs of sodden turf lashed to my feet. But, shut off by the weather from the hurtling city about me, I achieved a sense of primitiveness and wildness, a sense that I was in a world I didn't know everyday. And when I watched a green winged teal spring out of our vernal pond, I could have been lurking by a beaver pond in Montana. But it wasn't only Montana I was feeling connected to. It was something larger.

This sometimes happens at night. I remember an August evening last summer, right after sunset. I sat at my desk doing serious business, when I heard a fox bark. I went outside to our office parking lot, and following the sound, was able to discern where he was. He was down in the swale that forms between the Portiuncula Chapel and the slight ridge to the east where the wood-chip trail runs. Our drainage creek runs through there, and that's where our vernal pond sits. It was dark, but all around the perimeter of Mayslake were lights and noises.

Chicago was a dull rose wash to the East. Oak Brook Center was a sky scraping wall of office lights. Traffic lights flickered green, yellow and red into the night. Headlights swept down Route 83. Dark new houses risen on the denuded hills - above Second and Third Lakes - cast houselights down into the still dark waters like cruise-ships in port. The noise of jets ripped through the sky, and trucks thundered across rumble bars on the East-West Tollway just a mile to the North.

But down there in that dark, watery and grassy swale, another life was in charge. The fox barked loudly and at persistent intervals, moving up and down the swale as though patrolling it. He may have been warning off rival fox; he may have been giving fair warning to predators after him. But to me, his yipping seemed more like a cry of possession, as though not satisfied with urinating on all the boundaries of his turf, he was anointing them with the mark of his voice as well. Running up and down, yipping and barking in the dark bowl of earth, he acted as though none of the lurid and noisy encroachment about him ever existed. Each of his cries seemed a further claim on the sanctity of his little range. And each of his cries brought me away from the garish lights and noises to touch again another part of reality.

We get overwhelmed by what we ordinarily choose to call reality. Reality is the job, making money, having problems in the family, securing ourselves against crime and death, the erosion of our souls by the roaring speed of the fast track. We smile wanly about gulls in the fog and foxes in the night, and, although we may wish they were so, we dismiss them from reality as an aberration, however pleasant, in a life where reality is acknowledged only when we hold our silken souls grimly to the abrasive grindstones of "making it". What we require is the knowledge that the fox and gull are as real as the rubbery roar of traffic down Route 83. Even more, we need to know that while the traffic is more immediately a sign of humanity, the fox and gull are more reality as a sign of the creator of humanity.

And so, just as much as we have to pay attention to Route 83, just so much do we have to pay attention to the fox and gull. If that means we have to strain to do it, so be it. You know how it is when you are trying to sleep in a room when someone else is reading with the light on or when there is a stereo or TV or a party in the next room. If you can't do anything to change the situation, you pull the blanket over your face and cram pillows around your head. You do what you have to do to get some rest. In the quest to keep afloat in the reality we have created, we need to get in touch with the deeper reality of Him who created us. That's why there are places like Mayslake. That's why Mayslake tries to keep the land it has, and keep it serene and quiet, and at least partly wild. Because we want you to see the gull in the mist, hear the fox in the swale, help you understand that they are as real as a Marshall Field's store, but more importantly, that none of it - light, noise, Marshall Field's, fox or gull - have any meaning at all without the Creator.

Life in the Slow Lane
Spring 1987

Mayslake is a slow spot surrounded by speed.

To the East, where it passes us, Route 83 has been for some time now a high speed, six lane highway, whose narrower shoulders north and south of us are now being pushed back to the same width from Roosevelt Road to I-55. Thirty-first Street, which runs along our northern boundary, is already a fast moving four lane artery. Even now we continually worry about being picked off as we slow to negotiate the turn into the grounds. East and west of us 31st Street is still only two lanes wide, but pressure is building to pry these sections even wider so that from Highland Avenue to York Road it will cease being a street and become a highway. The result of all this is speed, noisy, roaring speed - cars, trucks, busses, motorcycles, vans - so that wherever you walk within the quiet of the retreat house grounds, you are assailed by the rubbery whine of speed.

After a respite from speed and its mayhem, occasioned by the oil crises of the 70's, Americans are once again restlessly fingering their way back into the fast lane. Right now there are bills in Congress - backed by our own governor - to push the speed limit up to 65 on most of our interstates.

This, of course, will mean a return to the unnerving speeds of 75 and 80 that were commonplace before 1973. Already the law-abiding driver has become a hazard on the highways. With this comes more highway butchery and death, more smashed up junk, more bullying by speed freaks, more tension and stress, more headaches, and more of the bone-weariness that drags out of the car with us after yet another harrowing trip on our nation's roadways. It will also mean missing more of America as we hurtle by, our eyes fixed only on the car or roadbed ahead of us.

It strikes me that most of the beautiful things in life are those that happen slowly. The mellowing of a marriage or a friendship, making love, dining with those you care about, drinking good wine. Babies, flowers, trees, things that are grown from seeds take their time. A goose gander waits patiently for thirty days, doing nothing but hanging around - never checking his watch - while his mate faithfully broods their eggs. The only time, it seems, that birds and animals in nature move fast - by their terms - is when they are attacked or threatened themselves. Speed is the child of fear, appetite, and insecurity. The fastest I ever move is when that same gander thinks I'm getting too close to his nest or his little family, and comes flying low and furious at me! The only plant I know of that pops up quickly is the mushroom, and it dies just as fast. There is a grace about going slow, a grace that enables us to see and experience more of the world more deeply as we are passing through.

Even medicine recognizes this. It distinguishes Type A and Type B personalities among humans. The former are pushy, quick, fast-moving; the latter, quiet, more passive, slow to move. Type A's, researchers point out, are much more prone to early death through heart attack than Type B's. If the mushroom is the Type A of the plant world, then the high speed driver is the Type A of the traveling public.

That is why I have been thinking a lot recently about the "Sunday Driver". We all know who this is, and we by and large despise him or her. These are the people - often, but by no means exclusively, elderly - who poke along our roads, highways, and interstates at speeds at or even below the posted limit. If we were able to keep track, we would, I suspect, find that we have hurled at them more curses and directed at them more obscene gestures than we have at any other segment of the population, including politicians and communists. But whatever other problems they may cause us, the "Sunday Drivers" enjoy the trip much more than we do. They are less rattled; they see more; they connect with the corridors through which they move. They are, God bless them, the monks of the highway.

Mayslake is definitely home for "Sunday Drivers" because Mayslake clearly means life in the slow lane. When people come here, they leave their heated cars panting in the parking lot, and trundle their luggage hurriedly into the building. But, because there is nothing "to do" here, they begin to slow down. They begin to walk slowly. They stand with their hands in their pockets reading things on the bulletin board. They pick up books and magazines to read that they would never give a second thought to elsewhere. They sit quietly by a window or lake and watch geese slowly sail across the water and graze the lawn. They stroll reflectively through the cemetery. They look at summer carp hanging lazily in the ponds, or raise their eyes to a hawk lifted gracefully on thermals. They don't talk as much and have slowed down so that, like "Sunday Drivers", they can see and listen more.

They sit in chapel, watching candles flicker in the semi-dark, and realize that there is no real prayer in the fast lane. So they just look at the crucifix, aware of Jesus' patient presence, realizing that he waits for them, when and if, they ever slow down. They learn that a twenty minute Mass, or a rapidly ejaculated rosary, or brisk stations of the cross are not signs of mature Christian prayer. They learn that when they don't rush prayer, they can simply sit quietly before the Lord and begin to hear him in ways they never thought possible before.

God himself is very slow; he moves like a stately procession of endless blue sky, and the brief rush of our lives is like a dry leaf blown across his face. A thousand years of our frantic lives are as but a single day in the eyes of God. Our life is a dandelion - here today, gone tomorrow. But he is there, not inert like a granite cliff that never crumbles, but as a faithful friend and lover he stands forever at our door, knocking patiently while we, unheeding, peter away our lives in frenetic triviality. He is always hanging around, never away on important business, waiting, waiting for us to slow down.

The beautiful thing about Mayslake - and slow places like it - is that it continues to exist in our speed-addicted world. The sad thing is that for most of us it is only an exception to life and never becomes a model.

Lawns and Weeds: Who's Really in Charge Here?
Summer 1987

To most urban people, Nature is like New York City. Nice place to visit, but you wouldn't want to live there. Nature makes most city and suburban dwellers at least a little uncomfortable. It's too cold, or it's too hot. It's too wet, or it's too dry. It's often messy and dirty. It's frequently dangerous. But, most of all, they know they can't do much about it. Nature is beyond their control, and they'd rather spend their energies on that part of their lives they can control. Despite Mark Twain's complaint, nobody has yet done anything about the weather, except to predict more accurately just how uncomfortable we're going to be and for how long.

Because we live in an urban setting here at Mayslake, we are constantly running into trouble with Nature. We are - at least by suburban standards - stewards of a good sized chunk of it, and, outside of its 20 acres of lawn, it's pretty generally unkempt, wild, yes, natural. That's all right, it seems, for forest preserves. But since almost all privately owned land around here is nicely groomed and manicured, we tend to stand out like an enormous, scruffy dog, badly in need of a bath, that has wandered into someone's living room. And so we get complaints - sometimes from our guests, sometimes from our neighbors, sometimes even from official sources. Our geese have untidy toilet habits. The unmowed parts of our grounds are unsightly and support noxious weeds. There is the scum of algae on our ponds. We have dead and partly dead trees standing in the woods or toppling into the water. Our woodchip paths aren't smooth and clean like asphalt. Clearly, even this small bit of Nature isn't everybody's cup of tea.

There are, of course, many good reasons for living this close to Nature, and there are more than a few people who are satisfied with these reasons, but there is one reason for living this close to Nature that I suspect even Nature lovers don't give much thought to.

Living with Nature is a lot like living with God. When you live with Nature, you have to live much more on its terms than you would really like to. I first became aware of this when I started doing wilderness outings a few years ago. I learned that if you're careless, you get hurt. There's no Emergency Room nearby, and if you're confronted by a grizzly bear, there's no 911 to dial. So, you go carefully. You wear the right clothes and shoes. You go at the right pace. You don't trust the water. You respect the space of the wild creatures there. You go on Nature's terms, not your own. Thus it began to dawn on me that that's the way I'm supposed to live my life with God - on His terms, not my own. Living close to Nature reminds me of that.

Take lawns, for example. We have 15-20 acres of lawn here at Mayslake (though most true lawn enthusiasts would probably refer to it as little more than well-mowed pasture). But I'm satisfied, even proud of it. It gives the place a finely sculpted look, especially where it borders the more wild parts. But, it's not a "good" lawn. It is continually breaking out with epiphanies and surprises. We get a buttery smear of dandelions in the spring, thistles in the summer, fleabane, creeping Charlie, crabgrass, clover and even aggressive little brigades of poplar shoots. It is also tunneled and chewed up by woodchucks and chipmunks, carpeted with goose droppings, and festooned with molted duck feathers.

It has been said many times - and the lawn enthusiasts among you will nod in agreement - that a lawn is the most unnatural piece of agriculture ever invented. Nature hates the controlled monotony of a lawn, takes every opportunity to wreck it. You can never turn your back on lawn. You have to seed it carefully, give it the right soil, and make sure it gets watered properly - especially when Nature doesn't want to. You have to douse it with chemicals, some to make the grass grow, some to kill everything else. You have to defend it against moles, woodchucks, even kids. Whenever I think of human beings taking care of lawns, I will always think of the elderly Japanese gentlemen I saw sitting right down in the midst of residential lawns in Honolulu meticulously picking out every little blade or shoot that didn't belong there. They know Nature is forever lurking behind the wall, just waiting for them to relax.

Lawns raise the question, however mildly, of just who's in charge here. I always think of what Thoreau said about our need for the "tonic of wildness". In *Walden* he wrote, "We can never have enough of Nature ... We need to witness our own limits transgressed and some life pasturing freely where we never wander."

That's the way it is with God. We should like to control our lives the way we control our lawns, and we expect God to help us do both. But God wants control too. He transgresses our limits, and never lets us relax. He is always reminding us of our limits by visiting us with unexpected surprises into our well-trimmed lives. Sometimes he sends daisies. But sometimes he sends thistles. And eventually, despite all our efforts to keep control, he gets His Way. Just like Nature will eventually take over even the best kept lawn in town.

So, I am grateful for living next to Nature. It's not only because I am romantic about woods and fields. It's a constant reminder to me of just Who's in charge here.

The Gatehouse Goes Down and Trees Go Up
Autumn 1987

There are many things that Mayslake Retreat House doesn't have. We don't have air-conditioned bedrooms, our heating system is cranky. We don't have large guest rooms with telephones, radios and TVs. We don't have fancy furniture and fine works of art. We lack a swimming pool, golf courses, and exercise rooms. And our dining room doesn't offer gourmet food. We certainly can't compete with the glistening new hotels springing up in Oak Brook.

But there is one thing we do have that they don't, and that is one of the prettiest pieces of land in the area. Sixty acres of it - rolling, green, watered, and tree shaded land. We have well-groomed lawns, flower gardens, lakes and ponds, meadows, a restored prairie plot, an apple and pear orchard, gingko trees, natural Illinois woodlots, and a well-tended cemetery. People who come to Mayslake as guests, either for our retreats or for their own programs, tell us that what they like best about Mayslake is the grounds. I have been told by more than one person that as soon as they enter our winding driveway, a feeling of peace begins to come over them (which is partly, I'm sure, a simple matter of relief that they managed to make a safe turn off 31st Street without getting rear-ended by its rocketing traffic).

Yes, Mayslake is defined to a great extent by the land on which it sits. And the good news now is that we will be keeping it all! The Franciscan Provincial Office in St. Louis has made two important decisions recently that insure the future integrity of the retreat house grounds.

The first was a decision not to sell any more land out of the commercially tempting northeast corner of the property where 31st Street and Route 83 intersect. And as if this weren't enough, the Province in order to make it entirely clear to the real estate community, encouraged us to enclose that piece of land with landscaping, and made us a generous grant of $25,000 toward accomplishing that end. If you have been out here recently you noticed that this has already been done. A relatively mature stand of fast-growing trees - maples, oaks, crabapples, Austrian pines, and hawthorns - have been put in place, running along the frontage road and forming a visible boundary between the retreat house and the adjoining grounds of St. Paschal Friary to the South. Within that boundary screen, we are enlarging our network of walking paths and have included a bridge (now in place) across the drainage creek that empties Third Lake. Eventually benches will be placed along these paths. So, the land is not only saved, it has become the backyard of the retreat house.

The second decision made by the Province was to tear down the Gatehouse that sits by our front entrance. The Franciscans have had no use for the Gatehouse for several years now, and it has sat empty since 1983.

Extensive efforts have been made to sell the 2 acre plot it sits on, but to no avail. Many developers were interested in the Gatehouse plot but insisted on several more acres to put in more homes. (One proposal would have run right up to the edge of the cemetery.) But the Province, concerned about further invasions of the retreat house grounds, resisted all such offers. Consequently, the property went unsold. Therefore, the decision was made early in October to raze the entire complex and to hand the grounds over to the retreat house. You will notice something is missing the next time you come out. But that empty space simply enlarges the reach of Mayslake.

Why were these actions taken? As you might imagine, considerable financial sacrifice is entailed by not selling. Developers have been offering as much as $140,000 per acre. In an age when Religious Orders labor under considerable financial burden, why did they pass up this opportunity?

The principal reason was to provide the serenity that the ministry here at Mayslake required. As it does with other islands of peace and quiet left standing in the area, the crushing growth of DuPage County presses heavily against Mayslake. This is a county where whole towns and subdivisions are being sold off to developers to put-in new office and commercial buildings. This is a county where skyscrapers rise higher and higher, beginning to match the Loop skyline itself. This is a county where the increasing crush of traffic leads to ominous talk of gridlock, and where a massive new tollway even nips off a corner of beloved Morton Arboretum. This is a county where developers even try to buy golf courses to put more buildings on, where dumps are placed in forest preserves, and where even the few serene places left are stared into by the office buildings and residential developments that swarm up to their borders. This is the county where Mayslake has always stood. It will now continue to stand, holding a serene line against the juggernaut of progress. We do our work better here at Mayslake when the land gives a hand. It's as simple as that.

Franciscans also understand the sacredness of land. Our founder, Francis of Assisi, found God constantly in his creation. Franciscans try to do the same. Therefore, they recognize the sacredness of land, that the Lord abides there, as well as in the chapels and tabernacles. And some of that land must be left free of human creation so that God may be more readily found in his.

It is the season of Thanksgiving. We here at Mayslake have special reason for thankfulness this fall. We owe a great debt of gratitude to the wisdom and farsightedness of the Franciscan Province of the Sacred Heart who share with us a vision of the land, and have made that vision possible. We are grateful to you, our guests, not just because you have provided us with some of the money needed to ensure the salvation of the land, but because you tell us how much you love the land here, and because you complain bitterly to us of your fears that it may continue to dribble away. And we are grateful to God for the grace of this land. For in the final analysis, it came to us, not from Peabody, not from you, not even from Provincial headquarters, but as an undeserved gift of God. He gave it to us. It is our grateful task to continue to help people to find him there.

The Pope is - So to Speak - For the Birds.
Some springtime reflections on a new encyclical.
Spring 1988

Holy Saturday - April 2 this year - was a foggy, misty, even rainy day. Nonetheless, a friend, Conrad, and I rose early for a few hours' sojourn in the forest preserves of Cook County to see what birds had come back from the winter. As we stood in the wet grass near McGuinness Slough, I said to him, "I'll bet the tree swallows are over at Buttonbush (a small, protected marsh at 95th and La Grange Road). It's time for them to be back." When we got to Buttonbush later that morning, there they were - distinctive white-bellied swallows sweeping and darting vigorously over the waters. The next morning, Easter Sunday, I saw them here at Mayslake as well.

It wasn't the sort of bet you can easily get a bird-watcher to cover. Tree swallows, like most migratory birds, are pretty predictable about their times of return. We're all familiar with the famous cliff swallows that return to Capistrano (California) every year on the same day (although it should be said that the folks at Capistrano, for the sake of the town's image, have stretched the birds' punctuality a little beyond credibility). And little Hinckley, Ohio, is so sure of their reliability, that it is bold enough to set a Festival Day in advance to mark the return of the turkey vultures (buzzards) to their town.

Earlier that week, on Holy Thursday evening, I had watched the Paschal Moon - full and lustrous - swim in the clouds of the eastern sky. It struck me forcibly that that was the **very same** moon which had appeared the night Jesus celebrated the Last Supper, showing us the **very same** face. I thought that night that the moon is a sign of the abiding faithfulness of God as are the tree swallow at Buttonbush, the cliff swallow at Capistrano, and the buzzards at Hinckley. In a world in which we have managed to change just about everything else, the swallows come back on time, the moon is full at Easter, and God is always present to us.

Nature has much to teach us, as the little homily above suggests. But there is far more to Nature than metaphors. Nor is Nature just a set of interesting and colorful phenomena that we can visit in a national park or watch on public television. Nature is not separate from us. We are part of both its rhythms and mysteries. We are as much a part of it as the swallows.

And yet we are steadily isolating ourselves from the experience of Nature. We let the sprawl of urbanization crush out anything but gelded remains we call lawns. With stolid thoughtlessness we litter the rest of the countryside with the leftovers of our consumptive lifestyle. We work, take our leisure, and even pray in cycles that have little to do with night or day or the turn of the seasons. Our TV weather and anchor persons brightly, and stupidly, bewail the rain, the snow, the heat, the cold - oblivious to the fact that in a world of perfect sunshine and 80 degree temperatures, the great circle of life on which we depend would cease to turn. We rifle the pantry of Nature for still another luxury in our relentless addiction to stimulus and gratification. We are in danger of allowing Nature to become a combination grocery store and zoo which exists only to feed and entertain us.

Sadly, Catholics haven't been any better than anyone else at paying attention to Nature. Some years ago the United Nations approved a very impressive "Charter" on Nature. Local environmental advocates wanted to showcase the new Charter with a news conference here in Chicago. I was asked to recommend a Catholic environmentalist with name recognition who might be called upon to grace the occasion. As well connected as I was with the local environmental movement, I was unable to come up with such a Catholic.

Well, now I can. He isn't local, but he's visited here before. His name is Pope John Paul II. This past winter, December 30, 1987, the Pope issued his latest encyclical *On Social Concerns*. In this encyclical the Pope stresses again the familiar social concerns of papal encyclicals - economic justice for the poor, materialism of both the East and the West, unemployment, the arms race, and so forth. But in this encyclical, for the first time in that magnificent procession of such documents since Leo XIII's *On the Rights and Duties of Capital and Labor* in 1891, has also come a ringing call to Catholics to begin to pay attention to the natural world!

The Pope places his discussion of Nature in the context of what he sees as "true development", which includes not only economic development but also moral development as well. He tells us that we cannot "develop" if we "exclude respect for the beings which constitute the natural world." And then he summarizes with academic precision what have always been the three main concerns of environmentalists since the movement's beginning at the turn of the century

First, we must respect every existing species of life. We cannot see plants, animals, and land as simply economic and human resources to be harvested and used at will. They - each species of them - have a dignity of their own as part of God's creation.

Second, the resources available to us in nature are limited. Many of them are not renewable, and will simply play out like an exhausted oil well. Hence, it is important that we avoid wasting them. There are hundreds of stories around the world of careless devastation of natural resources to the point of extinction.

Third, the Pope solemnly warns us against our terrible habits of pollution, which appear, despite the apocalyptic warnings of environmentalists and governments, to get worse rather than better - with frightening consequences for our health.

Calling to mind God's prohibition to Adam and Eve about eating the fruit of the tree of good and evil, the Pope warns us that we cannot simply, without limit, pick and gorge ourselves on the fruits of Nature. There are limits, and we must learn to observe them.

At last then, a Catholic spokesman for the swallows! A respect for Nature is now right up there on the top shelf of papal concerns. Along with advocacy for Labor, for Freedom, for Peace, for the Family, for the Unborn, for Human Rights, for the Poor, the Vicar of Christ has now taken up the case of the Swallows and Buzzards, the Land, the Water, and the Air.

I remember a number of years ago writing a piece for our friars about environmental concerns. One of my fellow friars raged at me for this, and asked why I wasn't writing about abortion instead. Well, now he knows. Now, the Pope knows too, and he reminds us that we cannot continue to live in the manner to which we have become accustomed. He reminds us that we must live more in tune with God's creation. He reminds us, indeed, that we are part of Nature.

Which brings us back to the homily above about swallows and the Paschal Moon. We can never learn from nature unless we let ourselves become a part of it. A couple of decades ago sociologist Peter Berger cast an inquiring eye over the emerging landscape of current events and thought he heard signs of a revival of religious experience. He called these signs "rumors of angels". There are rumors in nature, too, not only of angels, but also of God, and ourselves as well. Just step outside and listen.

About those faithful swallows, I would bet Conrad again that the chimney swifts will return to Mayslake on April 30, but I know he won't take the bet.

Rain - Grace
Summer 1988

It was Monday June 20, the 27th day in a row without rain, in this dry and barren summer. It was the summer solstice, too, when the sun burns brightest and longest. He reminded us of his power this day by blazing to a record high of 104 degrees.

I run in the late afternoon, usually without regard for the weather. But these temperatures were just outside the range of the reasonable. So, not having appointments or meetings that evening, I delayed my jogging till after supper. As I set out, thin, sun-bathed thunderclouds stirred about in the hot bowl of the evening sky. Meteorologists had not called for rain, but slowly a few drops spattered down on the baked earth and my sweaty face. As I ran, the rain teasingly stopped and started, then settled into a light steady shower - the kind the Irish call a "fine, soft rain". Near the Eighth Station, I ran into Bill Bush, one of our volunteers, showing a friend the grounds he works on. They were both dressed neatly in street clothes, but making no effort to escape the rain, we stopped to chat. A few minutes later, I came across

Brother Myron from St. Paschal's across the pond. The rain was coming down harder, but as his habit slowly dampened, we too stopped to talk. As we spoke, a neighbor from Trinity Lakes came by, and he too stopped, equally oblivious of the shower enveloping us. Clearly, whatever the clothes we were wearing, we were all as thirsty for the rain as the grass beneath our feet. When I got back to the house, the rain was strong and steady, but I could not bring myself to go back into the building. I usually pray at this time of day, out of doors when the weather is nice. I hesitated, halfway in the house, then, impulsively, headed back out into the rain and to my prayer bench by the Portiuncula.

I prayed without book, breviary or Bible. I prayed, not just in the rain, but with it. I prayed till my leather watch band was limp with wet and I could wring the water out of the sleeve of my old green jogging shirt. My binoculars, which I always carry with me when I run, I carelessly allowed to get soaked. Someone had said something to me about colds and pneumonia when I left the building, but I didn't care. I gave myself in prayer to the rain. I felt refreshment as the cool air coursed with the rain over my skin. I felt relief that the dry punishment of drought had relented. I felt gratitude. It was a time of grace, was grace itself. And I was drenched with it, even a little tipsy.

The next day, the air heated up again to 101, and no more rain came. The grass was still brown and crunchy, the hot winds provided little relief, and the joy of Monday evaporated with the moisture. I prayed that night too at my bench, but broke teeth on dry bread. The Jesuit poet, Gerard Manley Hopkins, wrote once on a similar day: "My heaven is brass and iron my earth." That was my prayer the day it wouldn't rain.

Weather is always a powerful parable for me. I dislike cold spells, heat waves, heavy snowstorms, rain that lasts for days, drought that dries the wells and streams. I also fear them. I don't seem to fear what they can do to me at the moment, for I will hike, jog, and even travel in heat waves, torrential downpours, blizzards and cold snaps. I even enjoy the challenge these offer. I do fear, however, the effect they can have on my life if they persist, like this summer's drought and heat. I imagine the worst - flushing toilets only once a day, food prices rising, my farmer cousin driven out of business, the return of the feared "Dust Bowl" of the Thirties. Mingled with this fear, I perceive the full meaning that the parable of the weather unfolds for me. For weather confronts me with the essential lack of control I have over my life. Like most people, I live with the illusion that I manage my own life and control my own environment and destiny. I plan, discern, decide, deal, arrange, even enter into relationships as though it were all up to me, and could all be held in line with my own agenda. Then comes the endless grip of weather, a heat wave for example. Headlines that scream, "No relief in sight" stretch tight across my gut. There is nothing I can do, and so I fall into depression, even anger.

This may seem trivial for you who read this. I am not afflicted with chronic pain, illness, failure, or loneliness, and must appear to whine as I take up arms against a sea of weather. And so, in a sense, I do. But in another sense, that of the parable, my obsession is significant for us all.

Despite rain dances and prayers, weather always wins. So does God. But I submit to neither gracefully.

Sometimes I think that I even try to control the weather by the obsessive attention I pay to it. That first day of summer, after I had come in and changed into dry clothing, it continued to rain. But every chance I got, I ran to the window to make sure it hadn't stopped, peered anxiously at the sky looking for more, checked the size of the raindrops on the driveway and even - out of earshot of course - vocally urged it on. Even sitting to pray in the downpour was in part, I think, a faintly shamanistic attempt to keep it coming. I do not trust the weather enough to leave it alone.

I do this with God too. I am supposed to trust him the way the lilies of the field do, and I am given to understand that if I put him and his kingdom first, all the things I worry about will be given to me. But, I don't much act that way. I scheme to make things come out right, as though it were all up to me. And when they don't turn out the way I want them to or according to my schedule, I get depressed, and even blame myself. As I do with the weather, I keep my eye on God and his world to make sure they do their jobs. I tell my Finance Committee, as they cast skeptical eyes on my budget, that they have to trust - God will provide. But there are butterflies in my stomach when I do.

There is also some incurable greed involved in all of this. When I go for a long time without getting my way, I can get accustomed to and even develop some disciplined resignation toward deprivation. Forced to lower my expectations, I begin to be satisfied with the little I am getting. But, once I start getting my own way again, all this discipline turns out to be little more than a stretched rubber band that, at the least relaxation of tension, snaps back to its usual tight and narrow grip. So, when we finally got that nice rain, I was pleased, humble and grateful. But, it wasn't enough. I wanted more. And as I watched the heat and aridity return in the following days, all my virtuous exhilarations dropped to sullen disappointment.

I do this constantly in my work here. I keep a careful eye on the ebb and flow of success in our ministry - numbers of retreatants, expressions of satisfaction or dissatisfaction, rising or falling income. And my spirits gyrate on these gauges as much as they do with those that measure the weather. I have not yet learned deeply that Grace is given by God freely, at his discretion, not mine. So, lacking the calm of real acceptance, I ride the roller coaster of my own self-trusting illusions.

Weather then is a relentless parable for me about my relationship with God. On the evening we got the rain, our community had assembled for the Eucharist before dinner. Fr. Kieran was the celebrant, and he worries about rain for a much more practical reason than I do - he raises all the flowers around here. He chose for the Mass liturgical prayers for rain. As we emerged from chapel, the thunderclouds were beginning to heap up around us, offering some promise. And when the rains came, I congratulated him on his prowess as rainmaker. He responded that he'd been praying every day for weeks! So, God does not jump at the liturgical snap of our fingers or the other rain dances we do. He sends his gifts when he sends them. We can do little more than sit patiently at the window and wait. My prayer is that I learn to wait better. As a special gift, though I'll probably never get it, I'd like to wait with a little less anxiety. I really envy the lilies of the field!

Let heaven and earth praise Him who is glorious:
Let us praise and glorify Him forever.
And every creature that is in heaven and on earth
and under the earth and in the sea and those that are in them:
Let us praise and glorify Him forever.
 - Francis of Assisi

A Bloom of Asters
Autumn 1988

The Village of Oak Brook requires us to cut our open fields at least once a year. Their concern has to do with what they call "noxious weeds". This year Harold managed to mow down most of the fields, but due to a combination of difficult terrain and lack of time, one section went uncut. The result has been stunning. The mowed portions - including walking paths cut through the unmowed areas - are a flat, mono-colored green stubble. But, the unmowed section carries the most spectacular bloom of fall wildflowers we have seen here.

There are three kinds of wild aster - the deep blue New England aster, the sky-colored arrowleaf aster, and creamy white plumes of heath aster. Patches of each tumble loosely through luxurious old gold swaths of goldenrod. White waves of daisy fleabane sweep through and around this melange so colorful that it would challenge the deftest of Impressionist painters. Drawn by this tangled garden, our guests and retreatants, who otherwise stick timidly to woodchip paths and asphalt driveways, have begun to venture into unfamiliar parts of the grounds.

This wildflower field is a tiny example of the delights that can happen when, deciding to live with, not against Nature, we leave it alone. It is proof of what Nature can produce when we do not frustrate it and try to stuff its big life into the manicured lawns, formal gardens, and golf courses that satisfy most people's taste for natural beauty.

This past summer all of us experienced something about living in harmony with nature and what happens when we don't. It was a summer of Big Environmental Events. Heat and drought of historic proportions touched in some way every one of the fifty states. It sucked up our water, killed our crops and lawns, and strained our energy resources as we clutched desperately at our fans and air conditioners for relief. The worst forest fire in recorded history smudged the postcard beauty of our favorite national park. The most powerful hurricane in decades splintered lives and plundered economies in several Caribbean countries, sending thousands of tourists fleeing from smashed Cancun to the quieter shores of Hawaii. Unbelievably, two-thirds of one entire country, Bangladesh, drowned beneath some of the worst monsoon floods in memory. Millions of visitors fled the beautiful beaches of New England, Long Island and the Jersey Shore, driven off as the grisly offal of offshore dumps crawled onto the sands. As if all this were not enough horror for one summer, scientists gathered gloomily in Toronto to announce the onset of the "Greenhouse Effect". This friendly sounding word describes a scenario in which human pollutants gather so densely in the atmosphere that they threaten to shut down the sky that protects and nourishes us. The ominous advent of the "Greenhouse Effect" gives fair warning that in addition to all the problems nature delivers on its own, we are creating a new "nature" with toxic effects potentially far worse - and far more persistent - than the occasional hurricane, monsoon, drought, or forest fire.

Some of these disasters are nature's own. Some are of human making. But, whatever their source, they confront us with the reality that despite all our technological achievements, we cannot afford any longer to live in contempt of the laws of nature. Earth, Air, Fire, and Water - the elements of the Ancients - rule our planet with a far tighter grip than the clumsy manhandling we try to force upon it with our little pushbutton tools.

For decades most of us have scoffed at environmental concerns as the doomsday whinings of elite nature lovers. In President Nixon's administration, for example, environmental activists were dismissed contemptuously as the "bird and bunny crowd". But not any more. If the events of this summer have not spoken the message loud enough and clear enough already, perhaps the following will. In 1988, three very conservative organizations, none of which has paid more than scant attention to environmental issues, have scrambled in alarm aboard the environmental bandwagon.

The first is the papacy of the Roman Catholic Church. As 1988 opened, Pope John Paul II issued a major encyclical, *On Social Concerns,* in which for the first time in the history of papal encyclicals, a Pope made clear environmental demands upon Catholics. He tells them "authentic human development requires that they respect the integrity and connectedness of all created beings; that they respect the limitations of natural resources; that they abhor activities which pollute the environment."

The second is the Republican Party. Not since the very different days of Teddy Roosevelt has the GOP shown leadership in this area. The current administration has indeed been regressive, but in the summer and fall of 1988, its presidential nominee stood on the polluted Jersey Shore and on a boat in polluted Boston Harbor, pledging to "clean up America".

The third is prime time television. Prime time television, of course, governs every one of its minutes by the bottom line of what people will watch and what advertisers will pay for. This summer, the least daring of all these networks, ABC, read the mood of American public and business community well enough to calculate that it could get away with a prime time show on the environment. When the Catholics, the Republicans, and ABC Television join together to express alarm over the same issue, you can bet it's not some wild-eyed leftist cause favored only by a well-heeled and overly sophisticated elite.

Environmental concerns have therefore passed over from issues of aesthetic preference to human survival. Here at Mayslake we like to see this concern as a religious commitment. We take our cue from our patron, Francis of Assisi. He saw all creation as a family - brothers, sisters united through a common mother (Earth) to a bountiful Father-Creator. We struggle, therefore, to keep our land out of the hands of developers. We plant new trees and save old ones, even dead ones (herons and woodpeckers love them!). We restore long-dead prairies. We don't poison our lawns with herbicides. We protect our fox, our geese, our muskrats, our raccoons, our skunks, our possum. And we are at least beginning to notice the tremendous amount of plastic we use in our dining rooms.

Mayslake is many things. It is a place to encounter God and each other. It is a place of peace, quiet and rest. It is a lovely place. It is also, praise God, a place where we can practice saving the earth. It was indeed a blessing that Harold never got around to finishing off the fields. We not only had the grace of the asters, but we saved a little bit of that earth as well.

Jerusalem
Spring 1989

February 14 this year was not one of my good days. It featured a late afternoon meeting, involving confrontations over values, with Franciscan colleagues. It was not an agreeable exchange, and left me a little surly. What followed immediately was the drive home, punching my way through rush hour traffic. I don't do this often and so have not developed the coping mechanisms adopted by other more frequent travelers to maintain their equanimity. What it often does to me - especially when I am in a hurry - is rub all the sore spots of my relationship with urban society. As I poke and crunch along, I am abrasively massaged by the endless billboards, the rude drivers, the noise and careening speed of trucks, and the congestion of factories and apartments that coils itself tightly along the roadways. All of this makes me headachy and foul and that's the state I arrived in back here at Mayslake.

I was rushing home to be present for the opening of our Lenten series of evening prayer, and to greet our first guest homilist, a Lutheran pastor. I bolted down a couple of warmed over pork chops, shaved rapidly, greeted Pastor Berg, worried - needlessly - about everything, and finally slid, rattled and still surly, into a pew for the services.

Then came the grace.

Mary Jo had chosen as part of the service Psalm 137. This psalm is a brief song which expresses the pain of the Hebrew people exiled to Babylonia in the 6th century B.C. As punishment for their resistance to the invading Babylonians, and to make sure they didn't continue a guerrilla warfare under the occupation, the leading Hebrew citizens and craftsmen had been carted off to Babylon. There, far from homeland and Temple, they became classic homeless people. Psalm 137 therefore begins as a funereal dirge. It presents the Hebrews sitting by the many canals of Babylon, wistfully recalling and longing for home. Adding to the indignity of their exile, their captors come like tourists, to ask the Hebrews to sing for them the songs of Jerusalem. White folks did the same thing to the Negroes of the Old South, sitting along the levees and in the music halls, asking them to sing their songs of longing, the blues. But the Hebrews would not sing, chucking their harps instead onto the poplar trees that lined the waterways. They protested that they could not sing the songs of God in a foreign land.

But then whoever wrote the psalm seems to remember that if they stop singing they might forget Jerusalem. To forget Jerusalem! This was a fate worse than a withered arm or a tongue muted by becoming stuck to the roof of the mouth. And so he abruptly changes his tune, calls upon his people to pluck their harps off the bushes, keep on singing, and never forget Jerusalem.

"My life exactly", it came to me, as we prayed evening prayer that Tuesday night. Of late I had come to feel like an exile, in steady conflict with the values around me. I had come to feel that I do not live in a world that shares Christian values. Indeed, I live in a foreign land.

It was no comfort to me that last winter the Republican Party in Arizona adopted a resolution assuring me that I do not live in a foreign land, that America is indeed a "Christian nation". I need only glance beneath the surface of American life to realize what an awful illusion that is. I hear official Christian language from time to time, and I note that we observe some Christian holidays, usually with more commerce than piety, and that we fuss over Christmas cribs and crosses in public places. But these words, holidays, and symbols are not what really drive us as a people. What really drives us is what shows up on those billboards I see along the Stevenson Expressway and elsewhere - consumer goods as the rewards and sign of success. Sadly, what many Christians have done is to baptize all this. For they have made the frightening suggestion that all this stuff is also the reward and sign of good Christian living. With the addition of such powerful motivation, these consumer and success forces in our society have come to dominate our lives every bit as much as Babylonian princes dominated the poor exiled Hebrews. They have seized control of and laid waste to our landscape, reduced our churches to mere shells of the Gospel, and taken us, far more willing than the Hebrews, into a captivity where our songs sound funny and the memory of Jerusalem has begun to fade.

But the Hebrews survived in their foreign land. Historians tells us that they built communities of faith, put up, if not temples, synagogues, and told stories about Jerusalem. Because they did all this, they made it through exile and got back home seventy years later. As the psalmist might have put it, they plucked their harps off the willow trees and kept on singing.

That's the grace that came to me during evening prayer. The more the values of the world conflict with mine, the more I feel the need to draw closer to God, the center of my life. I need to stand at what T. S. Eliot called "the still point of the turning world." I need to remember Jerusalem. In practical terms, this means that I need to spend more time in quiet, more time in solitude, more time in prayer. It has finally become clear to me that what I need is not more renewal, not more growth programs, not more therapy, indeed, not more theological updating, but simply more faith rooted in God.

That's what we all have to do when we live in Babylon. When we do, we realize that Jerusalem isn't far away across burning deserts. It's in Babylon too. And it is only because Jerusalem is there too that it is possible for us not to sink into slavery to Babylon. Like the Hebrews, we need to pluck our harps off the poplars and sing the songs of our homeland!

The Goose as Neighbor
Summer 1989

One of the occupational hazards of living at Mayslake - and a hazard for guests as well - is the geese.

I am writing in June when the ten families of geese that hatched in May are gathering together into a clan. They do this every year in June, and one of their preferred loitering spots is our lawn where the old asphalt path leads down toward the bridge. Idleness, of course, leads to untidy results in the form of messy globs of goose droppings in various stages of sodden decay. This does not just happen in June. Residents and guests must place their feet carefully on our grounds during most of the months of the year.

The geese are pretty quiet in June, but that only makes the racket of earlier spring more dramatic by contrast. That's when they fight over mates and nesting sites. Geese mate for life, but every spring there are a few permanent relationships just getting under way, and the competition and courting can be thunderous - as are the consequent battles over the best places to build nests. It is not unusual for the din to go on through the night, and almost never does it wait for the grace of dawn when most of us begin to stir.

Once the nesting is under way, a new peril confronts us. The male is extremely protective of his brooding spouse, and even the slightest suggestion of a disturbance brings him, often from a spot out of sight, honking wildly and flaring his powerful wings to drive off the aggressor, whether fox or jogger. Sometimes this happens after the couple has chosen a nest site, but not occupied it, so that even the most innocent of visitations to its vicinity can bring the two of them screaming at you as though you were engaged in pillage. As a jogger, frequently subject to such attacks, I know that they always aim right for the back of the head.

It is a relief therefore when the young hatch because the male, while still protective, restricts his defenses mostly to hissing and neck wagging. It is also a peaceful sight to see the little goslings strung out on the water between their parents like yellow balls of fur on a clothesline. They call out the maternal in most of us. But not all of us. For what these new little geese want more than anything else is a lot of new little plants. And their parents know right where the best and freshest ones are - in the gardens and flowerbeds planted about the same time their parents went to nest. It is not an easy thing for even the malest of males to see a gosling carelessly wrench a blossom from a spring flower or rip a young carrot unfeelingly from the soil.

Our reaction to these noisy, cantankerous, thieving, and untidy birds, is not surprisingly a mixed one. Their charm, eclipsed by the annoyance they cause us, wears off quickly and we begin to look for ways to fight back. Most of these ways involve getting rid of them. Around here it can mean birth control by stripping eggs from the nests, or even shooting the goslings. At the very least, it means constant bitter complaints as though geese were some kind of vermin not fit for human presence. Our response to the geese is to do almost anything but learn to live with them.

But, suppose we take the long view of geese? What are they really but another kind of neighbor? Neighbors are always a mixed bag. They too, like geese, can be noisy, intemperate, possessive, messy and contemptuous of private property. And we do take the effort to rid ourselves of the inconvenience and discomfort they cause us. We call the police, complain to the alderman or village manager, mount petitions, and even resort to open confrontations.

In these attempts to control or even dislodge unsavory neighbors, we run the risk sadly of committing two kinds of sin.

The first sin is one we commit against ourselves. It is the sin of depriving ourselves of something very beautiful. Goose droppings mess up my shoes too. But there are few sights that excite me more - even after 20 years of it - than watching a graceful line of trumpeting honkers circle in from the sky, sweep in over the treeline, then settle with great contented splashes into our little ponds, there to pose quietly in the still waters like a fleet of Clippers riding at anchor. That sight is worth every bit of manure I've had to scrape off my shoes, every time I've been driven off my jogging path by a hissing gander.

A human neighbor whose differing values lead to offensive behavior offers the same opportunity for beauty. He may stand out glaringly like a wildflower in a manicured suburban lawn. But when we forget that he doesn't *fit*, what loveliness we will see in that very fact. It is a lesson we learn the hard way. Every new surge of immigrants to our land has met fierce resistance because they were so different from those of us already here. But once we relaxed and let the newcomers be, how interesting, indeed how beautiful, they turned out to be. They are like dandelions. Because we have been taught to hate them so, it has become impossible for us to admit how pretty they really are. Just so with neighbors who aren't quite like the rest of us.

The second sin we commit when we try to rid ourselves of the inconvenient and offensive life around us is arrogance. Arrogance means I set myself apart from and above everyone else for whatever reason - intelligence, education, skin color, income, success, religion. The opposite of arrogance is humility. The difference between the two is that the arrogant don't know who they really are, and the humble do. The arrogant feel, for example, that they should not have to put up with the likes of geese with their noise and predatory attacks on the garden. Their projects and lawns and sense of what is fitting are far too important to expose them to geese. They feel the same way about foreigners and other outsiders. The humble on the other hand do not think their lives and projects are so important as to justify ousting everybody else, including the geese. They know who they are. Far from desiring to be apart from everything and everybody else, they will to be part of them, indeed recognize that they really have no other choice. They, far more than the arrogant, are likely to learn to live with the geese.

Jesus, of course, was on the side of the humble. After all, Son of God though he was, and not at all required to change, he took on our human nature with all its untidiness. He even seemed attracted to its most untidy elements - thick-skulled fishermen, whores, corrupt public officials, even criminals. His biggest enemies were Pharisees, one of whose principal characteristics was arrogance. We will never forget those damning words spoken by one of them in the Parable of the Publican and Pharisee: "I thank you Lord, that I am not like the rest of men."

I doubt if the Pharisees, just as they kept their skirts clean of prostitutes, publicans, and even the Gentiles, would tolerate the geese. But it's very easy for me to see Jesus, who sought out even the Gentiles, stepping without complaint around a pile of goose droppings and giving a nesting female an affectionately wide berth.

Jonathan Foster, O.F.M.

"There is Not Enough Silence" - T.S. Eliot
Autumn 1989

There are times here - especially, it seems, in the autumn - when the woods stand still and quiet. They are rare times. No noise bullies in from the highways or bombards us from the skies. There is even no wind. The leaves and plants and trees and water sit motionless. A bird may sing, but this is just counterpoint. I, too, join the leaves, stop walking, even thinking. I listen as though in the stillness I might hear something new. There is nothing; but the fragile beauty of the moment slowly expands, and I do not move lest I break it.

The moment ends, of course, but without fire and wind, it is a Pentecost.

Occasionally, in the pages of our more literary magazines, I see advertisements for a little gadget that drowns out background noises by making another noise, usually that of a whirring fan. It does not produce quiet, but a noise you can tolerate so all the noise outside your bedroom or study won't disturb you. It is a strange solution, not unlike the "hair of the dog that bit you" that heavy drinkers are familiar with the morning after. It is surely a sign of the desperate state we have arrived at that we must make one noise to stifle and mask another. I like to think that the reason why people wear Walkmans when they jog or bicycle is to drown out the clash and din they glide through. But when I see the Walkmans in the quiet of the woods, I'm not so sure. If they really wanted quiet, earplugs would do. No, I think we have gotten addicted to noise.

It is not surprising. It is a noisy culture. Even here in this quiet spot where I live, noise skirmishes along our perimeter. Above lie a couple of flight paths along which jets rip loudly in and out of O'Hare Airport. Route 83 to the east of us now has six lanes, 31st Street to the North has four, and they are always full of rush, rumble, and squeal. Draglines still sound from the neighboring subdivision, and for five years now we have heard that cacophonous mix of hammer and rock music that appears to be an inevitable part of housing construction these days.

But your noise is worse than mine. I spend some time in homes with children. Children are always noisy, but now they have state-of-the-art techniques to amplify their din. From the moment they rise until the time they go to bed - and that may be deep in the night if they are older - they fill the space around them with electronic racket. And the end is not in sight. Advancing close behind the woofers and tweeters, videos, and speakers that make up the present generation of bedlam are the spreading battalions of cable, big screen, and high definition TV that promise to suck up the last remaining corners of silence we have left to us.

Ironically, even prayer has gotten noisy, especially the Mass. From beginning to end we have sound - words preached, prayed and chanted; songs (more verses than there used to be) and background music when we're not singing; greetings, introductions and hearty dialogues between presider and congregation; and sometimes even applause for the choir. Some moments of silence are allowed, but they are not real silence. They are instead brief, awkward pauses that are more like the stunned hush that comes over us when the TV blacks out than they are moments of prayer. One easily gets the impression that we feel as compelled to fill our prayer with noise as our kids do their play.

> T. S. Eliot asked us:
> "Where shall the word be found, where will the word Resound? Not here, there is not enough silence."
> *Ash Wednesday*

Silence. We need some silence in our lives. If for no other reason than to settle ourselves down, to loosen and relax the snarling of our nerves that comes from too much exposure to noise. But there is a more important reason we need silence, and it is found in a story about Elijah the Prophet.

Elijah went up to a mountain cave to wait for God's word. Like most people of his time, he figured God would present himself in a big ostentatious, noisy event. So, when the first big sound arrived - it was a great wind - he rushed out to greet Him. But it was just crashing noise. Then came an earthquake. More noise, just noise. Then a firestorm. The same. Finally, there came a soft breeze, almost soundless. To his surprise, God was in the breeze. He spoke to Elijah from the quiet.

Elijah was like us. Because of his fascination with the Big Sound, he almost missed the word of God. Our addiction to noise is a similar barrier. T. S. Eliot also wrote that there is "no grace for those who walk in noise." We will hear no word of God unless we find ourselves some still place and still time in which to walk.

Despite the airplanes and Route 83, quiet is what we do best here at Mayslake.

Homesick
Winter 1989

I write this just two weeks after getting back from four weeks in California. I spent that time, between Thanksgiving and Christmas, at one of the old Franciscan missions there. (The Province gave me the time off to do some reading and writing that I don't have time for here at Mayslake.) It was also a time to "get away from it all". What I found, to my surprise, was that almost from the day I got there, I wanted to "get back to it all". I was homesick.

When I told people out there that I missed Chicago, they shook their heads in amazement. It was December. The sun shone and the temperatures rose past 70° every day. Ripe oranges hung from trees in the mission's back yard. People walked the beaches in shorts, and surfers steadily addressed the rolling swells up and down the coast from L.A. to San Diego. Why would you miss Chicago? I checked the weather in Chicago. I considered the ice, the snow, the cold. I remembered the bulky clothes and balky overshoes of winter. I thought about the cranky heating system at Mayslake, the dark, barren trees, and the dried up sticks of last summer's grass and flowers. And I still wanted to go home.

"Home" is the key. Some of the reading I had been doing in California spoke of the sacredness of being at home in a special place. Simone Weil, contemporary French mystic, writes, "To be rooted is perhaps the most important and least recognized need of the human soul." Wendell Berry, farmer and poet, dismisses today's fascination with becoming "global citizens" in a "global village". "One can only live fully in (the global village) by living responsibly in some small part of it." Belden Lane, theologian at St. Louis University, deplores the "deliberate placelessness" and "innate restlessness" of Americans, and yet sees their very frantic moving about as a nostalgia for "the perfect place", for home.

I thought of this last comment as I looked about my surroundings in southern California, a place truly stacked with the rootless: the hordes of retired Midwesterners huddled in trailer parks; tens of thousands of military personnel, both active and retired; the omnipresent throngs of migrant field workers far from home, sleeping in makeshift shelters, even in holes dug in the ground. "Deliberate placelessness" indeed.

Home, I reflected, is important because it is where I can best be myself. It is where my friends are, my family, my coworkers, those I minister to. So, it is where I am best known and understood, where people are more likely to judge me by what I really am, not by what I appear to be or by what kind of service I can perform.

Home is also familiar and predictable. When I am home, I don't always have to be anxiously preoccupied with the unknown, even the threatening. A soul, I think, grows best when it has great long stretches of the familiar to nourish it. As I say this I wonder what else people leave behind when they sell their houses and set out for the warmth of the sunbelt. In surrendering houses for a place, however pleasant, is something of the soul left up North as well?

Home is also a sacred place. For one thing, I pray better at home. I have my favored bench on the east wall of the Portiuncula Chapel for the warm weather, and the first pew on the left in the main chapel when it is cold. I find too that I pray more regularly when I am in the more predictable routine of home.

Home also becomes a sacred place because I know more about it. Have you noticed that the more you know and understand about a person, the more respectfully, reverently you treat him or her? The person's soul begins to reveal itself to you, and you walk and talk more softly when you see that, just as you are more quiet and reverential in church. Familiarity breeds contempt only in the insensitive. This is true of place as well. The better you know a place, the more it reveals itself to you, the more sacred it becomes. You can only do this if you stay at home in one place long enough, and pay close attention to it.

For example, I know every kind of bird that has ever been through here in the last ten years because I pay attention and even maintain a list. There have been 178, to be exact. Last summer we had a Franciscan seminarian with us for a month who also happens to be a skilled botanist. When he asked what he could do, I suggested something I have long wanted - an inventory of every grass, flower, shrub, and tree that grows on our grounds. He did it - and generously. I now know them all, including, no less, the technical Latin name of each. I also know all the different kinds of animals that call this home. We vigorously protect them all from those who would mindlessly mow, trap, hunt, or, in the case of the geese, rob eggs from their nest for breakfast. And so the land gradually shows me its soul. As it does, it teaches me how I can know God. I just need to stay home, pay attention, and I won't miss Him.

In all these ways, a place becomes a home. We never get placesick. But in California, I got homesick.

Jonathan Foster, O.F.M.

The Meaning of Squirrels
Spring 1990

This winter here at Mayslake we were preoccupied with squirrels.

What we were trying to do, of course, was to feed birds. Four friars on the staff this year maintained bird feeders. The largest, most elaborate, and busiest of them is Fr. Bonny's. It stands in the front yard near the north entrance. You might think it a cage were you to give it only a casual look. It is a homemade affair with round platform and ceiling, completely contained by chicken wire mesh small enough to fend off the larger birds and squirrels. Bonny also fed in a variety of other ways: casting seed and bread on the ground; hanging suet from wires and strings; from time to time even putting out peanut butter covered bagels. Protected from the northerly winds by a loose flap of old canvas, the large, ungainly feeder platform - twice blown away by high winds - stimulates almost constant street activity by the foraging birds, and gives his operation a homey, ragged feel like that of an old fashioned barnyard. Fr. Kieran's feeder on the other hand is a prim finch feeder, a tubelike affair with neat perches next to neatly drilled feeder holes. It appealed only to finches, who apparently like to eat sideways, but the feed they kicked out was grazed by mourning doves and juncos. My feeder is named by its manufacturer "Hylarious," a name that refers to the antics of squirrels attempting to pierce its nearly squirrel-proof construction. Its feeder box opens onto a narrow trough. The platform where the birds perch to eat is weighted on a spring. When anything heavier than a cardinal alights, the platform sinks and at the same time throws up a baffle over the feeder trough, making it impossible for heavyweights to clean out the seed. I also spread seed regularly on the ground since there are birds, e.g., juncos, who prefer to feed there. Fr. Paul's feeder eventually attracted the most attention, if not of birds, at least of the staff here. Paul mounted his feeder directly on his study window so he could watch the birds and at the same time deprive all other seed predators of a favorable perch. As winter relaxed into spring, neither Paul nor anyone else had seen a single bird nip a single seed from his feeder.

His problem was squirrels. The feeder was mounted on suction cups in the midst of window glass in the hopes that the squirrels would be foiled in their approach by the lack of purchase. The squirrels, however, solved the slick glass in the way the Germans solved the Maginot Line in France in 1940. They simply bypassed it. They climbed up the brick wall and hung by their toes to feed upside down from the top of the window. One entrepreneurial rascal simply dropped into the feeder and curled up, as on a chaise lounge, to eat in comfort.

We all had similar confrontations with squirrels and we all worked creatively to thwart the clever rodents. Bonny's chicken wire mesh effectively sealed out most of them, but not all. I once stood face to face with one of them, I outside, he inside angrily gnashing his teeth and thrashing his tail. Moreover, many times adventurous squirrels repelled down the strings and wires from which he suspended a variety of goodies, and adopting often unbelievably acrobatic positions, proceeded to strip them clean. My squirrel-proof "Hylarious" was pretty effective against these marauders. But one inventive critter solved it. Instead of sitting on the sinking platform, thus shutting off the feeder, he shinnied up the platform pole, avoided the deceptive perch, and, albeit at what appeared to be an uncomfortable angel, managed to twist his head in such a way as to feed from the end of the trough. The squirrels were never tempted to solve Fr. Kieran's finch feeder, but they too were quick to profit from the seed kicked out onto the ground.

We were not seriously offended by these inroads on our efforts to feed the birds. We were in fact quite amused, both when foiling them and foiled by them. What strikes me, however, is the serious lengths we undertook to bar the squirrels from the bounty we provided the birds.

What is this partiality we have for birds, and this bias against squirrels? Could it be that it is a matter of preference for a kind of wildlife that does not challenge us? Squirrels after all are pretty smart, adaptable and enterprising. Most birds are not. Just as we have systematically gotten rid of the wildlife that threatens us bodily - bears, wolves, wild cats - do we surreptitiously harbor a resentment against those, like squirrels or coyotes, who challenge our intelligence, indeed, those ingenious enough to make themselves comfortable with our lifestyles?

It is interesting, now that humans have overwhelmed the environment, to observe the wildlife we still have close around us. They are the bright, entrepreneurial ones who have survived the waves of human invasion, and have set up camps behind the lines of battle so to speak, to profit like a Fifth Column from our lifestyle. They are usually not the most attractive of the lot. Among the birds are the starling, the house sparrow, and pigeon, foragers on human garbage that you will find even in the most distressed of urban slums. Among the animals are rats, mice, coyotes, raccoons; among the insects, cockroaches. And yes, squirrels.

Ironically, we seem to dislike and resent the very wildlife that prove to have the same triumphant and dominating survival skills we have. We like wildlife, but by and large, except in zoos and remote National Parks, we seem to like it tame and pretty, dumb and weak. These we feed. The rest we shoo away, kill or otherwise try - vainly it must be said - to extirpate. In other words, we wish our wildlife to be unthreatening to us at all levels. We are unwilling either to be mauled or outfoxed by it.

But, as is rapidly becoming clear, we cannot continue to pick and choose our environment according to personal tastes. If we do, we will eventually destroy it, because to pick and choose is to ignore the inner bonds between us and the environment, bonds St. Francis recognized when he called all creatures brother, sister, even Mother. When we rip out from the familial fabric only that which pleases us, we tear the fabric apart. Squirrels, furiously and persistently undoing our efforts to keep them out of our bird feeders, are but one reminder, however small, that we need to live, not selectively with the pieces of creation we like and control, but in full harmony with all of it.

I will continue to feed birds in ways that by and large foil the squirrels. The poor dumb birds after all might not make it on their own through a tough winter. But I will also cast seed freely on the ground where squirrels and birds can have at it together. And I will be glad, not angry, when they solve my "squirrel-proof" feeder.

Dispatch from Guelph - Woodchucks
Summer 1990

(NOTE: Fr. Jonathan made the 30-day spiritual exercises of St. Ignatius during the month of May at Guelph, Ontario, Canada. This is an occasional piece he sent us from there.)

The cattle here on the Jesuit farm and retreat house grounds would be well-advised to be wary. Today they were let into one of the previously gated pastures that had grown rich and lush from recent rains. From their current venue - a mixture of trampled mud, cow-flops and stubby chopped grass - they could see and smell the thick new grass, and had begun to bawl mightily, like a baby in sight of an inaccessible bottle of milk. But they need to restrain their joy in that new pasture. For should they gambol about heedlessly in pursuit of the best grass, they are quite likely to break a leg in a woodchuck hole.

The pasture till now has been the private preserve of a few Canada geese working their way upslope from the pond below, occasional retreatants adventurous enough to climb fences - and woodchucks. Especially woodchucks. Their dens stud the pasture like foxholes. Indeed, everywhere on this 700 acre farm I get the sense of an army invading from the underground. Alert heads pop up from secret holes as I gaze around. Low, fat, furry bodies scurry back into the safety of their defense works as I approach. New escape routes are added to existing networks. There are literally hundreds of these raggedly dug and unkempt holes about. I find them in open fields, along fence lines, under clumps of trees, in the deep woods, in the midst of the flowering orchards, right in the middle of the lawn. I should think they outnumber the 45 of us retreatants and all 250 cattle nicely. Someone asked me the other day what the farm must look like from underneath. I can only imagine the New York City subway system.

Except for this slovenly indifference to landscaping and their grass eater's fondness for growing things, they are harmless and timid creatures. They have no attack, and but one defense - flight to the safety of their dens, no matter its location. I happened once to get between a woodchuck and his den before startling him. He literally ran right at me to get to what was safety to him, and I, the source of his fear, had to sidestep nimbly to keep from being bowled over.

Woodchucks show up wherever humans leave a few undisturbed acres, and so they are part of the world of wildlife that gets along with us. Much to the chagrin, unfortunately, of many of us. Some trap them, humanely or otherwise (here at Guelph the Jesuits are humane). Others shovel dirt into their holes and pack them shut in the hopes of burying the beasts alive, apparently forgetting that what these animals do best is dig. Some are even known to plug up all the alternate entrances after they have cornered their prey, then build smokey fires or even run auto exhaust into their dens to suffocate them. All of this is done, of course, in the name of protecting garden, lawn or flowerbed. I suspect much of it is our ancient instinct of predator and prey. No more wolves to shoot, so we hunt woodchucks.

Though partial to lawns and fresh vegetables, I temper my partiality with a preference for living at peace with woodchucks. And for that matter, with all the wildlife I travel with aboard Planet Earth. One of the small but constant sorrows I have in life is that the woodchuck - though he has no cause - is terrified of me. I wish we could both just sit up and get a good look at each other. I have similar cringes of disappointment when a bird or animal I simply want to watch misinterprets my intentions and flees into a thicket or wood. Annie Dillard speaks of an "innocence" some people have with wildlife, a presence about them that allows critters to let their guard down and go about business as usual when they are present. (It is not a coincidence that the Latin root of "innocence" means "intending no harm".) Francis of Assisi apparently had this kind of "innocence".

We can all, however, have some degree of this "innocence" which allows intimacy with wildlife. All we need to do is "intend no harm" and we do that best when we go among wild things on their terms, not ours.

Just this past spring at Mayslake I woke up one morning to discover that a pair of mourning doves had chosen my study as their nesting site. They had selected the track between the inside window, which was closed, and the storm window which had been opened. I was immediately smitten with the intimacy of the situation.

Doves are far prettier and appear more fragile, indeed smaller, on the nest than they do shooting rapidly around the countryside, and so they called up from me whatever protective instincts I have. This intimacy however put my study on a completely different rhythm. I could move nothing that was near them. For a time I couldn't even open the adjoining two windows, and then only the more distant one, and that very carefully. I always moved slowly in the study, and was even reluctant to turn on the light at night. Every time I did so, he or she (they alternate brooding) raised a questioning head as though ready to caution me about unbecoming behavior. The price we pay for intimacy with wild creatures is that they make their pace ours. Fortunately, before I left for Guelph I was blessed to observe the hatching out of the first of their two little white eggs.

Such intimacy evokes the "golden age" imagery of Isaiah II, wherein he describes the messianic era in terms of harmony within creation. Natural enemies, above all human and animal, live at peace with each other in a vision of a restored Eden. "They do no hurt, nor harm on all my holy mountain." Throughout Christian history, with but odd exceptions (like Francis of Assisi), this vision of harmony between humans and beasts has been a romantic's dream, indulged in mostly by idealistic writers and artists, and the occasional mystic and natural historian. The rest of us could take it or leave it - cute, uplifting, like Bambi, stories for kiddies. Serious grownups, about the serious business of life, need not be concerned.

The time when we can dismiss Francis of Assisi and his kind as harmless nature lovers is rapidly ending, for it is becoming clear that the fate of the human race is inextricably tied up with that of the wildlife around us. Planet Earth is not a stratified class structure where the lower forms lie in supine submission to the needs and humors of the higher (read human) forms. The earth is a community of interdependent life forms. Touch one, you touch them all. John Donne noted that "no man is an island" to any other. We need to understand, and soon, that neither is the human race to its fellow species.

Jonathan Foster, O.F.M.

Clare and the Red Fox: A Cautionary Tale
Autumn 1990

Mayslake once again has a resident dog. Her name is Clare, and she is very tiny and fragile-looking, a skittery little Chihuahua about the size of a teddy bear. Clare came to us this summer with a new member of our staff and community, young Fr. Michael Jennrich. She is slowly overcoming an understandable timidity and is gradually getting used to the rest of us.

She is also gradually getting used to her wild brothers and sisters outside on the grounds. Quite a civilized and urban girl, she was at first even terrified of the occasional bug she would encounter in the house. But, having screwed up her courage to the sticking point, she now, on her daily sanitary walk with Michael, dashes prettily at chipmunks, birds, even squirrels. They all - needlessly, one thinks - run away from her. But one day there was a critter which didn't.

Michael and a visiting friend were sitting on a stone bench by the Portiuncula Chapel, and Clare was frisking freely about out of sight. When they got up to return to the building, they came around the front of the chapel to the main driveway. As they did so, they were stopped in their tracks. There was Clare, quivering with excitement, as she stood nose to nose with one of the red foxes that live here on the grounds. Neither appeared to be threatened or threatening, neither was running away. They were exploring each other, two members of the dog family, totally unfamiliar with each other as individuals or species, one exquisitely manicured by domesticity, the other rank with wildness; but beyond their differences, they sensed a bond that had united their kind for over fifty-million years.

Michael's first reaction was understandable. The fox was so much larger than Clare, and so much more used to the red tooth and claw of survival in the wild that he feared for her safety. He called out sharply. The red fox spun away and sped off to the woods. Michael later acknowledged that he had overreacted. There was little danger for Clare, and the moment of encounter was so poignant that even in the retelling of it, his eyes glowed with excitement.

Indeed. Such moments of encounter between the tame and the wild are rare. And while they are a little scary, they fill those who share them with an indefinable eagerness that calls them out of their customary world to one hidden and unknown, yet not felt to be hostile. So it was that the Little Prince tamed the fox he met in the desert. He did not simply dismiss him as a wild animal who brought nothing of value to his own world. He sat down at a respectful distance and watched the fox patiently, moving a little closer each day till their worlds, though unchanged, finally met and found their oneness. This, I like to think, is what Clare and the red fox sought.

What was true for Clare is true for us humans. We are proud of our civilization, but far more than we like to believe we have been shaped for the better by the mysterious forces of wildness that surround us. Wendell Berry, farmer, poet and university professor, is but one of many who speak of the "necessity of wildness" in our lives. Civilization stands for the ascendancy of the human endeavor over the throbbing intensity of the life the Creator has put into Nature. Civilization thus breeds in us not only a temptation to arrogance that seeks to dominate Nature, but perhaps even a promethean instinct to steal fire from the God of Sinai, Tabor and Calvary. In Berry's words: "The most dangerous tendency in modern society . . . is the . . . severance, once and for all, of the umbilical cord fastening us to the wildness of the Creation. It lies in the willingness to ignore an essential paradox: the natural forces that so threaten us are the same forces that preserve and renew us."

We are heirs, however forgetful we may be of it, of a long tradition of intercourse with the wild and mysterious that has provided the "forces that preserve and renew us". The Chosen People of the Old Testament found their purity during the forty years they spent as a nomadic people in the wilderness of Sinai and the Trans-Jordan. There they had been closest to God and farthest from human arrogance, and their prophets would often call them back to that wilderness time. Jesus himself sought out the same rocky wilderness to prepare himself for his ministry. Christians throughout history - from the Desert Fathers to Thomas Merton - have always sought wild and untamed places to escape to the clear wonder of God's face. Francis of Assisi passionately took possession of fierce Mt. Alverna to which he often fled for renewal.

The Puritans, though at first they hated the brooding wilderness of New England as symbolic of sin and evil, came to recognize it as something quite else. For they discovered that it was their labored striving with the reluctant wilderness that formed their character and spirituality - and was to shape American society for three centuries. They found grace in the woods as well as in the towns. Thus it was that Thoreau, who came from all these traditions, could write his famous lines:

> Our village life would stagnate if it were not for the unexplored forest and meadows that surround it. We need the tonic of wildness - to wade sometime in marshes where the bittern and meadow hen lurk and hear the booming of the snipe; to smell the whispering sedge where only some wilder, more solitary fowl builds her nest and the mink crawls with its belly close to the ground. At the same time that we are earnest to explore and learn all things, we require that all things be mysterious and unexplorable, that land and sea be infinitely wild, unsurveyed and unfathomed by us because unfathomable. We can never have enough of nature. We must be refreshed by the sight of inexhaustible vigor, vast and titanic features, the seacoast with its wrecks, the wilderness with its decaying trees, the thunder and cloud, the rain which lasts three weeks and produces freshets. We need to witness our own limits transgressed, and some life pasturing where we never wander.

All the above is written by way of yet another verse in the Requiem for Mayslake. There are at Mayslake none of

Thoreau's "titanic features, and seacoasts with wrecks". It is not Yellowstone Park. The red fox that Clare encountered is about as exciting an animal you'll meet here. But smallness is no indicator of wildness. The poor city cousins of wilderness, the forest preserves and Mayslake, are the only truly natural sources of mystery left to us in this part of the country. Music and art, human love, even worship, though often divinely inspired, are human contrivances. Even such relatives of nature as pleasant lawns, pretty flowerbeds, trimmed hedges, pet dogs and cats, are not enough, for they reveal the human hand more than that of God. Alongside them all, indeed, encroaching upon and even threatening them all, we need that part of God's creation that "pastures freely" and forces us to "witness our own limits transgressed". For wild nature alone is the unique preserve of God. He awaits us there as much as he does anywhere, and we strip away this sacred ground at our own risk. Thus, even the small wildness of Mayslake provides a place for us to come up against God.

I pray that the loss of the Mayslake land, however reasonable it may appear from other perspectives, will give pause to all of us - sellers, buyers, brokers, displaced users - that we might consider how to ensure that this be the last piece of sacred wildness to be lost. At the very least, we need to grieve the loss of mystery that these few acres bring to so many people.

When was the last time you had that same sense of shivering wonder Clare must have known when she stood nose to nose with the wild fox from the woods?

Bridges, Not Piers
Winter 1991

One of the experiences of my boyhood that still comes pleasantly back to me is the crossing of old swamp bridges in the family car. We would always have to cross one or two of them in order to get to the fields where we picked blackberries or huckleberries, or when we took a Sunday evening drive to look for deer along Minnie Creek or Bear Creek in my native northern Michigan. There remain clearly in my memory the rattle and clump of loose boards as we carefully made our way across the dark waters of the swamp-fed streams. I do not remember a fear that the bridge would collapse beneath our weight, but simple excitement of anticipating what lay beyond the stream the bridge opened up to us.

Since then my love for bridges has continued, and I never come to a stream of any kind that I do not look for a bridge across it, or, at least a convenient place to make a leap for it, or hopscotch across on rocks and fallen timbers. And I still love to hear the rumble of loose planks as I drive across, and the hollow thump of footsteps as I walk. I have to cross streams because there is too much on the other side to miss.

Much later in life I learned something else about bridges from a nun named Roberta. She was the first person to introduce me to that bridge between human beings we call love. In the summer of 1967 we worked and lived together with a team in New York State as part of a pastoral project. I remember walking with her out onto one of the bridges that span the Hudson River nearby. A far cry from one of my swamp bridges, it was a great engineered wonder of steel that arched smoothly up and over that great river. Besides us two pedestrians, it carried an incessant flow of gas powered traffic that did not bump over loose planks but whined over unyielding concrete. I was self-conscious out there in mid-river with this nun, but she, unembarrassed, walked the bridge as a metaphor. As it bound together two remote banks, so love bound together two people distant for many reasons from each other.

Thoughts of bridges remind me of another body of water that constantly stretches, unbridged, before me. It is the sea that stretches between me and God. I have been satisfied most of my life to let Him remain on the other side, only dimly seen and heard, signaling to me with a kind of mystic semaphore, while I mess busily around over on this side. I have not been anxious to build a bridge, or even find one.

What I have been satisfied to build is only a pier. When I was a boy, I regularly saw a mute symbol of that effort. For years, just outside St. Ignace, Michigan, on the north side of the Straits of Mackinac, a pier-like ruin jutted out forlornly into the waters. One could see it from the ferry which crossed the Straits. Built in 1941, it was in fact the first attempt to bridge the Straits. Only in the 1950's was it finally incorporated into the splendid bridge that now proudly unites Michigan's two peninsulas. But for years it ran perhaps only a few hundred feet out into the water, then stopped. What it offered was only a marginally improved view of the other side. What it did not offer was a union. Like that ruin, my "bridge" to God unfortunately has only been a pier made of self-indulgence, promises, and good intentions.

Bridges and piers have been very much on my mind this year. There is the bridge our staff, the Board, and I must build as our ministry here at Mayslake ends next summer. There is the bridge thousands of you must build as you look for another sacred place like Mayslake to spend sacred time with God. And there is the bridge which each of us is called to walk as we listen to God's steady invitation to love.

What kind of bridges will these be? They probably won't win any architectural awards. Last spring when I was on my 30-day retreat in Canada, I used to cross every day the kind of bridge that is the most likely metaphor for the spiritual bridges you and I must build.

Upon confronting this bridge for the first time, a sensible person would pause and calculate his chances. Its deck is simply two sawed-down tree lengths thrown across some 20 feet of open water. They are aged, unfinished by saw or adze, still bearing dried and curling bark, and supported by only a few triangular steel fence posts which themselves have settled askew under the weight of the logs. For most of its length, the bridge is planked with lengths of board unevenly cut, firmly nailed, but crudely spaced so that the water beneath can be seen. Halfway across there is a bump in the bridge, created by a six or eight inch high timber, squared by hand, and firmly fixed to the deck with railroad spikes. This surprising elevation appears to be an obstacle of some kind, but to what is not clear - cows, bicycles, joggers? Perhaps the bridge builders just ran out of boards. At another place rusty pipe, like those in cattle gates, takes the place of a board. And at the near end, on top of the boards, has been nailed a three foot square piece of plywood panelling, its paint a faded blue, and parts of its wood warped. What raises the most caution, however, in the first time stroller is that the entire bridge is warped, twisting gently down, then up, from near to far end. Consequently, it sways when crossed.

It is this precarious bridge that is my metaphor. It reminds me of the ones of my boyhood in the Minnie Swamp. Like those bridges, it at least gets you to the other side. Like Roberta's bridge, it unites, binding bank to bank. But mostly it is rough and ramshackle. Building this kind of bridge is usually all we saints and sinners can manage. The rest is in the hands of Him whom Paul called the bridge named "Peace" (Eph 2:14). But he does not come to us if we are content only with piers.

Soil for the Ministry
The Flowering of the Mayslake Community
Autumn 1993

    This spring and summer, as never before in my life. I have been intensely aware of the succession of flowers over the land, the "Parade of Flowers" as I have come to call it. Why now and not when I was at Mayslake? It's probably due to the fact that I have to drive 12 miles to the office and 12 miles home every day, sometimes twice a day. I am impatient with driving, the radio usually bores me, I can't listen to tapes, and so I watch the passing scene. There, what columnist Bill Stokes once called "the glory in the ditch" caught my eye. Beginning in early Spring and extending right on into the late Fall, each species blooms prettily, has its day, then yields to the next in line. And so this year I watched the bright yellow daffodils in their extravagant growths at the Morton Arboretum yield in turn to the vast delicate carpet of blue-eyed marys at Will County's Messenger Woods. Next came the lush and fragrant lilacs, both wild and domestic, which handed on to the equally fragrant honeysuckle. The deep blue wild iris bloomed next in their remote marshes, and were followed by white dancing fields of daisies. Then, pale blue chicory - a weed to most - took over the roadsides, and it will stay a long time. But, it makes room for the almost odorless, warm pink bushes of wild roses that bloom in late June. Finally, with the advent of high summer - when I write - the brown eyed susan has sprung up in the fields, and sturdy queen anne's lace has taken its throne as regent of the summer.

It is the same soil, sometimes even the same plot, that produces this restless and relentless blossoming of life. All this colorful variety of plants has roots in the same soil. Despite the clever genes of each, despite their variable response to air and wetness, despite their creative adaptations to environment, none of them can survive without good soil. And so this succession of flowers is a parable for one of the critical issues of our times. What is more important: the individual or the community? The individual's responsibility for the community or the community's responsibility for the individual? Does the individual exist to serve the common good, or does the community exist to serve the individual? Are the flowers in all their flashy display more important than the dull and unpretentious soil in which they grow? Philosophers and theologians, political leaders and poets, generals and popes have struggled with this issue since the dawn of the human race. Different periods in history, different cultures and religions have stressed one or the other of these two, always seeking a balance, rarely achieving it.

Does the flower exist for the soil, or does the soil exist for the flower? The urgency in our days arises from the widespread perception that the pendulum has swung too far in the favor of individual rights over the rights of the community. Individualism, it is feared, has gotten out of hand. In their scramble for what they feel they've got coming to them, people are dangerously neglecting that which sustains them all and makes possible the unique and colorful life of the individual - the common good. The war over abortion is a good illustration of this. On the one hand, there are those who favor abortion. They stress the right of the individual woman to self-determination concerning her body. On the other hand are those who oppose abortion, especially abortion for convenience sake. They protect not only what they believe to be the more fundamental right to life of the unborn. They are also concerned about this jagged rip in the moral fabric of community caused by the legitimating of abortion.

The conflict over the individual vs. common good exists within the Church too. Here the debate swirls about the authority, and even the person of the Pope. On the one hand are those Catholics and their, more or less, liberal theologians. The heart of their teaching is the rights of the individual Catholic - both the right to his/her own moral decisions and the right to interpret scripture and doctrine according to their own lights. On the other hand are those Catholics and their, more or less, conservative theologians who rally around the Pope. They see him desperately trying to hold together the center of Roman Catholicism by his worldwide preaching of orthodox Catholic belief, especially as it affects the common good.

The problem with too much individualism is that it tends to disengage us from our communally shared roots. And without roots there is not much possibility of life. If you've ever driven across the sagebrush deserts of the West and encountered tumbleweeds, you know what I mean. These are plants severed from their roots, and they are simply blown about at the mercy of the wind.

I mull over this issue constantly as we build our new ministry. Since we are not part of the classic communities of the Church, a diocese or a religious order, I am concerned that we not become tumbleweeds, rolling about at the whim of whomever is in charge, relying only on ourselves, answerable only to ourselves. It is for this reason that we have undertaken a bold experiment. We call it, for now, the *Mayslake Community*.

The *Mayslake Community* has as its purpose to support Mayslake Ministries. This it will do primarily in two ways. First, members will be asked to recruit retreatants for our various retreat offerings and, in general, to promote the ministry. Second, members will be called upon to function as a "Town Hall" for the ministry. Since we will be feeling our way for some years, if we are smart, throughout it will be important that we solicit our constituency about the nature, usefulness, and timeliness of our programs. Thus, for example, this Fall we will assemble as many of the members of the *Mayslake Community* as possible, to brainstorm and evaluate the development of our Faith and Work ministry. This kind of assembly will take place several times a year. We may also call upon the *Mayslake Community* to perform other services in support of the ministry such as making calls in the event of a capital fund drive. It is not, however, a dues paying organization with expectation of annual contributions. Special programs and offerings will be made available for the members of *Mayslake Community* which will not only be spiritual in nature, but celebrative and community building as well.

Who belongs to the *Mayslake Community*? Currently it is an invitational membership. Last Spring we selected 88 names from our mailing list. Each of these were contacted by mail and by phone inviting them to join. Of these, about 50 have accepted our invitation. We held our first convocation at St. Margaret Mary Parish in Naperville, June 26, and about 30 of these were able to attend. As time goes on and the community develops, further invitations will be considered and sent out. Former Mayslake sponsors will recognize in this concept some of the elements of the old Mayslake Retreat League. Indeed, it was the success of this program that inspired the *Mayslake Community*. Just as there was a real sense of "moral ownership" of Mayslake by the members of the Retreat League, so it is our conviction that the same kind of ownership on the part of the people we serve must characterize Mayslake Ministries. In a sense, this is what called us out of the collapse of the old Mayslake to initiate this new ministry in the first place.

Community, if I may say so, is the good soil in which the individual grows and without which, like the tumbleweed, it simply bounces around till it dries up and dies. As it is beginning to do, the culture needs to reexamine its lopsided commitment to the individual and work to restore a healthier balance. So does the latest blossom in the church's "parade of flowers" - Mayslake Ministries. It too needs a soil in which to root itself. This soil for us, we pray, is the *Mayslake Community*.

Jonathan Foster, O.F.M.

Time for Christmas, But Not for Christ?
The Incredible Shrinking Retreat
Winter 1993

Every year, Advent is the same frustrating experience for me. Like many of you, I am drawn by its simple warmth and simple holiness. I put up an Advent wreath and light the four tall candles of waiting. I eagerly sing the ancient hymns, read the familiar and encouraging stories about Isaiah, John the Baptist, Mary, Joseph, Elizabeth and Zachary. I listen to the silence of Advent, and hear once again with gratitude its promises of home and harmony. That lasts for maybe a couple weeks. Then, the reality of the approaching Christmas Day crashes through everything like a bulldozer. The parties, the shopping, the decorating, the Christmas cards, the cookie baking, the noise, the hype, the visiting of relatives, and since I am in ministry, the preparation for the lavish celebrations in church. Suddenly, and sadly, the waiting hours of prayer are over with, plowed aside by the demands of the season. Suddenly, at this most prayerful time of the year, I don't have time to pray. It isn't surprising that what I often meet Christmas Day is not Jesus - only Christmas.

At any time of the year, not just Advent, the most frequent reply we get when we invite people to retreat is the plea, "I don't have time", or "I don't have enough time for a weekend retreat", or, as in the following query submitted to us recently: "Do you offer a one hour retreat?" One Hour? Considering that the first retreat, designed by St. Ignatius of Loyola in the 16th century was to last *thirty days,* this request has to represent bedrock in the downward spiral of the public's commitment to retreat making. The thirty day retreat was never the norm for the length of a retreat. It was designed by Ignatius for Jesuits, and even they quickly cut it back to eight days for the normal retreat for religious and clergy. Religious and clergy have found that even eight days is too long, so that the normal length today is more like five or six days, and often less.

Lay people of course had different problems. Because of their commitments to family, and because their employers did not look kindly on them devoting work time to prayer and contemplation, and because they weren't expected to be as "holy" as nuns and priests anyway, the good Catholic laity had to confine their retreats to weekends. But they were full weekends - starting, at a minimum, Friday after work and ending late Sunday afternoon. Some even squeezed out an extra day of work and began on Thursdays. For example, the Cursillo weekend opens on Thursday night and ends Sunday night. Most retreat houses today still try to hold on to at least some Friday to Sunday retreats, but it is a struggle.

First, people really do perceive themselves as having less time. It is one of the great ironies of our time that as fast as we are handed labor and time saving devices, just as fast do we soak up newly liberated time in a frenzy of new work and activity. "Work *does* expand to fill the time available." We do appear to be too busy.

Moreover, business has picked up the term *'retreat'* and now frequently refers to any workshop or training program for its employees held away from the office or plant as a retreat. Since these are frequently but one day or part of one day in length, with no overnight, a broad segment of the public is getting the idea that a retreat is just a brief ducking out of the daily grind of work.

Today many Catholic parishes are offering truncated programs of spiritual renewal, usually at the parish center, and calling them 'retreats' or 'retreat days'. Some of these last only a morning, or an afternoon, or an evening. Some parishes are now calling their missions 'parish retreats'. So, you can go out for about an hour, three or four nights a given week, hear some talks, attend a prayer service, and tell yourself comfortably that you "made a retreat this year." Some parishes do a little better and offer their parishioners one overnight, e.g., Friday evening and Saturday. (The popular Christ Renews His Parish program is a modification and downsizing of the Cursillo mentioned above.) Some parishes do not require the overnight, but simply offer a Friday evening and Saturday morning and afternoon program, and call it a retreat.

Downtown churches, which do not have residential parishioners are also getting into the "mini-retreat" business. Recently, we received a flyer announcing a *retreat* downtown at a Catholic center. Readers were assured that it would last only "three and a half hours" - including an evening meal.

It is tempting to dismiss these programs as just one more example of this culture's preoccupation with slimming down and shortcuts through such products as "lite beer", "mini-donuts" and "weekend getaways". And, of course, to a certain extent they are. But there is nothing wrong with these programs in themselves. They are in fact signs of a renewed interest in lay spirituality. They are particularly valuable if they are seen as the first step to something deeper. Unfortunately, the impression is often created that these experiences are what a retreat is all about and that you can get all the advantages of a retreat by participating in one of them. This is especially pernicious when parishes do not promote other, more extended kinds of experiences.

We at Mayslake Ministries are proponents of what we call the *long weekend.* We believe a retreat requires a minimum of two overnights at a place away from the parish and the work-a-day world. Our reasoning is simple and is based on experience. Unless there is this commitment of time, it is not likely that people will find their way to the center of their lives.

Our world today is so filled with stimulus - sound, sight, information, color, uncertainty and change - especially change - that it takes increasingly longer to shed these, or get behind them to find a quiet place. A few hours, a day, even one overnight rarely allows us to achieve that state. The mild euphoria of a mission certainly does not allow for this. Even two overnights is regularly insufficient. One of the most frequent reactions we get from retreatants as they prepare to leave after two days is their reluctance to go because they are "just getting into it".

One of the favored features of the Christmas story is that of "gifts". The Magi were the most famous gift-givers. They brought gold, frankincense and myrrh. The shepherds are said to have brought a lamb or two. We are asked to give God something at Christmas also. Money, usually. But before and after money, we are also asked to give something else - *time*. Time to be with God in prayer and celebration. We are asked to do this, not only at Christmas, but throughout the year.

So, right in the face of all the demands being made on your time, give time to God. Make a retreat! A long weekend retreat. But, for right now - give some time to Christ this year, not just to Christmas.

"Stupid Galatians" and a Walk in the Snow
Spring 1994

For most of us who are not children and do not ski, there were few moments this past winter when we could really enjoy the out-of-doors.

I had one of these moments early in February. It followed a couple days of snow that had given us 5-6 inches of cold new powder. It was still snowing when I got up, but by the time I settled down to pray, the clouds had retreated before a cold front, and a dazzling sun had burst out of the blue sky into the bright new wintry coat. It was an irresistible summons, so I put on parka, hat, muffler and boots, and walked out into the shiny cold to continue my prayer on the streets of the town.

I stayed away from the main arteries, edged past the school where bright patches of children were being loaded from school busses and Mom's vans, and after a few blocks came to the Forest Preserve woods that edge three sides of the town I live in. Picking out a faint, snow-filled game trail, I struck off into the woods. It was a walk of Grace.

I was praying over Paul's letter to the Galatians. "Stupid Galatians", he called them because they still did not understand what Jesus was all about. They were not Jews, and Paul had taught them the simple gospel that God loved them no matter who they were and what they had done, and that this was enough. But some *faux* Christians - more Jewish than Christian - had gotten among the Galatians in Paul's absence and managed to convince them that they must also live under the old Jewish law. This law was said to be God's, but it had become a maze-like thicket of human prescriptions. These Jewish Christians - or, judaizers, as they were called - taught that you could win favor with God only by observing that law in all its minute particulars. But, because most people could not meet its demands, it had become a burden, a yoke, and a source of great anxiety. Most perniciously, it suggested that even in the matters of God, human works are more important than the works of God. Paul, on the contrary, was trying to teach the Galatians that this is not the way it works. Jesus' ministry sought to free them from that burden, and to let them know that God's love for them was far more effective than their love for God, far more important than their observance of the law, or 'good works'. Paul reminded them that it was God who had freed them from the Egyptians, not Moses. But, like the Hebrews of the Exodus, who didn't want to let go of the "leeks and melons and garlic" of their slavery, the Galatians apparently preferred this Law to God's. "Stupid Galatians", indeed.

As I shuffled quietly through the woods, the new snow became for me a metaphor of what Paul was writing to the Galatians about. Snow, like Grace, comes unbidden on its own time, often unpredicted. It democratically falls everywhere, not confining itself to deserving neighborhoods. It appealingly covers dirt and garbage. (Luther once called humankind "a dungheap covered with snow"). It softens harsh edges ("stiff rails softened to swan's down", as James Russell Lowell put it) - and puts graceful curves on harsh angles. Because of the snow and because the leafless trees stand bared to the sunlight, wintry woods are filled with a brightness they never otherwise have. And snow is quiet, making no sound of its own as it falls, and muffling all others. So quiet was it the morning of my walk that I could barely hear the street traffic of people en route to work, and was startled by the sudden shriek of a red bellied woodpecker. The woods, unsightly on their own time, had been made lovely by the snow. Just so, the work of Grace on us all.

It is Paul's conviction about Grace - illuminated by a snowfall - that guides our work at Mayslake Ministries. We do not presume, like the judaizers in Galatia, to understand how God works. Nor do we assume that our knowledge and skill in preaching, worship and spiritual direction count much towards making you more pleasing to God. That's his business, and we trust that he will get it done.

Jonathan Foster, O.F.M.

Nighthawks: A Personal Observation
Autumn 1994

The summer ended for me this year on August 22. That morning, when I looked out the window of our offices in downtown Downers Grove, I saw four or five nighthawks dancing through the sky. Because they are among the first, and certainly the most visible of the migrants heading south, nighthawks are the robins of fall, marking the last days of summer.

Nine inches in length, their long wings prominently barred with white, they look a little like hawks, but they aren't really. They get their name from the graceful way they dart and sweep around the sky "hawking" insects. They're actually first cousins to the whippoorwill, with whom they share the practice of flying around with their large mouths hanging open, the better to inhale the myriad of insects they consume each day. They hunt mostly during the nocturnal hours, and because they like to roost on flat roofs of urban areas, their loud plaintive call, "peent, peent" is often heard in cities after nightfall. For all these reasons, "Nighthawks" was the name Edward Hopper gave his famous painting (now hanging in Chicago's Art Institute) of three men and a woman sitting in silence in an all-night cafe.

I look forward every year to the return of the nighthawks. I don't see them much the rest of the year, probably because of their nocturnal habits, and I miss their beautiful flight, in which, sweeping up and down from side to side, they seem to dance rather than fly. Their numbers in migration can be very dramatic. I remember encountering an enormous flock of them one late summer day as I drove up Route 83 through the Forest Preserves. Flying low, by the thousands, they swerved and flickered just above my car so that I seemed to be driving through a flock of giant insects.

Nighthawks also announce the coming pleasures of fall. The damp heat of high summer yields to cool, dry, sunny days. Patchworks of scarlet, orange and yellow break out helter-skelter through leafy woods. Apples and pumpkins. Indian corn and Indian summer. Sky-blue asters. Goldenrod. Yes, even football. Of all the four seasons, fall is the one I like best.

But the coming of the nighthawks is also a bittersweet experience, for I am saddened too that summer is over. I will miss the lush greenness of it all. The warm waters and the cold drinks. The fresh green vegetables and the red roses. The bare arms, the shorts and sandals. The relaxed pace. Vacations at the sea shore, in the mountains, in the north woods of Michigan and Wisconsin. The early dawn, the lingering dusk, the long sunny days. All drifting away. The schools are open again and people get on with the serious business of life. And I am only too aware that after the interlude of fall, will come the grey, leaf-stripped and cold lifelessness of winter, the year's chilly death.

Lately, the coming of the nighthawks has been especially poignant for me. I have turned the corner of three seasons in my life, and life each year feels far more like fall than summer, even late summer. I agree with C.S. Lewis, who wrote in one of his letters that, *"Yes, autumn is really the best of the seasons."* And I like it when he goes on to compare old age to fall, suggesting that like fall it may be the best part of life, though, as he dryly points out, *"of course, like autumn, it* (old age) *doesn't last."*

I certainly want to believe this is the best season of my life, indeed, I suppose I have to believe that now, though I didn't 20 years ago. But when the season in which I am living is clearly the last season before decline sets in, the coming of nighthawks heralds a mixed message. It is a little unnerving to realize that fall is harvest time, when farmers bring in the apples, potatoes, the corn and the soybeans. And so it is time for me to bring in the sheaves and bushel baskets of my life and set them down before the Master of the Harvest.

A great part of this harvest will be the coming to fruition of the project we have undertaken with the Benedictines at Marmion. It comes not in the summer of my life, but in the fall, and so I am tempted to think of it as some kind of dramatic climax. The Big Bushel. The Giant Pumpkin. The blue-ribbon winner at the County Fair.

But, making a success of Mayslake Ministries is not God's primary interest in me. Time after time in the Scripture I read about God telling me that it is not the temples I build, nor the sacrifices I offer that he looks for. *"For you are not pleased with sacrifices"*, the psalmist says of God, adding: *"my sacrifice, O God, is a contrite spirit; a heart contrite and humble you will not spurn."* (Psalm 51:19) The harvest, the yield, the crop, the fruit that God waits for most anxiously is not what I have achieved, not my success, not even Mayslake Ministries. God waits simply for myself. From spring planting, through summer's sun, and in fall's harvest, God waits a whole lifetime to get back the one thing he gave me in trust in the first place - myself.

For those like me who think that pleasing God depends on being successful, this is a hard lesson to learn late in life. But I am learning it, however slowly. And it is a message that more and more informs my ministry.

Please pray for the success of this ministry. But pray mostly that no matter how empty the hands I - and you - bring before the Master of the Harvest, we can all be at peace if we bring our hearts.

The nighthawks have all gone south by now. Look for them again at the end of next summer, when, another season in your life has turned.

Christmas and the Electronic Sun
Winter 1994

    We have no idea of the real date of Jesus' birthday. The date we celebrate - December 25 - was not revealed in the bible, and indeed did not come to be celebrated until 200 years later. One of the reasons why the church chose the current date is that it approximates the winter solstice (December 22) when here in the northern hemisphere night throws its dark cloak farthest over the hours of the day. Christmas is celebrated on one of the first days in which light begins its six month journey to seize the day from darkness.

    The rest of the church's liturgical year also follows the sun. Thus Advent and Christmas are the feasts of winter. Lent and Easter are the celebrations of Spring. Ordinary time is the celebration of the summer growing season. Appropriately, the feasts of All Saints and All Souls, the remembrance of those who have died, are observed in the midst of the autumnal harvest. This entwining of worship with the course of the sun reflects the church's wisdom of integrating faith with everyday life by establishing a rhythm between the two.

One of the most ancient practices of prayer in the church was also based on the course of the sun. It is the Benedictine practice - dating from the 5th century - of punctuating the day of work in a rhythmic fashion with periods or 'hours' of prayer, or, as we have come to call it, "the Divine Office". "Ora et Labora" - "Pray and Work" - was St. Benedict's mantra, and he sought to do this by interrupting the day eight times with communal prayer. Benedictine monasteries still do this today.

This kind of seasonal and daily rhythm is important, indeed critical for the Christian life, because it emphasizes that faith is part of daily life, the "everyday spirituality" and "the spirituality of work" that we talk much about here at Mayslake Ministries. The opposite of rhythmic spirituality is "Bookend Spirituality", in which faith is separated from daily life the way book-ends are separated from the books they enclose, or, as is the case for many of us, the way Sunday Mass appears to have little to do with the rest of the week.

The problem with following this seasonal and daily rhythm is that our sun, which has set the rhythm for so much of the church's prayer, is being replaced by a new sun. The new sun is the Electronic Sun, and it has its own rhythm. It artificially lights the night, communicates live images instantaneously across planets, continents and seasons, and gives us, for example, the strange phenomenon of professional athletes ice skating in southern California in June. Environmentalists, and the spirituality which emerges from them, are urging us to hold onto the kind of natural, solar based rhythm that has formed the basis of the church's traditional prayer. And they are right to do so. But we cannot ignore the rhythms of the electronic sun, which seem to affect more of our lives than the natural sun.

The rhythm of the electronic sun is formed by the radio alarm clock at 5:30 AM, the morning news, rush-hour to work and school, the morning talk shows, the afternoon soaps, after-school activities, the rush home again, the evening news, prime time, and the late night twin giants of triviality, Leno and Letterman. Our seasonal rhythm also follows the electronic sun. It includes the artificial light of daylight savings time, Christmas in October, football in February, basketball in June and baseball in November. Rhythm therefore has not disappeared from our lives. It just follows a different sun.

It is for this reason that Mayslake Ministries' collaboration with the Benedictine monks at Marmion is so providential. The 300 acres of Marmion Abbey where our new home will be located is just about a mile north of I-88, and just about a mile west of Farnsworth Avenue. This makes it a place of quiet within one of the most booming commercial and industrial stretches in Illinois, the "Loop", one may say, of the western suburbs. It punctuates the rhythm of the Hi-Tech Corridor both symbolically and in reality. The symbolic value lies in the fact that it will occupy very valuable real estate that proclaims nothing more than the value of 'Sabbath rest' to men and women frantically carrying out the work of the other six days of creation. Its real presence will be realized in a number of ways: as a quiet, restful place to drop into for a visit; as an alternative, prayerful lodging for those who travel into the area on business; for retreats throughout the year addressing the need to establish rhythm between faith and work; as a place even for certain kinds of meetings not at odds with the sacred nature of the retreat/guesthouse space. What better way to re-establish rhythm in our own spiritual lives than by spending time in a place where men and women still stop their work several times a day to pray and reflect?

There is another rhythm that will be obvious to those who come to our retreat/guest house. The monks grow and sell Christmas trees that green not under the electronic but the natural sun. These men praying in rhythm with the day, growing trees in the rhythm of the seasons will now be joined by a retreat house that will proclaim rest and quiet to the busy men and women who live and work under the electronic sun.

Trust: A Cardinal's Song, or A Walk on the Lake?
Spring 1995

Sunday, February 19, was a soft, luminous day. I had celebrated Mass the day before as a part of a retreat I had given, so I rose a little later, put on old clothes, skipped shaving, and headed out to the canal trail near my home for a long, contemplative walk. The woods were filled with sunshine, mild air, and the first colorful outbreak of joggers, dog-walkers and rollerbladers of the year.

It wasn't long before I heard what I knew I would hear that morning - the song of the cardinal. I hadn't heard it yet this year, but I was sure this would be the day. Before my walk was finished, I had also heard the lonesome song of the dove, and the sweet languorous love-call of the chickadee. It was clear to me from that moment that Spring was coming to Chicago. For the song of cardinals, the doves and the chickadees, hardy veterans of the winter that never go south, are the true Gabriels announcing Spring. Only weeks later do the red wing blackbird and the robin, those popular, but fair-weather heralds of Spring, show up.

Because I tire easily of winter, I always wait eagerly for these songs. Sometimes they come earlier - sometimes later. But I always know they will come.

I can always trust the cardinals. He may sing a little early or a little late, but you are absolutely sure, as sunlight fills more and more of the morning sky, that he will sing announcing Spring.

Indeed, I trust the cardinals more than I trust God.

God is never so predictable. Years may go by before God does what I think he ought to do. In the meantime, things may happen to me, things, I say, that would be unimaginable if there is a truly loving God. But then suddenly, I am blind-sided by grace, and there he is. Trusting God can be like waiting out a century of winters without a cardinal's song, then unexpectedly hearing it loud and clear in the midst of a bitter January blizzard.

This matter of trusting God is one of the most frequent problems people bring to me in spiritual direction. Who wants to give up control of her life and trust such an inconsistent, unreliable and unpredictable God? It's not easy. Indeed, it is the first and most difficult challenge of the spiritual life.

There are alternatives of course. We can trust in ourselves, our skills and hard work, our charm. We can trust our fellow humans. We can trust in our technologies. We can trust our genes - good teeth, good bones. Some of us even trust the stock market, or, more recently the casino riverboats in Joliet and Aurora. But of course our track record with this kind of trust doesn't produce a very convincing bottom line. None of this cocky self-confidence gives us the kind of control we'd like to have. The belief that we are in control of our lives is unquestionably a myth, but it is one of our most cherished myths.

I like to talk to my untrusting spiritual directees about the story of Peter walking on the water (Mt. 14:22-33). I take that story a lot more seriously today than I did ten or fifteen years ago. In those days I assumed that if there was to be any walking on water in my life, it would be because I was clever enough to know where the stones were. Today, I realize, after considerable research, that there aren't any stepping stones out there. But, I also think I still see Jesus out there, the spume and spray of the storm whipping about his face - and mine - and I think I hear him calling me to walk to him. On the water. Without the stones. So, whom do I trust? Jesus? ... or me?

If I trust myself, I most likely will take the conservative approach and stay in the boat. But Jesus isn't in the boat. Or I might stick one foot into the cold water, and pull back in terror. What happens in all these cases is that I never get to Jesus.

So, what does it mean to trust God? Let me say first what it doesn't mean. It doesn't mean I never have butterflies in my stomach; that I'm never anxious; that I feel good about trusting; that I am never in darkness. Trusting is not always a feel-good experience.

On the contrary, *trust is as trust does*. We must act on what we believe God is calling us to, even though we are frightened and confused. Trust means we continue to pray for peace and justice in this world, though it never seems to arrive. Trust means that we continue to spend time in prayer, though we rarely experience the presence of God. Trust means that we continue to pray for deliverance from an affliction though nothing ever changes. Trust means that we continue to live according to the Gospel though more and more people think it absurd of us to do so. Trust means that, if we are in Peter's shoes, we step out onto the water, not believing we can do it ourselves, but confident that Jesus will keep us from sinking.

All the great spiritual writers understood the importance of trust. Cardinal Newman, for example, wrote: *"Therefore, I will trust Him - if I am in sickness, my sickness may serve Him; if I am in sorrow, my sorrow may serve Him. He does nothing in vain. He knows what He is about. He may take away my friends, He may throw me among strangers. He may make me feel desolate, make my spirits sink, hide my future from me - still he knows what He is about."*

Trusting that the cardinal will sing in February is a lot easier than trusting in God. But then it's not nearly so important. I can survive a late Spring. I cannot survive if I refuse to walk on the water with Jesus.

The Illusive Iris
Summer 1995

We had a chilly, wet spring this year, and most of us groused about it. But a friend of mine who is a gardener emphatically rejoiced in it, claiming that it was the first real Spring - by which she meant cool and damp - that we had had in years.

It was certainly good for the wild iris that grow in the woods near my home. Wild iris are a marsh flower, and thrive only where it is wet. Not as big and showy as the typical backyard iris, they are colored a delicate lavender with a spray of veined gold at their heart, and are half the size of their royal purple cousins. But they are graceful, as all iris are, and have in recent years captured my heart. They also hold up well as cut flowers, sometimes even putting out new blossoms in their glass environment. So, for the last couple years, I have been plucking them from their damp habitats to grace my home.

But this year, they were almost unreachable. The rains were so prodigious that instead of growing up in damp spots, the iris in my woods stood in foot deep water. And they seemed to like it, since they bloomed profusely. Any attempt on my part to reach them would only have resulted in plunging into cold water to an uncertain bottom. So, except for one attempt - a precarious sortie onto a dead log that reached out into the marsh - I left the iris in the woods.

But I am glad for that one effort. I brought five iris blossoms home that day, set them in a vase of water, and placed them on the small shrine in my study where I spend my prayer time. A day or so later, I was praying with the book of Job, Chapter 38. Job is demanding an explanation for his misery, and God responds with an awesome description of his power and wisdom in creation. I was wishing and praying that I might have something of Job's experience of God, when I fixed upon the iris.

The iris is a very fragile part of creation. Indeed, the original blossoms on the stalks I had picked had already faded, and I had snipped them off. However, one new blossom had unfolded from its tight pocket, and another was in the process of doing so. I watched. It occurred to me that, if I wanted to see the petals move, I shouldn't take my eyes off them for a minute. But, the first petal fell away from its clasping leaf while my eyes wandered elsewhere. So, I decided to watch more closely, and brought the vase closer to me - just a foot away.

Since I have a limited attention span, I am not particularly good at this kind of concentration. Whether it is prayer, looking at beautiful scenery, observing great art, or listening to music, my mind tends to wander. Moreover, if I keep my eyes focused on anything very long, my watching turns into a glassy stare that might just as well be focused on nothing. So, occasionally, I would look away from the iris, but then quickly glance back to see if I was missing anything.

The petal did unfold, but so slowly and so imperceptibly that whether I stared at it or took quick glances, I never saw it move. After 10 or 15 minutes however it had clearly blossomed. Within a half hour, after I had finished my prayer time, the flower was as full and graceful as any that had bloomed before. But, I had seen nothing happen.

I found this a little frustrating. Maybe I had seen too much time lapse photography. Maybe the fast and highly stimulating pace of modern life has disposed me more to action than repose. Maybe, voyeur-like, I was demanding a peek into mysteries I had no right to see. But, I wanted action. I wanted to see those petals actually move, observe the sinews of life at work. The frustration, however, was an important experience for me. Watching for God obsessively, it occurred to me, like watching an iris petal unfold, is no guarantee that I will catch him in action. Long hours of exercise will automatically consume calories, but long hours of prayer - while important because he may come at any time -- will not automatically produce the experience of God. It made me realize that what is important about my experience of God is not actually seeing him at work, or even feeling his movement within my life, but simply acknowledging the results in the world and in my life.

Many of us do not 'feel' the presence of God in our lives. We often conclude from this that he is 'absent', and we wonder and worry about when he will return. So, the experience with the iris blossom ought be of some comfort for us. Our relationship with God, like my relationship with the blooming iris, does not depend on experiencing the blossoming, but of simply seeing the blossom.

Ripening
Winter 1995

Last August I spent a day in the Arkansas Ozarks, near the Buffalo River National Park. The Buffalo is the first and still the only river to be given the title "National River" and I wanted to hike along its banks. It was a very hot and humid day, with temperatures in the '90s, and so, wearing shorts and sandals, I showed up at the ranger station to seek directions. They were friendly, but they practically ordered me to put on long pants, socks and shoes, and to cover myself with insect repellent to ward off the chiggers and ticks that swarm in their woods at that time of year. Reluctantly, because of the heat I obeyed, then drove a couple miles to buy a can of "OFF". Thus swathed and slathered, I took off on a brisk jaunt up a wooded trail that followed the dips and contours of the river. What little breeze there was that steamy afternoon was effectively screened out by the trees, and that, combined with the exertion of a steady upward grade, stimulated every sweat gland in my body so that my clothes quickly became an oily mat of perspiration and chemicals that hung on me heavily like wet cardboard.

I did this for only an hour, and for the last fifteen minutes I was steadily obsessed with just one thing - relief, which was available close by from my car's air conditioner. I nearly ran the last fifty yards to my car, unlocked it, jumped in, closed the door, turned on the ignition and switched the air conditioning fan up to an arctic high. I toweled down, quickly changed back into shorts and sandals, sucked the juice out of an orange, and within ten minutes was tooling along in an artificial environment that left me, except for the dried sweat and caked dust, exactly where I had been 90 minutes earlier

Such sudden environmental shifts are not uncommon and certainly not unwelcome in my life. This time however a warning light popped on. Was the change of environment too abrupt? I could have allowed my discomfort to recede gradually, like a high tide. I could have simply sat under a tree and allowed my heart rate to slow down, and the breeze, what little there was of it, to lift some of the sweat from my body But no, because there was the chance for instant artificial relief, I rejected the natural process. I did not give nature time. I couldn't wait!

I do this a lot, allowing unnatural but quick patterns into my life that by-pass natural, but slower rhythms that require time. I am, in other words, rejecting the process of ripening. Plants require a certain time to sprout, flower and ripen. So do babies and small children. Communication is more effectively carried out when it is given time. Species require centuries of slow adaptation to new environments. We all know these things, but we persist in our "wisdom" of shortcutting the processes of ripening. Kids become adults too fast. They expect instant success after college. They mate too fast. Sadly, they divorce too fast. All of us travel too fast. We collect information too fast. We switch channels too fast. In our communication we rush too fast to the bottom line. Ripening is disappearing from our lives, replaced by artificial stimuli that offer a wide range of attractive substitutes. But these substitutes are also addictive. Each of them successively applied brings us closer to some unrealistically perceived utopia of total satisfaction and control, and so presses us to even quicker fixes.

This same phenomenon exists in the spiritual life. If our prayer does not provide satisfaction, we are ready to look for another prayer, or even to give it up altogether. Because computers have dramatically shortened the gap between request and response, we are coming to expect God to act in the same way.

So, here it is Advent again. Advent is hard to find beneath the thick, jungle-like overgrowth of Christmas festivity. Covering the four Sundays before Christmas, it is the season set aside by the Church to recall the long centuries the Israelites put in as they awaited the Messiah's arrival. Advent also commemorates the millennia that Christians have been waiting for God to put the world to rights. It is, if I may say so, the Season of Ripening, when we are reminded once again that things move ultimately not at our pace - much less that of our computers and air conditioners - but at God's pace.

What have we gotten for our waiting? The nation and the world, even the Church do not appear to be demonstrably better than they were last Christmas. Indeed, a case may be made that they are worse. For example, Lord and Taylor was putting up Christmas displays already in late August (now these are folks who understand 'ripening' - albeit of another kind).

What about the two of us? I know I am no better at faith and prayer than I was a year ago. You probably aren't either. Our new retreat house has a model and fund-raising plan it didn't have a year ago, but it's still far more a 'promise' than it is a 'place'. On a personal level, God doesn't seem to be any closer to me now than he was a year ago, and I expect your experience is similar. This waiting upon the Lord can get tiring.

What does it mean to "wait"? It doesn't mean that we throw up our hands in resignation and do nothing. Indeed, God expects us to use whatever resources we have. We wait, not passively, but actively. We act, as the old proverb says, as though everything depended on us, and pray as though everything depended on God.

What is most important to note is that waiting is not something we do because there is nothing else to do. Waiting is the most appropriate activity of human beings who believe in God. It is a recognition that God is creator of all, sovereign of the universe, Lord of history, and loving provider of the Grace that saves us. It is therefore a humble acknowledgment that the world and our lives run on God's time, not ours. **Waiting in a sense is an end in itself.** Waiting is not an inert activity, like the wait of exhausted commuters for a bus. It is ripening in a divine sun and rain. It is growing in God's time.

My prayer for you, then, this Advent is that you learn to live more in God's time than your own. That in your waiting upon the Lord, you ripen.

Jonathan Foster, O.F.M.

When Work Is Toil
A Lenten Message for Workers
Spring 1996

Recently, we asked a group of working people to function as a focus group, and advise us on our "Good Work" retreat. One of those invited was unable to attend, but sent us a letter. He is a middle-aged tradesman who has been very successful in his career. In part, this is what he wrote:

"I am afraid the "Good Work' retreat is a thing of the past. I think most people do not even want to talk about work for a weekend. The people I talk to seem to have a low feeling about the company they work for, all seem to be waiting for the axe to fall on someone, downsize the place - mergers lose jobs too. Just this week someone in my building barricaded themselves in the office because they were let go. I was in our main lobby last year when a lawyer was let go. He was taken out by security screaming, "You can't do this to me!" With this in mind, how can people relate to God's presence at the work place with this kind of hostility by company and workers?"

This kind of complaint is heard with dire frequency these days. "Work sucks" as another of our participants said. And it is not just the workplace that creates problems for people. Frequently, it is our own attitude towards work that makes it stressful for us. Many, especially males, so over-identify themselves with their work that when their positions are lost or threatened, they wonder emptily who they are - even when they have spouses and family. More and more people have such high expectations for a material standard of living that they work so hard and so long that other values are lost sight of - including family, and their own spiritual lives.

So what do you do when work is hard, stressful, anxiety-ridden and unsatisfying? The media are full of similar stories and a raft of helpful suggestions. Workshops on handling stress in the workplace have become a cottage industry.

But what does our faith have to tell us? How do you fit the time on the job, which consumes more of our week than any other activity but sleep - and some people tell me it even consumes more time than sleep - into the spiritual life? The simple answer lies in looking to the central symbol of Christianity - the cross. The long shadow of the cross, which falls over all of life, falls also on our working hours. Pope John Paul II, in his masterful encyclical *"On Human Work"*, notes that all work is sometimes "toil" and that "the Christian finds in human work a small part of the Cross of Christ."

What this means, in practical terms, is the following:

- First, that, even in the midst of the difficulties of work, we remain faithful to performance of the job. We do not slack off. We do not do just what is necessary to earn a paycheck. We do not dump our work onto others. We do not take out our frustrations on coworkers.

- Second, we do not simply whine about our situation. As exploited workers do in organizing unions, we work to correct what can be corrected.

- Third, we remain faithful in another way - faithful to God in prayer and worship. When God rested on the Seventh Day of Creation, he meant that humans rest too. This "rest" was not to be just a physical one, but a spiritual one as well. Unless we take time out to pray, it is very easy for us to lose sight of the reason why we work, and how even work that is "toil" can be a source of life. It was for this reason that Pope Leo XIII in his great encyclical *On Capital and Labor* (1891), so strongly resisted efforts of owners to make their employees work on Sunday

We can also learn from the Benedictines to pray ***during*** the workday. Benedictines, even the very active ones at Marmion in Aurora and St. Procopius in Lisle, pause several times during their workday for common prayer. It is not as easy for the laity to do this, but I know of more than one worker who closes the office door for a few minutes of prayer during the day. There are also a whole array of daily prayerbooks available now that help us introduce prayer into our daily life and work.

In sum, then, work placed in the context of the Cross makes all work, especially work that is "toil", a sacred arena where God's presence can be felt. It was in pain that Job experienced God. Paul eloquently describes his own suffering associated with work when he recites the grim inventory of his "boasts" in the second Letter to the Corinthians (11:23-28). Jesus spoke of the joy that is present in pain when a mother is bringing a child into the world (John 16:21). And it was on the cross, in the midst of the apparent wreckage of his own work, that Christ, faithful to his Father to the end, gave us the model of how we are to live, including how we are to work when work is "toil".

Many who have gone before us have been able to find meaning in the most degrading work. The African slaves in American, as they confronted the oppression of their work, developed a powerful religious faith that carried them right through the triumphal civil rights movement of the last 20th century. Exploited workers during the industrial revolution, rather than turning away from the injustices of the workplace, found solidarity with one another, and formed the other great human rights movement of modern times, the labor movement. Oppressed workers have even created art-forms. Much of the folk music of common people, including work-songs and chants, and especially the "Blues", were a response to harsh working conditions.

A contemporary, Chicago based social psychologist, M. Csikzentmihalyi (pronounced Chick-sent-me-high) has studied workers with a view to discovering what in their work gives them the greatest satisfaction, and allows them to enter into the experience of 'Flow' (the title of his book). To his surprise he discovered that when the proper attitude is present, a worker experiences great satisfaction even in the most menial jobs. It is his conclusion that it is not the work itself that is most critical in determining whether a worker is fulfilled, but the character of the worker and what he/she brings to the task.

Clearly, for the Christian, an awareness and acceptance of the reality of the Cross in life is crucial in approaching work that is toil. Remember this on Good Friday when we celebrate the dying and rising of our God, who not only understood, but experienced the same sufferings we all face, and from which we all draw Grace.

Learning What Trust in God Means
Summer 1996

The following remarks were made by Fr. Jonathan on the occasion of the signing of the lease with Marmion Abbey, and the announcement of Mayslake Marmion Ministries Capital Campaign, May 5, 1996.

It is just six years ago this month that we first learned for sure that Mayslake was going to be shut down. We were given a year of grace to wind things down, but the deed was done and published in the lovely month of May.

That decision, of course, caused within us a lot of anger, frustration, sadness, even a sense of failure. For me it raised another question - What do I do now? I had become committed to Mayslake, it had even come to define my life, my very being. What's next? I could continue giving retreats as an itinerant preacher. I could continue to do spiritual direction wherever I could find a room to meet people in. I could pursue something I had wanted to do all my life, something for which I had some skill - and that is be a writer. All of these were elements of my ministry at Mayslake.

But they were only elements, bits and pieces that I could not easily separate and break off. For my ten years at Mayslake had convinced me that all these pieces could only come together and be made whole by a special place that supported, enriched and gave life to them all. For me, the ministry of the spiritual life had come to mean something very simple - providing people with sacred time in a sacred place. Sacred time, sacred place - this is what Mayslake meant to me. And I just couldn't pull all the pieces apart.

There were enough other people in our ministry who embraced this vision - Mary Jo from the staff and members of our original Board - Sr. Madelyn, Mike Busse, Rich Pagliaro, Val Rand are among those still with us. So, this vision, "sacred time, sacred place", became our dream, a dream that we felt we were called to by God.

The thing about dreams, however, especially dreams you believe are from God, is that it isn't always clear how you are ever going to put them into practice. We had no site, no building, very little money. We were advised that we probably couldn't raise more than half a million dollars from our clientele, far short of what we would need to put up a new building. We had no religious order, no diocese, no foundation to provide us with a safety net in case we ran out of money. Much of our clientele had been alienated by the closing of Mayslake, and even some of our colleagues in retreat ministry in the Chicago area felt we were crazy to put up a new retreat house. We didn't even have office space till three weeks after Mayslake closed.

So, I have spent a lot of time and energy these past five years learning what trust in God means. I have learned more about trust in these years than I learned in all my thirty years of ministry before Mayslake Marmion Ministries began. And I have learned it with some difficulty. I have learned that when you trust God, you don't depend on your own resources, your own skills, your own education and experience, your own wisdom, your own networks, even on your own hard work. You use all these, but they don't always work. I have also learned that trusting God doesn't free you from anxiety, worry, doubt, fear of failure, even the temptation to quit. I have experienced all of these. Trusting God does not dispel the butterflies in your stomach. I have learned also that trust doesn't necessarily "work" - that is, just because you trust that this dream of yours is God's dream, too, doesn't mean it will come true. What you learn when you really trust is that in matters of the spiritual life, in all of life indeed, it is finally God's business and not yours. What trust really means is that you remain faithful to the call, no matter how bleak the future looks, no matter the failures, no matter the opposition. You keep putting one faithful foot ahead of the other, and let God lead the way. I haven't learned that lesson entirely, but it's slowly gaining headway in my headstrong heart.

But, I believe that it is because of this trust that we gather here today on the grounds of Marmion Abbey. In 1991 when we started, we certainly never imagined we would be working with Benedictine monks. We, after all, came out of a Franciscan tradition. Most of us didn't even know where Marmion was. Nor did we initiate the eventual collaboration. It was one of the monks of

Marmion who first whispered in our ear that we ought to talk to the Abbot about our project. That was the summer of 1993 We took his advice, and the rest is history. The contact with the monks of Marmion has been the clearest sign of Grace and Providence that I have ever experienced in my ministry. And it came not because we were so smart, but because we had no other option but to trust.

The other great sign to us that our dream is God's work is you, and the hundreds like you that are not able to be here today - people who have supported us by your prayer, by your volunteer work, by your participation in our programs, by your financial commitments. We thank you for all of this and because the dream is not finished, we ask you to continue to walk this way of trust until it is.

This trust is really another word for faith. The Letter to the Hebrews tells us that *"faith is the realization of what is hoped for and the evidence of things not seen."* (Heb. 11:1) The epistle goes on to offer the patriarch Abraham as a sign of that kind of faith/trust. *"By faith - Abraham went out not knowing where he was to go. By faith he sojourned in a foreign country, dwelling in tents. For he was looking forward to the city with foundations, whose architect and maker is God"* (Heb. 11:8-10). This is a pretty good description of Mayslake Marmion Ministries. Please stay with us. We have to dwell in tents for a little longer. But the "city with foundations" is within sight. We just saw it a few minutes ago.

(Ed. This last sentence refers to the ritual in which the building site was blessed.)

The Church as Chatty Cathy
Autumn 1996

Some time back, a young reporter called me for an interview about our ministry. In the course of our conversation, I mentioned that there is usually a great deal of silence in our retreats. "Silence," she asked, "like, people don't talk?" "Yes," I said. A pause. "Wow!" she responded. "What a neat idea! Where did you get it?"

I was amused that an intelligent and educated person like this reporter should find silence such a newsworthy phenomenon. I was also a little alarmed. But, I should not have been surprised.

If there is anything disappearing faster than the northern spotted owl, it is silence and quiet in our society. Like a massive sponge, dry and hungry, noise and sound are moving relentlessly over our cultural landscape, soaking up every vestige of quiet left to us. Every car, every motorcycle, every restaurant, every airport lounge, every department store, every grocery store, and sadly almost every room in our homes is rigged for sound with state of the art equipment. The increasing presence of cellular phones moreover is stripping us of the possibility of ever having a guaranteed moment of solitude and quiet

The garage where I get my quick oil changes has a tiny lounge in which to wait out your 10-20 minutes. They used to have a nice selection of magazines, which I enjoyed leafing through. But the last time I was there, a TV had been installed and was blaring out one of those god-awful talk shows in which complete strangers strip down to their private lives to entertain us. The magazines are gone, and I guess the owners felt they were doing us a service by turning on the TV. I had to take a book out into the garage proper in order to escape this noisy intrusion into my life.

Most of us complain about all this noise, but we are getting used to it, aren't we? Now however, I am getting alarmed about another area of life that noise and sound are invading, indeed taking possession of. The area of religion and faith.

Today's Church, while not given over to the racket of boom-boxes, has, I believe, some discomfort of its own with quiet and silence.

In a misconceived understanding of Vatican II, Catholic prayer and worship seem to have made a pact with noise. From the almost total silence of Catholic liturgy before the council, we have evolved a worship that seems to abhor silence as nature abhors a vacuum. Casual celebrants, zealous liturgists, folksy ministers of music rush to fill any gap in the liturgy with song, organ medleys, announcements, and public prayer. The faithful, perhaps taking their cue from all this liturgical camaraderie, have turned the body of the Church into a plaza for casual, even gossipy conversation. It's as though, having removed the Blessed Sacrament from its central place in the Church - for which, admittedly, there are good liturgical reasons - we act like the family that has removed grandma from the parlor so they can party there. Noise, not quiet, defines the ambiance not only of worship, but of the Church itself.

Noise has also come to define the retreat movement as well, although it is the gentler noise of encounter and conversation. Retreats were totally silent before the Council. It is no coincidence, however, that the most popular retreat movements in the post-conciliar period have been 'encounter' retreats: Marriage Encounter, Cursillo, Christ Renews His Parish, and their various spin-offs. Nowadays, silence on a retreat is usually looked upon as downright old-fashioned, "pre-Vatican", as many like to put it. Why? Some people are afraid of silence, perhaps because it requires them to look more deeply into parts of their lives they would just as soon not deal with. Others, perhaps because they are so unaccustomed to silence, don't know what to do with it. Some just think it's wrong to be silent when there is so much you can learn from interaction with other people.

It is becoming clear that the extroverts, who, according to Meyers-Briggs, are the majority in the population, have finally gotten hold of Christian spirituality.

Our ministry here at Mayslake Marmion is more friendly to silence. We recognize that the massive silence that pervaded Catholic worship before the council was unbalanced. We recognize that much of the noise generated in Catholic worship and retreats today is the welcome sound of community being built. We recognize that our relationship with God has a communal dimension. But we also recognize that our relationship with God, with others, and indeed with ourselves, has an individual dimension that requires solitude and silence. Husbands and wives recognize this. While they certainly do not hold back from some public displays of affection, their deepest love does not take place in the living room, but is reserved for more private chambers.

So also with God. We must celebrate God in the community. We must find him in one another. But, we do not find him fully unless we seek him also in the solitude and quiet of private encounter. Hence, we try at Mayslake Marmion to incorporate silence into most of our programs.

In doing so, we may seem to be going against the trends. But, I see other trends emerging in the culture. I was heartened on Good Friday this year to see an example of this countertrend - of all places, on TV. It was on PBS Channel 11, "The Newshour with Jim Lehrer". The final segment of that program was devoted to "Prayer as Divine Therapy". It featured the work of the Trappist monk, Thomas Keating, who has been introducing into this country the ancient practice of "centering prayer". This is a kind of prayer which transpires entirely in silence. There is no singing, no reading, no discussion, no oral prayer, not even much meditating. Participants are simply invited to empty their busy hearts and minds to make room for God. The cameras were invited into a couple such retreats and gatherings, and showed groups of 20 some people simply sitting in a circle in silence. And most of these people were lay people. Fr. Keating has also formed an organization called "Contemplative Outreach" to promote this kind of quiet prayer. It has chapters all over the country, including one here in Chicago.

So, perhaps both the Church and society are beginning to realize, to their embarrassment, that they have been talking too much, making too much noise, and are once again considering the ancient wisdom of silence and quiet.

Jonathan Foster, O.F.M.

Spirituality for Males
From the Christmas Shepherds to "Promise Keepers"
Winter 1996

Two thousand years ago, a handful of people gathered in an open field near the little town of Bethlehem and heard an evangelical message delivered by angels that sent them hurrying off to a nearby ox-stall. They were the first witnesses of Jesus Christ. This past summer, over 60,000 people gathered in Chicago's Soldier Field, heard more evangelical messages, and became the latest witnesses of Jesus Christ. The first were the familiar shepherds of Christmas; the latter were the "Promise Keepers". Both groups were all men.

Often overshadowed these days by the women's movement, and sometimes denounced as patriarchal chauvinists, males have nonetheless played a significant, indeed dominant role, in the history of Christian spirituality. Starting with Christmas.

This latest expression of men's spirituality, Promise Keepers, has become in less than five years one of the significant religious stories of the decade. A movement that is overwhelmingly Protestant, nonsectarian and evangelical, its signature is the great rallies held Friday evenings through Saturday afternoons at football stadiums all over the country. Last year, more than 15 such rallies, comparable in size to the one at Soldier Field, were held throughout the country.

Catholic leaders, looking hungrily at the stunning success of this movement in male spirituality, and noting that at least 10% of its registrants are Roman Catholic, have been casting about looking for a way to emulate it within the Catholic Church. As a result, we have such efforts as "St. Joseph Covenant Keepers" (Florida), "Mission of the Redeemer" (Canada), "Camp Emmaus" (Joliet), "Men's Spiritual Fitness Workout" (Chicago), and "Credo" (Chicago) - the last a clearinghouse and promotional center for what is now being hastily labeled *"men's ministry"*. I welcome, with some reservations, all these efforts. But it is important to remember that spirituality for males is not something new in the American Church, springing up only in our day in reaction to the success of Promise Keepers. There were the shepherds of Bethlehem, of course. But, I would not hesitate to assert that in modern times the most successful effort in spirituality the American Church ever made was carried out by men and for men. I refer to the retreat movement for men.

Begun in the first decade of this century - right here in Chicago at the Divine Word Seminary (Techny) in Northbrook - *retreats for the laity began with retreats for men,* and after a slow start spread like wildfire from the 20's, right into the '60's. It was a movement that not only provided retreats for men, but, unlike Promise Keepers which uses football stadiums, actually built retreat houses, hundreds of them, in practically every diocese in the US, and established its own national office, the National Catholic Laymen's Retreat Movement. Mayslake was one of the largest and most successful of these houses, and at its heyday in 1964, was hosting 144 men *every weekend.* Nationwide, it has been estimated that as many as a million men were making retreats every year (a figure that surpasses Promise Keepers best years!). There was a parallel movement for laywomen, but it started later and never matched the men's movement in numbers. In the aftermath of Vatican II, the men's and women's retreat movements were merged into one organization, Retreats International. During this time, retreats for men began to decline, as many became convinced that all retreats should be open to both men and women. I suspect too that the call by women, both in society and in the church, for equality and recognition, has played a part in this decline. But, there are still retreat houses where men's retreats flourish. One such retreat house, owned and operated by laymen in the suburbs of Philadelphia, still hosts *300 men almost every weekend of the year!*

Here in Chicago, the old Mayslake and the Jesuit retreat house in Barrington, were the principal centers for men's retreats, and such retreats are still sponsored by Barrington, and Mayslake Marmion Ministries.

It is a mistake to overlook this earlier movement in men's spirituality. Not only is it historically unjust to do so, it is, if it leads us to focus only on the model of Promise Keepers, risky. For if we look only at Promise Keepers, we ignore values emphasized in the retreat movement - values of quiet, of good preaching, of good worship, of sacramental confession and private spiritual direction, and the time commitment of 2-4 days in a remote setting apart from the everyday world.

But, what the success of Promise Keepers and other related movements do remind us of is that there is a role for distinct approaches to spirituality for men.

I don't have a lot of space here to go into what characterizes male spirituality. So, let me instead share a story that I think offers some insight. I gave an evening of reflection recently for a group of about 30 men at St. Joseph's Parish in Elgin, IL on the subject of spirituality for men. As a part of the evening, I read them the story of the Prodigal Son. I gave them 15 minutes of quiet to consider the three men in the story: the profligate younger son, the responsible but self-righteous older son, and the forgiving father. I asked them to reflect on which of these three men was most like the men they knew, and most like themselves. In the discussion that followed, a remarkable sympathy was expressed for each of the three men, including the prodigal son, but there was a pretty general consensus that most of them were more like the responsible, but self-righteous, older son than they were like the debauched and dissipated younger boy, and the generously forgiving father. I gave them credit for this kind of honesty. But then, one man, by all appearances middle-aged and blue collar, made this astute observation. He said that in the three men in the story, he saw a development of the typical male. "When we are young, we are like the prodigal son, recklessly and thoughtlessly sowing our wild oats. But, then we grow up, get married, have children of our own, become responsible citizens, but, in turn, become harshly judgmental of the faults of youth, especially if they are our own kids. Finally, if we are blessed, we become like the old man and learn the grace of forgiveness. This is the way God is. The parable is the story of our lives as men." There was a nodding agreement around the room. It was for me also a new and wonderful reading of that famous story, a story of men who can overcome their only too familiar proclivity for irresponsibility and arrogance, and become forgiving and loving.

Let's go back to the shepherds. There are other men, who in all their masculine strengths and weakness, appear in the Christmas story as well. There is Joseph, a devout, working-class Jew who feared humiliation as a cuckold, but whose gentle concern for his wife's reputation prevailed. There was Zachary, John the Baptizer's father and a minor cleric in the lower ranks of the Temple hierarchy. His common sense made him skeptical of the angel's words predicting his aging wife's pregnancy, but it also got him in trouble. There were the shepherds, the poor, illiterate and bad-smelling underclass of Jewish society, who despite their crude lives - they rarely went to synagogue or temple either - were the first to worship the infant. There were the pagan wise men from the East, who were led to undertake a strenuous and dangerous journey. They may have been motivated at the outset by detached scholarly curiosity. In the end they knelt to adore. These men showed up at Christmas in a typically masculine way.

Men today, whether in Promise Keepers or on a quiet retreat, need to feel welcome before God in a way that is just as masculine.

Sandpipers
Spring 1997

In the past six months (I'm writing in January). I have had the grace of spending some time close to both the Atlantic and Pacific coasts. What I enjoy most about such visits is the experience I have when I take out my binoculars, shed my socks and shoes, and go kicking through the surf in search of birds.

One bird I always find there is the sandpiper. Sandpipers - known to bird-watchers as 'shorebirds,' or 'wading birds' - come in many sizes, from the tiny 5" Least Sandpiper to the large, 19" Long-billed Curlew. The majority of them may be aptly described as flirting with the sea. On their long skinny legs, they dash along the lip of the incoming surf, picking at the prizes each brings in, running after it as it withdraws to the edge of the sea, then quickly darting back up the beach as the next billow piles in.

When they get caught in a few inches of swirling water, they fly up daintily, sometimes crying out - indignantly, it seems - as they shake the drops from their feet. But they are never completely taken over by even the most powerful waves. They master an ocean that always seems bent on mastering them.

The ocean is as close as I can come to an image of God. Vast, mysterious, powerful, fascinating, frightening, the sea is nonetheless intimate with us. In the ancient trail of evolution, the sea is the source of all life, which it continues to provide richly today. I think of this as I tread its edge, careful to let it wet only my ankles while I stare out over its rolling expanse towards Europe or Australia. I think at such times that I am like the sandpiper, safely skirting the edge of God while ravenously picking up the gifts he tosses my way.

This interest in the mere margins of God is a condition I think we all share to some extent. Few of us are hardy enough to let ourselves be swept out into the heart of God by the compelling undertow of God's desire for us. Our relationship with God is mostly an endless effort to protect ourselves from him. While we hop around on the beach waiting for gifts, we deny God ourselves. We operate under the illusion that we can control God the way sandpipers may assume they control the sea.

Many of us, for example, try to reduce God to a manageable size, an object we can carefully peruse at a distance and at our leisure. We deal with him as an oceanographer might research the mysteries of the sea. We know this and that about God. We read religious books. We even read the Bible. We enjoy the occasional theological discussion. We subject God to tests about his behavior in history and nature. Indeed, as some rabbis in the concentration camps are said to have done, we put God on trial and find him guilty. But unlike what they did after the trial, we do not turn to prayer. For we know without admitting it that while the finger of God that reaches up onto the beach honors our minds, it is our heart that God really wants.

But we also seek to trivialize God by avoiding the other channels down which he seeks to reach us - ourselves, and our relationships with others.

Thus, we refuse to plunge into the oceanic depths of our own being. We refuse to admit the truth about ourselves and our motives. And so we end up living, if not lies, at least distortions of the truth about ourselves. It is no coincidence that Jesus called "the Evil One" (Satan) "the Father of Lies" (John 8:44), suggesting only too frighteningly that it is off the shadows of untruth that evil feeds. Some of our reluctance to pray, to be alone, to be quiet, is expressive of this fear of our own depths.

We further shore up ourselves against truth by building high seawalls behind which we hide from God. We buy and collect things mindlessly. We obsessively groom our youthful appearances. We carefully nourish sanitized bigotries ("Haven't we done enough for them?"), acceptable addictions (e g., fashion), and socially approved sins (abortion, extramarital sex) the way a sunbather applies layers of sunscreen. Sufficiently lathered over, neither wave nor sun can get us.

We also stand a healthy distance from depth when we fiercely protect our grudges. At the very least, we breathe a cold silence toward those who have offended us. And frequently, we continue to pelt rocks and kick sand in their faces long after the hurt should have healed. In this unforgiving, ungenerous way, we create an increasingly smaller patch of beach for ourselves.

These are but some of the strategies we use to avoid God. Not entirely, to be sure. Just enough that God does not become inconvenient. We prefer a God who is more like the gently slapping wavelets of Lake Michigan in the summertime than when he is like the pounding surf of the ocean. ("Become our uncle" we plead, as the poet Auden wrote.)

That is the other thing about the ocean. My last trip there, I stayed in a home not fifty yards from the surf. The weather was sunny and warm the entire time I was there - no storm or rain or wind. The sea from high on the beach appeared calm, there were no whitecaps. But the long swells broke on the beach in boils of sand and white foam, exploding one after another in an endless cannonade. From inside the house, each wave sounded to me like the gusts of high winds in a howling midwestern blizzard that rattles windows and squeezes whining through the thinnest cracks in the roof. It went on day and night, at 10-15 second intervals, thousands of times a day. It worked its way into my consciousness. I heard it in the daylight when the beaches thronged with people. I heard it at 3:00 a.m. when they were empty and dark. After a while it came to suggest to me the endless, restless, ultimately unavoidable voice of God. I may do a lot of things to stop up my ears against it. I may try to explain it away. But, like the waves, God continues to roll in, and break with a thunderous roar onto the shore, reaching, searching on the beach.

If the sandpiper hears the waves, it is of no concern to him. But if we hear it, and do not heed, we do so at a price.

Visiting a Visitor
The View from Hale-Bopp
Summer 1997

The biggest outdoor event of this miserable spring was clearly the quadri-millenial visit of the comet, Hale-Bopp. The media covered it intensively. Garrison Keillor wrote a ballad about it on "Prairie Home Companion". For 39 people in San Diego it was tragically an omen for which they gave their lives. Most of us at least paused in our headlong and pedestrian lives, and blinked for a moment in wonder. The astronomers took some of the mystery out of it by describing the comet as it really is - a big ball of dirty ice the size of DuPage County, wheeling silent, lifeless, and aimless on a fixed track about the sun. Ball of dirty ice or not, Hale-Bopp is for earthlings a wonder. Surely it must have been for Abraham, who was just setting out for the Promised Land the last time it appeared.

Hale-Bopp is only the latest startling revelation from deep space. The great eye of the Hubble telescope sees so much out there that it makes me shrink back in awe, gasping for sanity against the staggering proliferation of the cosmic population to embrace the familiar hills and lawns of Earth. All this stellar aggregate gives me some sense of what the people of the Old Testament were trying to say when they spoke of the "fear of the Lord." They were not filled with cringing terror, but overcome by a deep sense of awe at God's mystery and power that cast them to their knees not in fear but in worship.

But I had another thought. What if there were some passengers on this comet and they were peering at us through their telescopes as they cruised by? Our earth doesn't have a million-mile long tail, but the astronauts tell us we are a pretty blue ball. That, I'm sure, would prompt a second look from Hale-Bopp. They, like us, would blink, murmur something appreciative, then return to business. But, what if they got close enough to see what lies beneath the swirling mass of cloud and atmosphere? They would find a lot more to marvel at than a blue ball.

One night, I watched the comet from the bluff I live on overlooking Archer Avenue and the DesPlaines River Valley. As I did so, I couldn't help seeing, and at the same time hearing, the rumbling swarm of the late rush hour traffic. My first inclination was to admire the serene heavenly comet and despise the congesting, noisy, polluting stream of traffic below me. But then it occurred to me: why is a comet that produces dirty ice and a long gassy tail more exciting than, say, a slick, self-propelled Corvette that seems sometimes to fly itself? Or, better than all Chevys, Dodges and Fords? They wouldn't appear as dramatic from outer space as a comet, but the ingenuity that created and built them could turn Hale-Bopp into a refrigerated storage place for frozen pizzas if we could just get close enough.

We are always ambivalent about our technology - does it do more harm than good? - but it is only we on Earth (so far) that even have a technology.

A few days later we were giving a retreat at Cardinal Stritch Retreat House in Mundelein. After a couple warmish, though cloudy days, a powerful cold front had blown in and scoured the sky and the air. That evening everyone rushed out after night prayer for the spectacular view. So did I. But I also remembered a walk earlier that day when the comet was not visible. Three deer had come out of the encircling woods to graze calmly on the retreat house lawn. They raised their heads when I came out the front door, but continued to browse. Only after it was apparent to them that I was not going away, did they slowly, with mincing steps, move off. Finally, like children full of glee, they ducked into the trees, kicked up their legs in graceful, earth-clearing leaps, flashed their white tails and disappeared. Deer are as common as rabbits in Chicago's suburban woods, but I never tire of catching a glimpse of their wide, wary eyes and sailing lope.

There certainly aren't any deer on Hale-Bopp. What comets and the Hubble telescope are calling forth from us is a sense of wonder and awe. But this is not a new experience. It is as old as the cave paintings of Lascaux and the stargazers who saw warriors in the starry night sky. It is what inspired Hopkins' *The Starlight Night* ("Look, look: a May-mess like an orchard bough"); Gustav Holst's 'The Planets'; and Annie Dillard's modern classic of wonder *Pilgrim at Tinker Creek*.

In this last work, Dillard wrote that she sometimes returns from the woods "scarcely knowing my own name. Litanies hum in my ears; my tongue flaps in my mouth, 'Ailinon, alleluia!'" There is in the Chicago area such a speech-defying place. It is called Messenger Woods, near New Lenox. Every May these woods unleash a 'May-mess' of wildflowers that rivals the galaxy-filled space caught by the Hubble telescope. There are acre after acre of closely massed blue-eyed mary, pink and blue cowslip ('mertensia'), white and shy prairie trillium and generous sprays of wild geranium, red ginger and columbine. I go there at least once each spring. It is a kind of pilgrimage.

Pilgrimage is the right word. A journey to visit a sacred place. Earth is a sacred place above all because it is created by God. It has been made even more sacred because God has entered deeply into its marrow and bone through the enwombing of Jesus in the body of one of Earth's creatures. Because it is sacred, Earth must be not only lived on, not just taken from, not just used, not just divided up and owned, but visited. As on a pilgrimage. We must visit Earth the way we visited the night sky this spring to wonder at the long-tailed comet. We admired the comet with its million mile tail. I hope we did not go to it the way we surf cable and the internet - looking for something to sate our curiosity and our appetite for entertainment - because we are bored. The dirty iceball and the pretty blue ball are not just titillating entertainment. They are sacred places.

Places of wonder for pilgrims. To visit.

The Prayer of the Mourning Dove
Autumn 1997

I have been trying to teach people something about prayer for many years now. This past summer, a mourning dove taught me something about prayer

I was conducting some directed (private) retreats at a retreat house on a bluff overlooking the Mississippi River near Red Wing, MN. One of my directees, making her first such retreat, was a late middle-aged laywoman, wife and mother. Our session took place in a little room overlooking the lawn and a line of trees behind which the great river rolled slowly south. It was late morning of a lazy warm day. In our opening session, I was trying to explain to her the difference between meditation and contemplation. Meditation, I said, is a process in which we analyze and think about problems, biblical readings, God, Jesus, etc. Contemplation, on the other hand, I was about to say, was quite different. I paused, searching for the right words. During that pause came the sound of a mourning dove off in the trees - loud, plaintive, haunting. Both of us heard it, and we both listened for a moment - in silence - as it repeated its call.

Then - inspired - I said: "Mary Ann, that's contemplation!"

It was, however simple, a contemplative moment. It was a moment in which we did not think, analyze, study, talk, journal, or plan. We just listened. We were just there. The inspiration came not from our inner selves, but from outside. For a moment or two it took us away from ourselves, bonded us to the dove, and even brought the two of us just a little bit closer.

If listening to a dove can be contemplation, what does this say about this kind of prayer? First, it says that contemplation is not the great mystery we make it out to be. Second, the people we call "contemplatives" are not a mysterious lot. Third, contemplatives are not very rare. You don't have to be Thomas Merton or a cloistered Poor Clare nun to be a contemplative. Indeed, there is a contemplative in each one of us.

Contemplation, therefore, is simply the act of giving my attention as completely as I can to an experience, an object, or a person. But - please note! - it is not a functional attention. A mother who watches her toddler like a hawk isn't contemplating her. She's making sure she doesn't walk into something that can hurt her. Nor is a student who is concentrating on a math problem or intently analyzing a poem acting in a contemplative manner. The man who asks his wife as they snuggle in each others arms: "A penny for your thoughts" is asking the wrong question. She isn't thinking anything. She's simply gazing with admiration on her beloved. That's contemplation.

I'm a bird-watcher. There is a kind of bird-watching that is contemplative, and one that isn't. Non-contemplative bird-watchers go looking for the birds.

They usually carry a field guide and notebook. They count the number of birds seen, catalog ones never seen before, observe and note behavior. The other kind of bird-watcher simply watch whatever birds come along. They don't count, note, or catalog, and frequently don't even have field guides. They wait for the birds to come to them. Indeed, this is done quite well from - thank you - the front porch or the kitchen window. These two species have in fact different names. The former, more aggressive type are now more likely to be called 'birders.' The latter, more laid-back type, are still called 'bird-watchers'.

This is a metaphor for the difference between meditation and contemplation. Both are important ways of praying. But, there is one critical difference. Meditation is ours. Contemplation comes from somewhere else. Meditation is the result of our own efforts. Contemplation is given to us. Meditation is work. Contemplation is gift. Meditation is where we begin the serious journey of prayer. Contemplation is where it ends. Meditation reflects humanity's search for God. Contemplation is God's response to us.

All the great spiritual writers, from Bonaventure through Teresa of Avila to Thomas Merton describe this same process, and they describe it as the natural evolution of human prayer. Hence, it should come as no surprise that Catholicism's latest official statement on prayer, The Catechism of the Catholic Church, assumes that contemplative prayer is not narrowly distributed - as among mystics and cloistered monks - but widely, as among us all.

One of my directees, who was not searching for or even concerned about the difference between these two kinds of prayers, told me recently that he began praying -

as he frequently does - one of the psalms. The first words of the psalm were the simple affirmation: "The Lord reigns ..." He told me he never got beyond that first phrase. For the entire period of his prayer, he simply sat in awe of that reality - "God reigns!" What began as meditation ended in contemplation.

What you might say is that he heard the song of the dove and he just listened.

A People Without Rest
Millennium Overkill
Winter 1997

    The millennium is still two years away, maybe three (we're not sure when the millennium really begins since there was no year 0 to match the year 2000). Like most things we do today, from browsing the internet to grief over the death of Princess Diana, we seem determined to greet it with excess. When it finally arrives, I imagine, we will be so exhausted and weary from all the ballyhoo that we will greet it with the same sad relief we greet the day after Christmas -- Thank God it's over, let's get back to real life.

    Last summer I talked this over with an old friend of mine who runs a small parish in Northern Michigan. He has what I call a 'sapiential bent' and shares my distaste for all the overkill. But he also made a positive suggestion. Instead of celebrating the millennium, he said, "Why don't we declare the year 2000-2001 a Year of Jubilee?" (Religious educator, Maria Harris, has also published a book on this theme, *Proclaim Jubilee*).

The idea of Jubilee has been taken over by married couples, priests and religious to celebrate long-lasting commitments. But originally, in the Bible (Leviticus 25) the Jubilee Year was a kind of period of rest, or sabbatical, for the people of God. In the Jubilee Year (every 49th-50th year), the land was not to be plowed and planted, the impoverished family was to have its land restored, and indentured servants were to be set free. It was a time, like the weekly Sabbath, when the country was to slow down and remember what it was, whence it came, and where it was heading. It was a time to remember that God is the true owner of the land, and that God, not their farms, was the center of their lives. The biblical jubilee is more about God than about us. It may be envisioned as a kind of year long retreat.

So jubilee, like its academic counterpart, the sabbatical, means rest. And that is something Americans seem determined to avoid. More than 150 years ago the famed commentator on the American scene, Alexis de Tocqueville, wrote this about Americans: "(The American) is always in a hurry. ... Besides the good things that he possesses, he every instant fancies a thousand others that death will prevent him from trying if he does not try them soon. This thought fills him with anxiety, fear and regret" (*Democracy in America*). That was 1840! Railroads had barely been invented! What would he say about us today?

We have so much to do that we are a people running the risk of a national nervous breakdown. Work, for example. It is not clear whether we are spending more or less time at work - a good case can be made for both. But clearly, as more and more women work outside the home, more of us are on the job. Moreover, by the increasing use of cellular phones, beepers, faxes, call-waiting, and all the other nervous fingers of the high-achiever world, we have allowed work to pry into cherished privacy.

But work is not the only problem, perhaps not the major problem for a restless people. Even more threatening to our "rest" are the multiplication of options available to us, the possibilities of things to do and experience, which rush at us in an exponential tide. The explosion of information and entertainment options on television (especially cable), radio, and the internet are just the most visible sign of the rapid proliferation of "things to do and see". There are a multitude of others. There are increased, lifelong educational options. There are options for a second career - for a third career. There are travel options. There are recreational options. There are options to "do good" through the increasing urgent appeals of a wide range of moral, religious and political crusades. Even the Church entices us today with tempting options for lay involvement, even leadership. These all surge into society like the flood from a broken dam rushing through city streets.

As the world dangles before our eyes these enticing new options for our lives, we, like de Tocqueville's American of 1840, seem hell-bent on trying out as many of them as possible. We are becoming a rest/less people, a people "without rest".

The key word here is rest/less. We are losing our capacity for rest. Rest is becoming for us merely a zonked out period before yet another frenetic foray into high octane activity. Perhaps we don't even want to rest. Perhaps, as Hamlet feared dreams, we fear rest because we don't want to know what we are really doing to ourselves.

This is the exact opposite of what spirituality is all about. Spirituality does not mean indulging in periods of withdrawal so that we can charge out to do even more and do it even better. It is not a pit stop for refueling. Spirituality is the time we take to simply acknowledge who we are - creatures called to adore and worship - and to acknowledge who God is, creator and center of our lives. Spirituality is about true Rest, Rest in God. Augustine wrote about our restlessness, and said that we would remain rest/less until we rested in God. Spirituality therefore means not necessarily doing more, but perhaps doing less. Spirituality means not making more noise (not even, necessarily a "joyful noise unto the Lord"), but courting more quiet. Spirituality means not going faster, but going slower. As Gandhi said, "There is more to life than increasing its speed."

Even the business world is becoming aware of this. As one consultant to Fortune 500 companies had advised her clients, the consumer in the new millennium will be demanding not more, but less. "If there is an American disease," she writes, "it is fatigue" (*The Popcorn Report*). A rest/less people must seek true Rest.

I write all this because "rest" is at the heart of what we do at Mayslake Marmion Ministries. It was what I came to understand that the old Mayslake was all about. It has characterized all the many retreats and days of prayer - and all the spiritual direction - we have done since 1991. It will characterize the new retreat/guest house for which we are raising funds to build in Aurora. We are not very confident that all the frenzy of our lives, including a lot of what passes for religion and spirituality, is doing our relationship with God any good. The motto we have adopted recently to describe our ministry is simply "Quiet, Please!" We need to be quiet, to rest, so that we can become aware of what God is doing in our lives. I like the phrase of a recent Catholic writer who stressed the need for rest and quiet "so that creation does not play to an empty house" (Thomas Hicks). Pope John Paul recently put out a call for Catholics to return to some kind of reverence for Sunday, the Lord's day. He called Sunday a "Day of Grace". We see our retreat/guest house as a "Place of Grace".

If we can build this place of peace, quiet, slowness and depth, we will have contributed mightily to a reversal of the frightening rush to rest/less smashup we seem to be veering towards.

What we hope to do is to turn a millennium into a Jubilee.

"Them're Geese"
Spring 1998

As you read this, one of nature's many exciting events may be taking place - right above your head.

This is the spring migration of the Sandhill Crane, one of North America's largest birds, and first cousin to the nearly extinct Whooping Crane. Every year during March and April, large flocks of these big birds (three feet tall with six and one-half foot wingspans) leave Florida to make their way to nesting grounds around the northern Great Lakes. And every October and November, they head back to Florida. If you care to, you can drive to the Jasper-Pulaski Wildlife Refuge south of Michigan City, IN, where you may see as many as ten to twenty thousand of them at one time resting on their trip south. As they fly, they sing, a wondrous trumpeting chorus that one noted author has compared to French Horns.

Although they fly right over Chicago, you've probably never seen or heard them, since they fly high, as high as 13,000 feet. Last fall, I was at the trailhead of the Illinois and Michigan Canal bike-path in Willow Springs, when I heard their call. I stopped my bike, and trained my binoculars on the blue autumn sky. I finally found them, circling slowly and musically, totally oblivious, it seemed, to the metropolis that milled about beneath them. The small parking lot was filled with people loading and unloading bikes. I turned excitedly around me expecting that everyone else would be gawking as I was up into the sky. No one had even noticed. Except for one old fella, who was shading his eyes against the sun and looking up. He had heard. I stepped quickly over to him. "Did you hear?" I asked, "Those are Sandhill Cranes." Without taking his eyes off the sky, he grumped back, "Nah, them're geese" (referring of course to the big pesky Canada geese that are found everywhere these days, and that also call as they fly, but whose cry is a trumpeting nasal honk rather than a mellifluous French Horn). "No, no," I pleaded with him, "they're Sandhill Cranes. They sound different. They're bigger and they're going to Indiana then to Florida." But, he was not to be persuaded. "Them're geese!" he asserted emphatically. "Here, look through my binoculars," I urged. But he turned me down. The identification was finished. There was nothing to discuss. "Them're geese."

Other than my few bird-watching friends, I seem to be the only person in my world that ever notices this biennial avian pilgrimage. I have stood in the midst of school children in Downers Grove and heard them. I have lingered on the steps of a townhouse in Oak Brook and heard them. I have rushed to my window at Mayslake when I heard them from inside the building. But no one else seems to notice. And now, the only guy who ever shared with me this experience of hearing them warble way up in the sky, says they're only geese!

I was not of course annoyed with the old gentleman, nor with the thousands of others who don't hear or see the cranes. I am after all a bird-watcher, and I am attuned to these things. But it led me to thinking about all the things we could see and hear, but do not.

Part of the reason is that we just don't look. It isn't always deliberate (though sadly enough this is often true). Mostly, it's because we get so absorbed in our own lives that we, as it were, train ourselves only to see that which immediately affects our lives. *We lose the sense of wonder and awe we had as children that is the basis of all religious faith.*

Just as frequently, *we reduce what is different and strange to something familiar to us.* We stereotype people and events, reducing them to something our small lives can manage. Arabs are terrorists. Democrats are big spenders. Republicans lack compassion for the poor. Baby Boomers are selfish. Generation X has no values. As the old gentleman pronounced definitively of the Sandhill Cranes, "Them're geese." He knew geese, and so anything that remotely resembled geese were geese. If it flies like a goose, it must be a goose.

We also reduce God to something we can handle. We see what we want to see, and if we like what we see, we accept him, and if we don't, we reject him. This is an ominous mistake. Not because God will swipe us with the back of his hand for our smallness (that's what we'd do, which is too often the measure of what we think God will do), *but **because we will miss so much**.*

But the saddest reason why we see so little, is that *we don't think we're capable of seeing anymore.* We accept our limitations too quickly. You, for example. If you are reading this you are obviously interested in the spiritual life. But you probably don't think you could ever be *a mystic*.

We admire mystics like St. Augustine, St. Francis of Assisi, St. Ignatius of Loyola, St. Teresa of Avila, even the 20th century Theresa, the 'Little Flower' and Mother Teresa. But as models, we dismiss them. They're out of our league. They're cranes. We can only be geese. But this is not true. We can all be mystics.

I have just finished working my way through one of the great classics of spirituality, Evelyn Underhill's study of the spiritual life, simply titled, *Mysticism*. Although published in 1911, it remains a standard work today, almost 90 years later. She describes mystical experience as within the reach of all. She defines it as an "innate tendency of the human spirit" that leads to complete knowledge of and union with God. Mystical experience is simply the highest and final reach of the spiritual journey you are now on. It is not alien to you. It is not rare. It is not reserved to nuns and monks. Mystics are not bizarre, unusual people. I know them in my ministry and you would be surprised at how ordinary they really are.

This is very comforting to me. It means that for all our spiritual lassitude, yes, even in the face of our sins, we are all capable of this highest experience of Truth and Love that we call the mystical experience.

There is much talk today about a spiritual renewal in our society. I believe this passionately, and it explains in part why I want to build a retreat house to facilitate this renewal. But let us understand something. Unlike what we read in the popular press and what is presented to us in so-called "pop spirituality", this renewal is not to be some kind of shortcutting religious self-help program to get us through a particular personal, cultural or ecclesiastical crisis. That kind of spirituality is merely self-serving. Spirituality may begin there. But it can only end when we open up our hearts and our lives to the great and mysterious, always loving being of God.

It is a call to attune our ears and raise our eyes so that we may know not just geese, but high-flying cranes.

God, Let Me Swallow My Spit
On Asking for a Break from God
Summer 1998

One of the familiar catechetical images of my childhood was that of the Trinity, in which, within a bare triangle, was enshrined a simple, staring Eye. This disembodied Eye represented the all-seeing God, who saw everything we did, and presumably made judgment on it all - "The Watcher" - Job's name for God. We are never out of sight.

I was reminded of this image in a recent conversation with a spiritual directee of mine. We had been talking about her image of God. She described God as someone who was keeping track of her all the time, watching her relentlessly, like the burning sun of a hot, blue, high summer day. She expressed her wish that God would give her a break sometimes, drop a lid over that fierce eye, turn off the searchlight, let her rest in the occasional, non-sinful, noncompliance with God's demanding Will.

I identified with her wish. My recurring image of God is not "The Eye", but it is just as relentless. I envision God as the driver of a car who has delivered me to a destination I am not anxious to go to. The motor is still running, and I am sitting in the passenger seat. My hand is on the door handle, but, like a kid who doesn't want to go to school, I am reluctant to get out. God simply sits waiting, and says to me - not threatening, not angry - but quietly insistent: *"Well?"*

This resentment of God's all-consuming attention is not a new thing. Job in the Old Testament or Hebrew scriptures felt it agonizingly. Job had suffered much at God's hand, and felt that he had had enough. And so, many times throughout the book, he complains to God. In one of his most eloquent complaints, he charges God: "You observe (a man) with each new day, and try him at every moment." He addresses God as "O watcher of men", and begs: "How long will it be before you look away from me, and let me alone long enough to swallow my spittle?" *(Job 7: 17-19).* This plea to let me swallow my spit, a phrase still in use among some Arabs today, is an eloquent expression of the exhaustion many of us feel in trying always to please God, not just by avoiding sin, but by always doing "the better thing". Indeed, when I was a seminarian, there was a minor heresy of the spiritual life, predominantly Canadian, known as "Meliorism", a doctrine teaching that whenever there was a choice between two goods, you always had to choose the "better one" ('melior' in Latin).

I would like to suggest that God does not always demand of us "the better thing". If God did, God would be nothing more than a merciless judge and relentless supervisor. And we know that isn't true. God is also merciful, forgiving, understanding. God allows coffee breaks and vacations and weekends - not for sin, to be sure - but to at least let down our guard and take care of ourselves for a while.

Another way of putting this is to say that while God is always present to us, he is not here just to criticize. God comforts as well.

Perhaps the most significant trend in Catholic theology to emerge in the last half century emphasizes just this point. This is a theme of "liberation theology" that has sprung up in Latin America. Liberation theology has arisen because of what to many appears to be the failure of Christianity and the inactivity of God. Despite, they note, two millennia of Christianity and a thousand promises by God to come to the aid of the poor and the oppressed, they have instead increased, not just in 'pagan lands' unclaimed by Christianity, but in the very Christian countries that make these claims. There is widespread, systemic and violent oppression in Latin America, the world's most Catholic area. There has been genocide in Germany, Rwanda (predominantly Catholic), and Bosnia. Where has God been for two millennia in these very religious, even Christian, Catholic countries?

The answer of the liberationists is that God has always been there. But God is not there as the Warrior/Judge lashing the poor for their sins and leading them to victory over their enemies. God is there in "solidarity" with the people. Solidarity. This means that God does not only comfort the people with promises of eternal life. It means that *God actually shares their sufferings.* The notion that God actually suffers seems scandalous to us until we reflect upon the reality of Jesus Christ. The culmination of the life of teaching and healing of the Second Person of the Trinity incarnate was not triumph and vindication over the enemy, but suffering and death. As the Letter to the Hebrews puts it, "he himself is beset with weakness" (5:2). The central image of the Christian religion is not a flag of triumph, but the cross of shame. If Christianity means anything, it means that God shares in our fate. Solidarity.

My colleague, Mary Jo Valenziano, commenting on the story of Job, puts it this way in one of her talks. Before the lecture to Job in the magnificent poetry of the book's final chapters, Mary Jo imagines God in solidarity with Job. Job's four friends have come to keep vigil. It is very companionable of them, but they stand outside the garbage dump and speak from a distance. They criticize Job - relentlessly. But God, she imagines, crosses the borders of shame, sits right down on the dump with Job and mourns with him. There is no criticism now. Just the comfort of God's presence. That is the meaning of solidarity, the heart of liberation theology, the cutting-edge of contemporary spirituality.

This, of course, does not mean passivity in the face of sin and evil. We are expected to confront and seek to overcome them. But we do not do it just because God rails at us about our sinfulness and spiritual lethargy. We do it because, aware that God shares our weakness and is present with comfort, we are emboldened, energized, given life and enabled to take up the burden of his teachings and commandments. These latter were given elsewhere and are ever valid. But, they are not the first word God speaks to us. God's First Word is simply presence in solidarity with our weakness, that 'first word' proclaimed by John: "And the Word became flesh and made his dwelling among us" (John 1:14).

And so the Eye sometimes blinks. The Driver sometimes says, "Relax." Job gets to swallow his spit.

And from this Sabbath-like respite, we take heart for the endless struggle.

Jonathan Foster, O.F.M.

The Standing Sabbath of the Sea
God and the Jersey Shore
Autumn 1998

In one of his poems, the Kentucky farmer, Wendell Berry, describes a visit to the woodlot on his farm as resuming "the standing Sabbath of the woods". It is his sacred place where he goes to worship, even on Sunday.

This past summer, I prayed at my own 'standing Sabbath' - the sea shore. As some of you know, I spent five weeks at the Summer Institute for Clergy in Long Branch, NJ - right on the Jersey shore. When I began to plan this mini-sabbatical, one of the conditions I set for myself was that whatever program I would take, it would have to be on a seashore, any seashore. For in recent years, the sea has grown in my consciousness as a metaphor for God.

The retreat house where the institute was held sits right on the ocean. A flower-lined path runs down from the main building to the sea where it intersects with a short boardwalk running parallel to the beach. A few feet past the boardwalk, the lawn ends and a sea wall drops about ten feet down to the beach. The wall is made up of a massive tumble of huge boulders, held in place by a thick stockade of wood and iron pilings driven deep into the sand. Beyond that lies a scrap of beach running about 100 yards between two rocky jetties that punch out into the sea. Onto this narrow beach, against this seawall, and sometimes spuming up onto the boardwalk, day and night, pours the Atlantic Ocean.

The face of the sea changes with the weather. It is sometimes iron gray beneath sullen clouds, sometimes a sparkling green with sunlight glittering off its waves. Near the beach it is a muddy tan from the sand it sweeps in, and sometimes black from the mussel shells it has stripped from the rocks and beaten into dust. But it is always in motion. It heaves, it pounds, it rolls, it swells, rising and falling, swirling among the rocks, crashing one wave on top of another, and at high tide dashing itself and anything in its path up against the sea wall in what appears to be a determined effort to throw back the shore and seize the land. Even on warm still days, when there is no discernible breeze from any direction, the sea, driven by a power no one can see, rolls in with a steady roar, dumping each wave on the beach with a drum-like thump.

Fishing boats gather every morning off the shore. For decades this spot off the retreat house has been favored as a prime fishing spot by the locals. There's a sunken wreck out there and a fault in the ocean floor that fish seem to like. Some days as many as sixty boats, including large party boats with as many as fifty fishermen lining the railings, gather within sight of us, all dipping their poles into the sea. Every day, some guys fish from the slick, uncertain footing of the jetties. Several species of gulls and shrill bands of common terns dive for the same fish as the fishing boats. A few starlings and house sparrows, too, fly into the jetties' rocks seeking some prey we cannot see. All creation searches the sea for something.

So do the priests. It is a favorite place to sit, to read, to pray. Some walk up and down the boardwalk reading their breviary. Some read books. Some kick contemplatively through the surf, or stand on the jetties looking out towards Europe. Some sit in the sand and wait for the tide to come in. I do all these things, but I also read poetry, and write in my journal.

We are drawn to the ocean, as to God. It is our 'standing Sabbath'. Like the sea that is so bountiful to gull and fisherman alike, God is the source of all the life we know. Like its cooling water and winds, God refreshes our souls and leads to green pastures. As the sea inspires some of the world's greatest art, music and poetry, God is the inspiration for our greatest deeds.

But there is this too, we know. God, like the sea, is a source of awe and not a little fear. Here at the Institute, we go only a few feet into the ocean, and experience just a few feet of its depths. The fishing boats cling timidly to its shores. We know there is far more out there than we can comprehend, but we do not let ourselves think about it. I have been told by friends who live by the sea that when I go swimming alone, I should never turn my back on it. And when I have failed to heed that warning, I have been knocked head over heels by waves. That can happen with God as well, and so we walk careful in the Presence, and not too deep.

But what impressed me most this summer about the image of God-as-the-Sea was its relentlessness. Francis Thompson wrote about God as a "Hound", tracking us down. But there is nothing like sitting there by the seashore, thinking about God, and watching those waves come in. They seem to be on a mission, hell-bent to take over the land that braces itself to meet them. They never stop, day or night. Sometimes, I sit safely up on the boardwalk and watch, and imagine God to be like them, and when I do this I fancy myself to be as safely out of his way as I am out of the way of the tossing waves. I even dashed off a smug little ditty about this experience:

The weariness of the sea -
It tries and it tries,
but it can't catch me.

Humans try to control the sea. We settle on its shores, right in the face of the marauding waves, and build jetties and dikes in an effort to keep it at bay. Last summer, we watched the Corps of Engineers in the process of rebuilding all the beaches along the Jersey shore by mining offshore sand and piping it up onto the shrunken beaches. The locals are glad for this, but they know sadly that it is only temporary, for the sea will eventually reclaim their beaches just as it will eventually reclaim many of the slim barrier islands that now support so many towns along the coast. Even so, we can act as though we are keeping God at arm's length. But it is only an illusion. I escaped the sea by returning to Illinois. I can't escape God. So, I had better keep an eye open for him.

One day, I watched a gull and a tern hunt for food. The tern, as all terns do, swept back and forth some feet above the water, head down, searching for prey. From time to time, it would hover, then drop straight down in the surf, disappear for a moment, then rise wetly into the air, to continue its frantic patrol. More often than not, its beak was empty. Most gulls fish like this too, though they don't dive under the water. The one I watched however, a large, black-backed gull, simply stood on the beach and scanned each wave that rolled in. Most brought nothing but empty mussel shells, but after some time, a wave threw up a large crab. The attentive gull was on it in a second. Without moving three feet.

I thought the gull had a better idea about fishing. He also gave me a better idea about finding God. Sitting and waiting is what God wanted me to do. God will show himself soon enough. Like the gull paying attention to each wave, all I am required to do is to pay attention.

So I return to Berry's 'standing Sabbath'. His is the woods, mine this summer, the sea. For all of us it is that special time and place where we can sit still and let ourselves watch God at work.

Francis of Assisi - 1999
The Relevance of Reverence
Winter 1998

St. Francis was born 817 years ago next year, and it may be something of a stretch for many to imagine that someone who lived his life buried in the midst of the 13th century could have relevance for us today. It is not such a stretch for us here at Mayslake Marmion Ministries. St. Francis after all was the motivating figure behind the old Mayslake Retreat House (1925 - 1991), and his name and spirit are still enshrined in the mission statement of Mayslake Marmion Ministries. (1991 -).

It is for this reason that we have chosen Francis as the central model for our scheduled retreats this year, and given it the title: Reverence: the Spiritual Journey of St. Francis of Assisi. We did not choose either Francis or this particular aspect of his life lightly. We are all more or less aware of St. Francis' love for nature - he is indeed the Catholic patron of the environmental movement. But this love for nature was only part of a deeper sense of awe, wonder, respect and reverence that Francis had for all that God had made, and above all for God the Creator and Lover of Everything. Gilbert Chesterton once described Francis as a man who saw himself *"not as king before a thousand courtiers, but as a courtier before a thousand kings"*. Everywhere Francis saw the creating presence of God, and so he ran stumbling in awe through all of life, constantly overwhelmed by its beauty, living constantly in a breathless state of reverence.

I feel it is important to call ourselves back to some of that same sense of wonder and awe - the reverence that Francis exuded through all his life. Our culture, whatever its other great and marvelous achievements, is one that seems to be steadily losing its sense of reverence. We are more cynical, ruder, more in-your-face, more inclined to mock than revere. I'm not sure why this is. But my guess is that it is partly because of the great improvements in the technology of communication. We are increasingly "in the know", we are insiders, who know more of "the inside story". We know about the private lives and doings of politicians, business leaders, celebrities, church leaders. We know how things really work - from government agencies to antibiotics to the origin of the universe. Are we becoming so familiar (the familiarity that breeds contempt), that we are at risk of becoming jaded? Whatever the reason, it is my conviction that it will help us to return to and dwell upon the great sense of wonder and reverence possessed by Francis of Assisi.

The reverence of Francis has a special significance in the Christmas season. Francis, you see, is generally given credit for the practice of building Christmas cribs or creches. Francis however had a distinctly contemporary approach to this devotion. He wanted desperately to experience the birth of Jesus as realistically as he could

So, he staged it - with a midnight Mass, in a real barn with real peasants, with real animals, real hay, and living stand-ins for Mary and Joseph kneeling before the manger. And legend has it that at the moment of Consecration in the Mass, a real baby appeared in the hay! "Virtual reality" before its time.

During this year of commemorating St. Francis of Assisi, we have something special for you. It is a beautiful 20 inch statue of St. Francis which is available on a limited basis.

Now, this is no ordinary "birdbath St. Francis" - the kind so often represented in cute and sentimental fashion. This is a genuine work of art, a truly limited edition. It is the work of a former retreatant at the old Mayslake, Robert Noonan, Sr., who in his spare time studied at the Art Institute of Chicago. Mr. Noonan has been dead for some years now, but he left to his son, Robert, Jr., a mold for this statue. Bob has offered to cast copies of this statue, and to donate whatever profits are to be made towards our building fund. The piece is made of ceramic with a glaze unique to each copy and can be located both indoors and out of doors. I think this is not just a great way to raise money, but I am delighted and excited to be associated with such a fine work of art. With Bob Noonan's permission, we have given this piece the name: "The Mayslake St. Francis".

I am grateful to Bob for this generous and tasteful gift. Although its offer came as a complete surprise to me, I should not have been. Francis of Assisi has always been known as "Everyone's Saint". Protestants, for example, have affection for him that they do not have for most Catholic saints. Bob's gift is simply further proof of Francis' popularity, and confirms the wisdom of our decision to offer a retreat based on his spirituality. I invite you to come for the retreat and take home not only something of Francis' spirit, but perhaps "The Mayslake Saint Francis" as well.

The Spiritual Life
Seeking? Or Surrender?
Spring 1999

Catholics were shocked recently to discover that probably less than 30% of them go to Mass every Sunday. This is a sharp decline from a 40% attendance that had held for about 20 years, and a catastrophic slide from the some 80% attendance before Vatican II. The decline among mainline Protestant Churches (Lutherans, Presbyterians, Methodists, et al) is even more pronounced. And yet, we are told, there is a great religious ferment afoot in the country, an ever-deepening "hunger" for spirituality.

So, what are all these religious folk doing? In several recent books on religion in America (e.g., Robert Wuthnow's *After Heaven: Spirituality in America since the 1950s*) they've all become 'Seekers'. Having loosened their ties to traditional faith and churches, they are casting about in a hundred different places "seeking God". The huge Evangelical mega-churches, such as Willow Creek (Palatine) and Calvary Temple (Naperville) in the Chicago area, profit from this nomadic spirituality, and indeed call themselves "Seekers' Churches". In the 'seeker' sense, there are probably more religious people not going to church than there are going to church. In this same sense, God is apparently hiding.

What shall we say about "seeking"? It seems a perfectly acceptable thing to do. Our conversation regularly and easily speaks about "looking for God", "seeking or searching for God", "looking for meaning". Even the Scriptures use this kind of language, e.g., Jesus' words, "Seek and you will find, knock and the door will be opened to you."

What I would like to suggest here however is that God is not hiding. Christian spiritual life is not about seeking, or at least not about us seeking God. But it is about another kind of search, God seeking us. The real question for spirituality is not 'Seeking', but 'Surrender'.

A rapid survey of the Bible, both the Old and New Testaments, show us a God who, far from hiding, is always initiating, always in passionate pursuit of us.

The very first words of the Old Testament depict God as Creator, an adventurous, creative entrepreneur, who for the "first" time wanders outside of himself in an act of love. God is the Maker and Owner of a Plantation in which he wishes to walk about with us. God is described after 'the Fall' as the Master of Creation, who descends upon us like 'Rain and Snow'. God is also the Deliverer and Savior - from slavery, from exile, from sin. God directs the life of the human race as 'Lawgiver' and 'Judge', protects us as 'Warrior' and 'Shield', falling upon our enemies like 'Brushfire', 'Boiling Water' and leaf-scattering 'Fall Wind'. God is described, frequently, as 'Jealous' for us, brooking no rivals, pursuing us like a lusty young 'Lover' or a 'Husband' wronged. In a gentler vein, God is a 'Farmer' or 'Sower', who plants us and encourages our growth, even a 'Potter', who shapes us with the intimate caresses of one who loves clay.

These are not images of a God sitting around waiting for us to find him. Indeed, God often reminds us that even if we persist in seeking, God is never far away. God is already there as Rock, Stronghold, Fortress, Tent, Shelter, Home, Refuge. He sends the Spirit-Advocate who continues to enlarge and teach the truth. Paul would summarize all of this by preaching vehemently that salvation and freedom do not come only after we have successfully scaled the great barrier of human law, but only from submission to Grace, from surrendering to God constantly coming at us and surrounding us.

In the light of this energetic God, our role as seeker seems pretty minimal. Often, what we are seeking is some convenient short-cut to illumination, something that seems to suit us better. Sometimes our search is aimed at some goal less worthy than God, like health, long life, prosperity, success, a kind of superior human functioning in which the center is me - not God. Sometimes, arrogantly, we are seeking a kind of perfection that gives far more credit to us than to God. And sometimes our seeking is really running away.

For most of us, comfortable only with getting what we work for, this is largely uncharted territory. Our instinct is not to be found, but to search. Such a spirituality, however, need not abandon the search. It only needs to realize that while we are confined to a short leash that never lets us get too far, there is no leash on God. Do not be surprised that God finds you before you find God. Be resigned to the fact that God presses the search even when we dawdle in our sin and laziness. Let us be resigned to our sinfulness and imperfection, and rather than persisting in the fiction that we can entirely overcome either, let God make up the difference. Above all, we need to learn that kind of praying which simply sits still and observes the work of God in the land and in our hearts. Sit down. Rest. Wait. That's what they tell you to do when you are lost in the wilderness. Someone - God - will find you.

No piece of spiritual writing captured this more dramatically than Francis Thompson's 'Hound of Heaven'. Here the seeking is indeed a running away, and the climax comes when the pursued 'seeker' collapses, exhausted, and lets the dogged Bloodhound find him. Finally, he realizes what we all need to understand, that the better metaphor for the Christian life is not 'Search', but 'Surrender'.

All this is not to suggest that our non-church-going seekers will only be found by God sitting in a church. God is no more confined to a church than we are. But, they have to sit down and 'Surrender' somewhere. It might as well be in church.

Esau and Email
Spirituality and the Computer
Summer 1999

Less than two weeks ago (I'm writing in early May), I was dragged out of the dark cave of prehistoric electronics and forced to stand blinking in the fierce bright light of cyberspace.

This came about because a group of men I work with, unhappy that I alone among them had no e-mail address, gifted me with a brand new computer with e-mail capacity And, just to make sure, they sent one of their own over to install it for me.

I am deeply grateful to my good friends for their wonderful gift. It is indeed a massive leap from my 1986 vintage Apple II, which for me was just a typewriter in disguise. And I do not wish that my remarks to follow make me sound like what we (in a less politically correct time) used to call an 'Indian giver'. I am still actually enjoying all the tricks I can do, and the little snippets of talk I can let fly into electronic space. But, I do want to take this opportunity to share with you some of the reasons why I am always a little reluctant to embrace a new technology. They have, I believe, much to do with spirituality.

Some of you will perhaps recall the scene from "2001: A Space Odyssey" where one of the apes accidentally picks up a dried out and sun-bleached leg-bone and realizes that he can use it to break other bones, and the heads of apes from a hostile troop. In such a manner, probably, the first technology emerged. For technology simply refers to any way in which humans (and sometimes animals) extend their activities artificially through the use of a tool. Buttons, electric lights, automobiles, hairdryers, tomahawks, and Tomahawk missiles, eye glasses and fire hydrants ... all are tools, all are part of technology.

Technology therefore is the natural, we may say God-given, result of human ingenuity and creativity. But, like the gifts of beer and tobacco, it has its bright side and its dark side. We do well to be cautious about any new tool or technology that comes on the market. Let me explain why I am cautious.

My first reaction to any new product that I am told I should have is to wonder, "How is this going to complicate my life?" I am no Luddite or Amish farmer who disdains all or most modern technologies. But I think they are to be commended for their concern that such technologies may unduly complicate or even compromise their lives. I choose to share in some of their reservations.

Although I could afford them all, I have no microwave, no CD player, no cable TV, and for 25 years I rode the same three-speed Raleigh bicycle. I still am not on-line, and, as you realize by now, it was just yesterday that I consented to post an e-mail address for all the world to hail me. I also drive a simple automobile that does not have automatic door locks and remote ignition. My rationale for all that is simplicity. The more things you have, the more you have to spend time taking care of them. The more sophisticated they are, the more they can break down. The better quality units you have, that is, the more technologically sophisticated, the more you have to protect them from thieves. And despite their claims of being user friendly you will notice that they all come with manuals and extensive 'Help' prompts. (My new computer comes with six manuals and two CD ROMs!) That was not the case with my old Raleigh bike. You didn't need manuals because the units were simple to operate. And unless you are willing to spend a great deal of your time, talent and energy hovering protectively and nurse-like over these various treasures - and I am not - the glowing promises of productivity and entertainment fade just a little.

Deeper than my desire for simplicity however is, I think, something in me that is akin to fear. Yes, fear of where this new technology might lead me. Most people I talk to about technology pooh-pooh my reservations. They counter that fear with one of the most naive statements that the human race has ever made. "Oh, not to worry. All technology is neutral. It's just a tool. You can do with it what you want." They make the statement, and in the face of overwhelming evidence to the contrary, they stubbornly adhere to it.

No tool is neutral. Every tool exerts demands on its user, requires its user to conform to its own exigencies. Consider an early tool - a hunting knife. It had to be kept sharpened. It required a handle. It had to be carried in a safe place, such as a sheath, which someone had to make.

It had to be cleaned. It had to kept away from children. Now these are small demands, but they are nonetheless demands, the Rules of the Knife, so to speak.

Some of our larger technologies have rules that do not just modify the work habits of their owners. They change the very culture in which they are put to use. Take the automobile for example. Because of its nature and potential, it needs long, wide, flat stretches of roads that flatten farmland, inner cities and national parks. Because it burns petroleum, it pollutes our air and water. Because it requires just one driver, it contributes deeply to the instability of the family and community. Hence, the Rules of the Car require that the very culture change its rules. This is hardly neutral.

All of this may be said in spades! of other great technological changes in our society - the electric light, the radio, movies, television. All have their own rules, and all have worked an enormous change in our society. We say that it is all right because we allow these things to happen. But, after a while, the technology outstrips our permission and simply makes its own headlong way. What began as a 'good idea' often turns out to be an unhappy bargain - like the one Esau made (Genesis 25).

Esau was one of two sons of the patriarch, Isaac. He was a hunter, while his younger brother, Jacob, was more likely to farm and hang around the family tent. Esau came home one day from the field, famished, and found his younger brother Jacob cooking a fragrant stew. When Esau, staggering from hunger, begged for "some of that red stuff' wily Jacob saw an opportunity. Guarding the stew, he demanded, in very unbrotherly fashion, that Esau forfeit his status of birthright to him as a price. Consumed with hunger, Esau recklessly agreed and gulped down the stew. From that day on, he lost his status in the family, and had to make his own way, becoming indeed the founder of a clan, the Edomites, that eventually became enemies of the clan of Jacob. The story ends with the sad commentary, "Esau cared little for his birthright".

It is a question we need to ask ourselves. *"How much do we care for the birthright God has given us, the life of the spirit?"*

The ingenuity and prosperity of our people have made many things, many technologies available to us - stuff! The spiritual person will not just reject them, may frequently adopt them, but will always ask:

"How will this affect the birthright of my spirit?"

Jonathan Foster, O.F.M.

God as 'Old Faithful'
Fall 1999

This past summer, I was fortunate to spend some time in one of my favorite parts of the country - Montana and Wyoming - with some of my favorite friends. We didn't spend a lot of time in Yellowstone National Park, but we did make the obligatory visit to watch "Old Faithful" strut its stuff. I had seen it several times, but to be there and pass it by would have been like visiting Chicago and passing up the Picasso.

We arrived at the famed geyser basin early in the afternoon of a very warm and sunny day. Already, thousands of people were forming a semicircle around the gray hump of crust from which the geyser spews. Some sat on the benches provided by the park, many just stood. Aware of its famed predictability, we asked those already present when it was scheduled to blow. "Ten minutes, give or take," they told us. So, we parked ourselves and watched the wisps of steam that continually drift from the geyser's mouth. Periodically, however, spouts of heated water would gush up, the crowd would tense, and a murmur run the length of the benches. But then the geyser would subside to mere wisps, and small groans of disappointment would rise. These gushes occurred several times, sometimes shooting eight to ten feet in the air. But the geyser always returned to quiet steam. She reminded me of an old fan dancer keeping up the crowd's interest with flashes of feathers, promising a look, but disappointing them with her carefully calculated placements of the fan. The crowd grew restless, babies cried, and the time pressed on to half an hour. I looked impatiently at my watch. An intense young man scribbling in a journal muttered to himself about keeping "those #$&* babies" quiet. Finally, from what appeared to be yet another false start, the water shot up, then up and up and up, flaring into that scene so familiar to all Americans, a full steaming, roaring fountain of water splendidly spilling into the sky above.

We hurrahed and applauded, and as we all got up to leave, I asked a bystander how predictable this geyser really is. He told me that on average it happens *about* every eighty minutes, but that it can burst out anytime between forty minutes and an hour and a half. And apparently, it's becoming less and less predictable. But, sooner or later, it always blows.

That's when I thought about God. We call God 'The Faithful One' and in the Scriptures, God is often referred to as such. But, if God is faithful, then God is sure a lot more like 'Old Faithful' than like London's punctual and predictable Big Ben. We may say and believe that God is faithful, but it's certainly not on our time. God does not come on demand; nor does God come in *any* reliable fashion that would make sense to us. Faithfulness happens on God's terms, not ours. The faithful God is more like 'Old Faithful' than we'd like.

Here at Mayslake Ministries, we are acutely aware of this divine serendipity now as our little ministry to the spiritual life enters its ninth year. Having lost the original Mayslake which we were also convinced was God's work, we set about in 1991 to begin a new ministry in rental space in a parish rectory, with the dream of building a new home for the ministry. Confident again that this is what God wanted us to do, we formed a partnership with Marmion Abbey, and set out to raise money to build that house. We did well in the beginning, but then the sources began to peter out, and concerned about encroaching deadlines set by our new partners, we have closed that relationship and once again are on our own. Once again, we are required to stand before the Faithful One as I stood before 'Old Faithful' this summer and wonder what God is up to. Have the successes we have had in fundraising ($2.3M) and ministry been just wispy spurts followed by disappointing collapses? Or have they been the slowly building pressure that someday will lead us to the full realization of our dream? Even as we pause to consider the options available to us, we are convinced that it is the latter. But, clearly, if God is being faithful, it's more like the 'Old Faithful' geyser in Yellowstone than we would like it to be.

One of the biblical texts that we have returned to many times in these years is taken from the little known prophet, Habakkuk. Habakkuk wrote in the years before the destruction of Jerusalem in 587 B.C. He could see the coming devastation at the hands of the Babylonians, and he feared for the survival of Israel. So, he challenges God. Scripture scholars tell us that Habakkuk was likely the first Jew to question what God was up to (he antedates Job). In ringing and colorful language, Habakkuk demands that God give an explanation of what's going on and intervene on behalf of the Chosen People. Then, like a sentinel on the ramparts, he stands by to await God's reply.

> This is what Habakkuk heard:
> "Then the Lord answered and said,
> 'Write down the vision clearly upon the tablet,
> so that one can read it readily.
> For the vision still has its time,
> presses on to fulfillment,
> and will not disappoint;
> > If it delays, wait for it, it will surely come,
> > it will not be late.' "(2.2-3)

This is what we in Mayslake Ministries hear as well: "Wait - it will surely come, it will not be late." When we started this project eight years ago, I boldly predicted that we would be in a new home in 2-5 years. I make no predictions now, other than to say that the time of the vision will come.

I know better now than I did in 1991 that God is faithful, but on God's terms, not mine. God is the increasingly unpredictable, but ultimately always reliable, 'Old Faithful'!

Jonathan Foster, O.F.M.

All the World's an Audience
A Spirituality of Praise
Winter 1999

In his comedy, 'As You Like It', Shakespeare wrote the famous lines, "All the world's a stage / And all the men and women merely players." With apologies to a much better poet, I take the liberty of recasting that line to read, "All the world's an audience / And all its players applaud."

When I look, somewhat pretentiously, for a simple way to summarize all of what spirituality is about, it seems to me that there is no better word to describe it than the applause of an appreciative audience - "Praise". Praise is perhaps the most basic of religious instincts - to stand before the mystery of the universe and its history, put our hands over our mouth - as the Bible frequently says - and simply give praise to God, its maker. It is the principal theme of the majority of the psalms, and appears in most of the other psalms not devoted primarily to praise. It is also frequently a part of other canticles sung by various actors in the biblical drama. Praise is also the theme of many of the popular hymns and songs of the church's worship. Francis of Assisi recognized the fundamental nature of praise perhaps more than anyone. His signature poem, "The Canticle of Creatures", written near the end of his life, and which I take to be his definitive view of what our lives and our world are all about, is simply a hymn of praise to God.

Francis also recognized something else about praise that we do not customarily think of. In his 'Canticle', he called upon all elements of creation to praise God as well. He invokes the sun, the moon, the stars, water, air, wind, fire, and the earth to give praise to God. In his other preaching, he often summoned non-human creation in his preaching to give praise, as in his famous sermons to birds. This was not a new idea with Francis. Biblical hymns of praise also call upon the non-human creation to praise God. Thus Psalm 148, for example, urges not just the angels and humans, but sun, moon, stars, rain, sea monsters, fire, hail, snow, mist, winds, mountains, fruit trees, cedars, and wild beasts to praise the Lord. You can find more of the same in the Song of the Three Young Men, in Daniel (3:52-90). This is not merely poetic conceit. These folks really believed that everything exists for one reason only - to give praise to God.

So am I coming to believe. I have lived long enough that I am allowing myself to be amazed not only at audacious and awesome claims of Christianity about God's intervention in our history, but even at the mystery of my own small path through life. Always an admirer of the flowers of Spring, the deep green of Summer, and the bright colors of Fall, I have more recently found my mouth - like the biblical awestruck - hanging open in amazement at the discoveries of astronomy. There was a day when people considered the earth to be the center of the universe, and when I was a child, I thought it was the sun. But now the almost frightening findings of the Hubble telescope reduce our blue planet to a cosmic trifle. We are a tiny grain wheeling helplessly through empty space, our fate to perhaps one day collide with something bigger and end our history as merely one more pulverizing indentation on some distant moon or planet. If we are not to reduce our planet to such a journey of meaningless absurdity, then the only way we can make sense of it is to invoke the biblical notion of praise. It is why we exist. It is why all the cosmos exists.

Some spiritual writers, including some of the Fathers of the church recognized that all creation participates in the symphony of praise. But, they called nature "mute", and said that it was our task as humans, with our power of speech, to give tongue to the silence of nature's praise.

Nature mute! Hardly! Nature has a billion voices. An ordinary bird may have as many as twenty different calls. The winds in their variety surpass the woodwind section of any great symphony orchestra. And this is to say nothing of the "voice" of color in nature, or the "voice" of shape and form. Why does a magnificent hanging valley in Yosemite or Glacier National Park require a human voice? Nature does not need us to speak for it.

Or, did they think that God can only hear the voices of humans, perhaps best articulated in Hebrew, Greek, Latin or whatever *lingua franca* of the day?

All nature requires of us is that we kneel down with it in adoration. This is what we may call a spirituality of praise. All things - human beings, angels, canyons, stars and galaxies, wolves, robins - when they are faithful to their nature and by that very fact, whether a hymn is written about them or not - give praise to God. Thus we give praise to God as humans by being faithful to God's call to union and Christ's call to discipleship. So also the moon praises God by simply hanging in the sky and reflecting faintly the light of the sun. And we may confidently say that those galaxies that no human eye has yet seen and may never see give praise to God by their wondrous existence.

Such a spirituality puts us in proper perspective. Before Galileo and Copernicus and Kepler, people believed that the earth was the center of the universe and that the sun rotated around us. Some spiritualities today similarly put human beings at the center of the moral universe, and require the earth and even God to swing around them. A spirituality of praise brings a much needed corrective to this.

Where is sin in such a spirituality? There is a small pond in the woods near my home called, because of its shape, Boomerang Slough. It is a good fishing pond. But, it is also a popular watering hole for the slobs of the community. On any given morning in the summer time, you will find their filth, 30 to 40 beer bottles floating neck up in the water, vying with the puddle ducks, who also like the pond, for swimming space. Those beer bottles detract from the pond's praise to the Lord. So also all sin, while it does not get us kicked out of the choir, makes our voice of praise weaker and off-key.

As you read these words, we are preparing for a special kind of praise. For the stage on which God performs becomes this time of year a simple manger. Angels and shepherds were the first audience. Get in line, bring your Christmas tree, and join in the applause.

In the words of one of our most beloved hymns, 'Venite, adoremus', 'Come, let us adore him'. It is the meaning of our lives.

In the Realm of Grace
Spring 2000

In 1991, I made what by now was clearly a rash prediction that in 2 to 5 years, we would be in the "new Mayslake", our permanent home for the ministry. That would have been 1996 at the latest. Since that time, one millennium has gone and another come, Bill Clinton has come and almost gone, the Internet has arrived in full array, the stock market has tripled in value, and, for us, our arrangement with Marmion Abbey has come and gone. A capital campaign that has raised a substantial amount of money ($2.4 million) has begun and ended. And there are those who have said, "That's enough. The signs are clear that God doesn't want you to continue."

Discerning what God wants you to do is at best a difficult task. And we admit that there is always the possibility that we are not reading the signs aright. But consensus among the interested parties also helps. Ninety-five percent of the donors to our capital campaign have told us go forward. And so has our Board of Trustees.

After we severed our ties with Marmion in March of last year, our Board met to consider its options. There were three. First, close up shop completely. Second, play out our hand as a ministry without walls and give up on the idea of a retreat house. Third, press on to achieve our original goal. There was no support for the first. There was some small interest in the second. But the overwhelming support of the Board went to the third.

So, Board and staff went to work. We called a special all day meeting in May to explore our assets and opportunities. We decided to suspend (not end) our capital campaign. We decided to put more effort into letting the public know about us, because we are tiny, little known, and have no high profile sponsor (viz., diocese or religious order). So, we asked our development director, Barbara Hess, to take off her fund-raising gloves and put on the glove of marketing, which she was quite happy and competent to do. We decided to hold all our gifts in reserve, to honor all pledges and contacted all our donors about this decision, including personal visits to major benefactors. We also saw that we would have to use some of the interest to enlarge our marketing as we had done for development purposes, and to this end we have hired a major bank to take over management of our portfolio.

Throughout the summer and fall we carefully crafted a new vision statement for the ministry. To help us achieve this end, we brought in a facilitator, Sr. Carol Jean McDonald, OP of Chicago's "Night Ministry". She has been an invaluable asset in the process. In October we called another special, daylong session of the Board, and finalized the Vision Statement. At our regular board meeting in November, this statement was approved unanimously by the Board with but one member expressing some reservations. The Board then charged me to put together a long range plan for the full effective realization of our dream by the year 2005. I, along with input from staff and board, have been hard at that work ever since. As I write (February 4), we have taken the first step towards realizing that vision by setting up a Site Committee to look for a new home for the ministry.

The site may include an existing structure that can be enlarged upon, or have acreage sufficient to eventually build a new facility. Any structure to be built will not of course precisely reflect the model we had designed for the Marmion site. However, many of the same features will be present.

What is also of interest is that people from several ministries have approached us informally about possibilities of collaboration.

2005! That would put us fourteen years after Mayslake closed. Do you measure dreams in years? In today's rapid growth culture - look at internet firms like aol.com - our dream will be seen by many as so ponderously slow as to be irrelevant. However, our dream is more like that which God revealed to the prophet Habakkuk - 'For the vision still has its time, presses on to fulfillment; if it delays, wait for it, it will surely come, it will not be late' (Hab. 2:2-3).

What is "too slow"? What is "too late"? In the realm of Grace, that is God's judgment, not ours.

Jonathan Foster, O.F.M.

The Little Brother
A Spirituality for Underachievers
Summer 2000

Where do you fit in the birth order relationship with your brothers and sisters? Where you fit in the birth order, according to many today, seems to have significance for the path your life will take. This was eminently so in biblical times. In the very traditional cultures reflected in the Bible, the "First Born" or eldest son was always accorded a special place in the family or clan. There were honors and positions that came to him by right of birth, a practice still seen today in the matter of succession to royal thrones. Prince Charles will become King of England whether he is qualified or not.

But there is also a subtext belying this tradition that forms a very significant pattern in the Bible and that was vigorously counter to the cultures of the time. This was the situation where the younger son supplanted the elder! I'd like to explore that pattern and take a look at what it means for Christian spirituality in general.

It begins right off the mark with the sons of Adam and Eve, Cain and Abel. Cain is the older of the two, but it is Abel's sacrifice that is pleasing to God, not Cain's. Cain, because he refused to accept God's preference for his 'little brother' has thus come to represent one of the darkest shadows of human existence (Genesis 4). God's preference for Abel seems to suggest that from the very beginning God was not going to do things the way humans do.

Also in Genesis is the story of Isaac's two sons - Esau and Jacob (Genesis 25-33). They were actually twins, but since Esau emerged first from his mother's womb, he was given all the privileges of the First Born - a triumph of biology over common sense. But Esau, by a combination of his own folly and Jacob's scheming machinations with their mother, Rebekah, lost the right of the First Born, and Jacob became the head of the great household that grew into the Judeo-Christian tradition.

Then, of course, there is the story of Joseph, the youngest of Jacob's 12 children. It was Joseph, least favored because last born, who became the savior of the family in Egypt (Genesis 37-50). We all know Joseph. How many of us know the name of the eldest son?

The best known of these "little brother" stories is that of David. When God told Samuel to look among the sons of Jesse for a king to replace Saul, six strapping young men were paraded before him, including the eldest son, Eliab. Samuel was impressed by them all, and expected God to single out one of them as the next king. But, no, it was David, the youngest, a mere sheepherder, too young even to join his older brothers in the war against the Philistines, who was chosen (1 Samuel 16). David, the little brother, became not only king, but a national, indeed messianic figure of the Jewish people. It is indeed the Star of David that is emblazoned on the flag of Israel today. And it is of some interest to note that it was not David's eldest son, Adonijah, who succeeded him as king, but the "little brother", Solomon (1 Kings 1). These are all Old Testament stories. The greatest 'little brother' story of them all however is in the New Testament, in a tale told by Jesus (Luke 15). Here there are two brothers also, the elder brother who was the model of familial loyalty, and the younger who brought nothing but shame on the family. Yet, whom does the Father clearly favor in the story - not the Elder, the "Good Boy" but, to the consternation of many of us, the Black Sheep, the younger son, "the little brother" who has nothing going for him but humility.

Take a closer look at your reactions to the story of the prodigal son. There is in most of us a swelling of resentment, small for some, but for some of us almost intolerable. It is very difficult for us to swallow this business of a besotted wastrel looking better in the Gospel than the upright and clean-living elder brother. I once made the real mistake of talking to a group of union men on a retreat about another parable that evoked similar outrage. It is the parable about the workers in the vineyard. You remember - the one where the guy who worked only an hour - at the end of the day and in the cool of the evening - was paid the same wage as those who had worked all day in the beating sun (Matthew 20). It is not a story - no matter that it was told by Jesus - that these union guys were willing to accept. But the story is really the same as that of the Prodigal Son, the same story as that of the "little brother".

God does not work the way we work. God does not abide by our standards of achievement. What this means is that this business of being saved does not depend on the hard work of our discipline and virtue. It depends only on God's generosity and love. This is why, in another of Jesus' stories, the poor publican who simply acknowledged his sinfulness was "justified" and the righteous Pharisee was not (Luke 18). The publican knew he needed God; the Pharisee, no matter how well he thought he observed the law, did not. What God asks of us above all is a humble acknowledgment of our sinfulness, repentance and trust in God's mercy. This is why Jean-Pierre deCaussade in his classic, *Abandonment to Divine Providence* could confidently cry out: "Rejoice every time you discover a new imperfection". 'Rejoice', because it gives further cause to trust God rather than your own goodness. It is indeed a spirituality for underachievers.

All this of course is difficult for Americans. We are, if nothing else, **achievers.** We are used to getting only what we deserve and work for. We are for that reason even a little suspicious of give away and welfare programs. And we hate it when some jerk scrambles to the top of the commercial or political world by means that are at least devious, if not downright immoral. Some of us, upon hearing of the kind of spirituality indicated by the "brother" stories, throw up our hands and say, "What's the use of being good?" But the answer is not self-indulgence in our own sins, expecting God's forgiveness.

The answer lies in basing our moral behavior on other grounds. We do not act morally in order to save our hides. We act morally because we are grateful God offers us his love. In return we offer him moral behavior.

In the offering of love, it makes no difference to God whether we are the big brother or the little brother. But it behooves both big and little brother to give love back to God.

Spirituality and Politics
The Tragedy of the "Naked Public Square"
Autumn 2000

Every four years, as a major election approaches, religious leaders are sternly warned against advocating one candidate over another. We live in a nation where Church and State are separate, and we might lose our tax exemption. But this separation does not mean that believers should vacate what Catholic theologian, Richard John Neuhaus, has called "the public square". According to Neuhaus, the "public square" is "naked" because religious viewpoints have been effectively, if unconstitutionally, kept from it. But the public square is also "naked" because many religious people have chosen to stay out of it.

One of the most appalling signs of decline in the quality of American culture is our failure to take the electoral process seriously. Only one in four Americans vote in the primaries, and less than half vote in general elections - numbers that fall steadily from year to year. Even more disturbing perhaps is the fact that so many people who do vote, vote in an uninformed way, relying on images and impressions that are shrewdly manipulated by the wizards of political consulting. Candidates are being sold the way a new brand of pet food is sold.

Our faith as Christians cannot tolerate this. Our faith not only encourages us, it **requires** - and I emphasize **requires** us to enter the public square, if only to vote intelligently.

Some reflections follow that may help us in this respect.

First, we have to shed the notion that those who seek a career as politicians are inherently suspect. The political career is not only a decent career, it is a noble one. The vast majority of politicians, whether local, state or national, are people who have taken the notion of public citizen to its highest level - a life of public service to the people. Perhaps this very high standard is the reason we despise politicians. Because of the relatively few who do not match this high standard, we lump them all together into a distorted stereotype. While the country is run by the literally millions of honest and public spirited political officers, the crooked politician makes the headlines and forms our image of them.

Second, we have to take a second look-at the standards of truth-telling we hold politicians to. They are not liars. Politicians in a democratic and pluralist culture such as ours are required always to make compromises. Politics has been wisely defined as "the art of the possible", or even "the art of compromise". Hence, sometimes politicians have to say things they don't mean, or embrace positions they would rather not. We call this lying. (We sometimes prefer a more earthy name derived from the barnyard). But it really isn't. Or, if it is, it is the same kind of 'lying' that car salesmen use. Even the very conservative moral theology I learned back in the late '50's made allowance for that. We expect them to use excessive and misleading language. They know it's excessive, and they know that we know it's excessive, so it becomes part of the sales dance. The same is true of politicians.

Third, politics is not inherently corrupt. Yes, there is a great deal of money available in the public square, and the temptation to pocket some of it is very real. The many Chicago alderman who have been or are serving time are a close at hand reminder of this. Yes, corporate funding is increasingly dominating the political scene. The current legislative furor over campaign finance reform has been a result of this phenomenon. Yes, there are many politicians who have behaved badly in office, by the excessive use of power, or by personal moral failings. Among the "great", Nixon, and Clinton come to mind. I suspect however that greed, power and philandering are no more widely distributed among politicians than they are among the captains of business. Politicians are certainly no less moral than many figures in the world of entertainment. Wilt Chamberlain claims to have bedded twenty-thousand women! Yet, there is no evidence that Americans have withdrawn their interest in the National Basketball Association because of this gargantuan display of promiscuity. Do we have a right to give up on politics because politicians are human?

Fourth, your vote does count. It counts because that is the only way democracy works. When more than fifty percent of us decide that our vote does not count, the other guy's vote counts more than it should. And that's what you make possible when you don't vote!

Earlier in the last century, Communists succeeded in many democratically held labor union elections because they stayed late and voted in their policies after everyone else went home. A minority prevailed because a majority lost interest.

Finally, politics really does affect your life. It is because of politics that we have both a pro-life and a pro-choice movement. It is because of politics that we have a movement both for and against the death penalty. Politics will determine whether we may someday have a school voucher plan. Politics determines our tax rates. It is because of politics that the law of the land prohibits discrimination on the basis of race, gender, age, disability and religion. It is because of politics that our air is cleaner, and our environment more pristine. Are you content to let all this happen without your voice?

If you are content to drop out of the political scene, then you are neglecting a significant aspect of your spiritual life. Spirituality is not entirely defined by what you do in church, what you do in prayer, how you live your private moral life, what you do in the personal life of your family. Spirituality also includes public responsibility, indeed citizenship. Jesus taught that you must render to Caesar what is Caesar's (Mt 22.15-22). Paul several times calls attention to the Christian's responsibility toward public officials (Romans 13.1-7, Titus 3.1), as does Peter (1 Peter 2:13-17). There was no democracy and there were no elections in those days, but public order was to be respected and observed. These biblical passages make it clear that such a responsibility flows directly from discipleship of Jesus. But perhaps the strongest argument we have about being engaged in the political world is the simple fact of the Incarnation. God became human in Jesus Christ. That means that God took on the whole of the human condition, all of it, not just the churchy and inner aspects of it. God **is** in politics. God **is** in the Public Square. So that's where our spiritual life has to draw us as well.

Further reading: *"Faithful Citizens: Bringing Moral Vision to Public Life"* - U.S. Bishops' Pastoral on Civic Responsibility, 1999. A condensed version is available in 'Catholic Update', St. Anthony Messenger Press.

Jonathan Foster, O.F.M.

Are You Bowling with Me Jesus?
Spring 2001

In 1965, Malcolm Boyd, an Episcopalian priest and civil rights activist, authored a best selling book of prayers called *Are You Running With Me, Jesus?* Written in the heat of the civil rights movement, many of these prayers expressed the need for Christians to march with the movements of modern society, especially involvement in social action. Boyd wrote at a turning point in American social history when social activism seemed to define the emerging generation. His urgent and buoyant appeal to this kind of Christian prophetic witness has received considerable dampening in a major book published last year by sociologist Robert Putnam of Harvard University called, *Bowling Alone: The Collapse and Revival of American Community.*

This book began when Putnam learned from proprietors of bowling alleys that, while people were continuing to bowl in great numbers, there was less and less traditional team and league bowling. He even found one bowling alley in Connecticut where TV sets were installed above each lane, thus effectively cutting down on the normal joshing and cheering among teammates and opposing teams as individual bowlers locked onto their favorite TV programs. People were 'bowling alone'.

He has amplified this original observation by studying and reporting studies of practically every form of social gathering engaged in by Americans. He has studied, for example, besides bowling: charitable giving, blood donation, card-playing among friends, TV, the Internet, the telephone (including, of course, cellphones), e-mail, urban sprawl, organizations such as unions and professional associations, the workplace, volunteering, church attendance and membership, prayer-groups, support groups (there are 130 different kinds of 12-Step programs!), protest movements (they are 'graying'), voting, blood donation, family life, racial relationships, "big Government", the market economy and so on.

What Putnam is looking for in all these studies is what he calls "social capital". We are familiar with "financial capital", the sum of financial resources a company has available to carry on its mission. "Social capital" is the sum of all the resources a community may call upon to carry out its mission, especially people. **What he finds is that in almost every category there has been a steady decline over the past forty years of the investment people are making in social groups and endeavors.** In the eighties, Robert Bellah and his associates (especially in their major work, *'Habits of the Heart'*) made this same observation in an anecdotal way and began to express a now widely shared feeling that Americans are becoming more and more individualistic. Putnam documents this decline in numbing detail - the book's 541 pages bristle with graphs of some kind or other (though otherwise very readable, the book's proliferation of graphs is a bit intimidating).

He sifts through all this information in search of explanations, and sorts them out scientifically. He first eliminates several factors that conventional wisdom might consider major villains in this decline of community. The decline is not due, he concludes, in any significant way to: the breakdown of the family; the role of "big government"; the market; or to racial tension (though he acknowledges a decline of tolerance in the last case). He then assigns a percent value to each of what he sees as the four major factors contributing to the decline of community in America. The first is the pressure on people today from the workplace, and the inroads it makes into the time available for social involvement. He notes that this factor contributes to a surprisingly low 10% of the decline. He assigns the same percentage to the explosion of urban sprawl which has created great distances between home and work, family and friends, and the time required to get back and forth. He ascribes a more significant role to all the forms of electronic communication and recreation, especially television, which, he believes, are responsible for 25% of the decline. But the greatest enemy of community, he says, is something a little more difficult to pin down, and a little more ominous.

He speaks throughout the book of what he calls the "long civic generation". This is made up of people born roughly between 1910 and 1940. No generation before them had shown such a sense of public commitment, and no generation since then has matched it.

Indeed, those over 60, even as they have aged during the last quarter century, show by far the greatest increases in volunteering. In Putnam's own words: "...generational change - the slow, steady and ineluctable replacement of the long civic generation by their less involved children and grandchildren - has been a very powerful factor." **When we speak of community involvement and public minded-ness, there do seem to have been some truly "good old days".** And if this generational shift represents a permanent restructuring of our country's values, what indeed lies ahead?

Putnam includes in the subtitle of his book the phrase "revival" of community. He does see some signs of hope. One of these is, of all things, the much maligned Generation X, those under 25. Where, for example, the generation before them - 'boomers' - have shown a steady decline in volunteering (the worst drop has taken place among those born between 1963 and 1967), Generation X has shown a sharp rise. It is not nearly as high as the over-sixties generation, but it reverses a trend and may be a portent of the future.

He also has an agenda for the future. He addresses six areas where improvement can and **must** be made - youth and schools; the workplace; urban and metropolitan design; religion; arts and culture; government and politics. Because our primary interest here is spirituality, it will be helpful to note what he says about religion.

"Faith-based communities remain such a crucial reservoir of social capital in America that it is hard to see how we could redress the erosion of the last several decades without a major religious contribution - (I)t is undeniable that religion has played a major role in every period of civic renewal in American history. So, I challenge America's clergy, lay leaders, theologians and ordinary worshippers: *Let us spur a new pluralistic, socially responsible 'great awakening' so that by 2010 Americans will be more deeply engaged than we are today in one or another spiritual community of meaning, while at the same time becoming more tolerant of the faiths and practices of other Americans."* (italics by author)

So, we religious people bear a heavy responsibility in the restoration of the social capital that has been eroding our own society for much of the latter half of this century.

A Million Signs
Summer 2001

I regularly travel to Quincy, IL on business. When I do, I usually take the train, four hours down, four hours back. The trip back to Chicago begins at 6:00 AM, arriving in the western suburbs about 10:00AM. Since I am busy with people the whole time I'm down there, when I board the lightly occupied train, I usually take a seat by the window and just sit there lazily watching the landscape go by. One of the benefits of living and traveling in Illinois is the lack of spectacular scenery, so you get to spend your tourist passion, of which I have a lot, on some very ordinary stuff. On a recent trip, it struck me that even these very unassuming sights seemed to demand that they too be noticed. And so, I paid attention, gladly.

I saw redwing blackbirds flare up to confront the rumbling train, in a brave attempt to shoo it away, as they might a hawk. I watched dozens of creeks wind their way across the fields and slip unstopped beneath our tracks. In the towns, I admired giant sycamores and tulip trees standing protectively over old streets like shading angels. Some of these towns are shabby. The signs on the old train stations, where the trains don't stop anymore, are weathered to illegibility, and new shops selling antiques occupy and then 'paper over' the fronts of old two storied buildings which once housed groceries and hardware. We passed hundreds of farms, some freshly plowed with geometric precision - black dirt golf courses. In one, I watched a farmer maneuver a tiny golf cart over his vast field, checking the soil for moisture. In another, rusted old equipment stood in the corner of a field near a shallow ravine that served as the farmer's dump. There are still some windmills in the farmyards, but they mostly don't work. I saw one in which all the panels had dropped off and the windmill was crowned with mere sticks of steel. I saw a red fox trot away from the train across an open field, a red tailed hawk hunched perching in a small grove, and starlings fluttering about tall grain elevators. I even admired a bale of varicolored aluminum cans, crushed, wired, and glittering in the bright morning sun near a depot in Mendota. It was a morning prayer of sorts.

People often ask me why God doesn't send more signs, like he did to folks in the bible and to some of the saints. My response is that God is probably sending a whole lot more signs than we think he is, but that because we have more or less got it fixed in our minds what kind of signs God ought to send, we don't see the ones that are always there.

In her lengthy poem/novel, 'Aurora Leigh', Elizabeth Barrett Browning has expressed this about as well as anybody since the Pentateuch. She writes:

"Earth's crammed with heaven
and every common bush afire with God.
But only he who sees, takes off his shoes.
The rest sit round it and pluck blackberries."

Browning evokes here the scene in Exodus where Yahweh-God requires Moses to take off his sandals before approaching the strangely burning bush. It is sacred ground. Yahweh is there. She is also evoking the fine old practice of picking wild blackberries. I did a lot of that as a kid. In the late summer, when blackberries fruit, our family would join one or the other family and spend the day out in the woods picking blackberries. This wasn't just for fun - as my brother-in-law and I do today, looking for enough berries so that my sister can make a couple of her wonderful pies. What we did in my youth was true harvesting. When we got the berries home, our mothers would heat up their stoves, can them, make preserves, then store them in our root cellars to feed the family throughout the winter. So, these were truly businesslike outings, complete with repeated admonitions to us kids not to eat more than we put in the one quart honey pails we had slung from our belts. Where I grew up in Northern Michigan, there were a lot more berries than there are today, and sometimes you could sit in one place picking from one particularly bounteous bush for twenty minutes or more. This burying one's head in one bush while we picked is what I think Browning must have had in mind when she described "the rest (who just) sit round it and pluck blackberries." Never to my knowledge did we ever think about these gloriously laden bushes as being "afire with

God". The point Elizabeth Browning is trying to make is that, despite our failure to notice, they are.

These blackberries are just some of the millions of signs God places before us everyday. They may not enclose some special instruction for our future directed to any of us individually, though I would not exclude that. But, they are signs that point to the God who creates, provides for, redeems, and even dwells among us. They are, as the poet John Donne once noted, the clothes God wears when she walks among us. They are, as has been so often expressed in our tradition, God's handiwork, footsteps, pottery, building, God's images - the innumerable array of stuff God has furiously and wastefully cast out into the universe, the trail he blazed throughout creation to call our attention to his presence.

But, of course, most of the time we miss all this. We are so fascinated by the signs, so attracted to their beauty and usefulness that we don't recognize them as signs. We don't get the meaning of the blackberries. We just eat them.

This is why even a train trip to Quincy can be such a revelation.

But in order for this to be so, we have to develop a side of ourselves that most of us neglect. This is our contemplative side. Contemplation is not a difficult exercise. It is simply the capacity each of us has to observe someone or something without trying to make use of it, make it our own, consume it, buy it or sell it. It is the capacity each of us has to accept the world out there just as it is without conforming it to ourselves. It is the same capacity each of us has to admire great art, be absorbed by great music, stand in awe of spectacular scenery, and in the end see God as God really is, not twist him into a caricature of himself that suits us. Contemplation is a gift, fortunately, not limited to saints, but it is a gift that requires some discipline on our part.

The discipline of contemplation does not mean of course that we never dare disturb the world by touching it, or using it for our own benefit. That too is part of God's plan. In Genesis God tells Adam and Eve that they may make use of all the seed-bearing plants, trees, animals, birds, "and all living creatures that crawl on the ground". God even gave them dominion over the earth. All he asks of us is that we recognize where they come from and to Whom they should lead us. This is, I assume, why the Plains Indians are reported to have apologized to the bison before they killed it. It is why some of us still say 'Grace' before meals.

So, eat all the blackberries you want. But remember Whose sign they are.

Does Prayer Work?
Fall 2001

Recently I visited everybody's favorite Catholic bookstore in the area, the Wheaton Religious Goods Store, and asked Lori, the doyenne of the book department, what was the hottest seller. She named a little book, called *The Prayer of Jabez,* only recently published. The book is about a brief prayer buried amidst the genealogical clutter of the First Book of Chronicles (4:9-10), uttered by an otherwise unknown character named Jabez. The entire passage reads as follows: "Jabez prays, 'Oh, that you may truly bless me and extend my boundaries! Help me and make me free of misfortune, without pain.' And God granted his prayer." It's a little book, and can be read in 30-45 minutes. It is the sort of book the stores stack on the check-out counter as a kind of impulse purchase. What is amazing is that it has become almost an instant bestseller, several million copies in the first months, with a cottage industry of follow-up booklets already available on how to use the prayer. I am sure that eventually there will be retreats and workshops centered on the book.

Why the excitement? Less than two years ago, religious pollster, George Gallup, described a very real religious revival in America, but one that is "a mile wide and an inch deep". This book appears to be part of that broad and shallow river. It's handy, it's inexpensive, and it promises that most American of hopes - results.

It also makes two important points that need to be looked at.

The first of these is that we should not be timid about asking God for blessings, not just for others, but for ourselves. God wants to bless us, and is apparently just waiting to be asked. The author would like to have us think that Jabez is praying for opportunities to do good, but since the original Jabez asks God to "extend his boundaries" (read: make me richer), the book, as though embarrassed by this typical Old Testament materialism, makes little of this.

The second point is that the book seems to make a guarantee that if we ask for something specific, God will give it to us. Although the author makes the theologically correct statement that God's response will not always be the one we are looking for, he tips his hand in a couple stories near the end of the book. There he slides over into the position that if you've got enough faith, you'll get just what you want. He gives his own example of getting stuck in traffic on the way to the airport and praying that his flight would be delayed so that he wouldn't miss it. It was delayed, and that was seen of course as an answer to Jabez' prayer. (He does not mention any concern about the other people on his flight who presumably did not pray for a delay.)

So, does prayer 'work'? Yes, but not exactly the way we would like to think. Prayer is certainly not a candle we light to lure God, like a great moth, to come to our aid, but Christians have always been tempted to use it that way. Think of the novenas, scapulars and medals Catholics have traditionally made use of. Even some of the more recent popular forms of prayer, such as centering prayer, walking the labyrinth, T'ai Chi, often guarantee that such prayerful activities will have predictable outcomes. Indeed, the *Prayer of Jabez* outlines a month-long discipline of petitionary prayer that is not at all unlike the Catholic novena. Believers have always looked for something that will wring a response out of God. Otherwise, we say, what's prayer good for? There's got to be, we think, a technique somewhere, a quick fix, if you will, that will make prayer a more productive exercise.

Jesus seems clearly to support this idea. Time after time in the Gospels, he makes this promise, "Again I say to you, if two of you agree on earth about anything for which they are to pray, it shall be granted them by my heavenly Father" (Matthew 18:19); or "Whatever you ask for in prayer with faith, you will receive" (Mt 21:22). The promise is uncompromisingly clear and frequently made. And yet we know from the experience of 2000 years that it doesn't happen that way. For example, in our ministry we prayed frequently for enough money to build a new retreat house at Marmion Abbey which seemed to us a noble and kingdom-worthy goal. But, our campaign did not achieve its goal in time for us to preserve that relationship. In the face of such anomalies, many people point to outcomes they have prayed for that *have* come true, and say to us, "See, prayer does work! Just like Jesus said", selectively forgetting the many times it hasn't 'worked'.

How do we explain Jesus' insistence on the success of prayer? This is especially problematic when we realize that it didn't always 'work', even for him. In the Garden of Gethsemane, Jesus asked God to "take this cup from me" (Lk 22:42), and yet God didn't. Jesus also prayed at the Last Supper that in the coming darkness Peter's faith might not fail. But Peter's faith did fail. Jesus' greatest disciple, Paul, begged God "three times" to remove "the thorn in the flesh" that bedeviled him, but God refused (2 Cor 12:7b-10). Clearly our understanding of Jesus' promises about how prayer 'works' needs to go beyond a literal interpretation of his words. I believe Jesus knew full well that not all prayers are answered as proposed. The certainty with which he seems to assert that they will be answered is not some kind of PR flimflam on his part. Rather, it reflects a style of preaching, familiar to people of his time, that freely used exaggerated language. Think of his call to put out an offending eye or cut off a hand tempted to sin (Mt 5:27ff). Jesus preached one way to the people of his time. It is not likely that, in our times, more suspicious of hyperbolic language, he would preach the same way.

But, two things are very clear from Jesus' teachings. First, he *wants* us to ask, to petition, to beg, much more than we do. Not, however, because prayer is the lever on the slot machine that turns up three cherries, but because we need to recognize our dependence on God, to acknowledge that he is the creator, the potter, and we only the clay. In Psalm 50, for example, God tells his people that he doesn't need all the oxen and bulls they bring in for sacrifice. But he does "need" for us to come before him as our creator, Father, or Mother - petitions in hand.

Second, God will always respond to prayer. He might give us just what we ask for. But, no matter how deep and virtuous our faith, he might not. The latter sometimes isn't always possible, even for God. I recall with some embarrassment my school days when before a big intramural game both teams in my very Catholic school huddled in prayer, and both ended their prayer the same way: "Our Lady of Victory, pray for us!" This was not a prayer for good sportsmanship or for protection against injury. It was a plea to help us beat the other guys, followed loudly by an intimidating threat shouted against them. God and Our Lady were, I am sure, both confused and amused. But they are surely not amused when Catholics and Protestants, Muslims and Israelis pray to God against each other in the same way.

But God will always, when we ask, give us something - something that we may not even imagine. For the greatest thing about prayer is that when we enter into it, we enter a world far different than ours. It is a world in which we are on God's terms, not ours. It is good to be there, and our presence there will always enlarge our souls. But we may not always expect to receive there what we had asked for. I hope this is what the Prayer of Jabez has in mind. But ... I'm not sure.

The Dark Side of Christmas
Christmas and the Cross
Spring 2002

As I write this (late January), my Christmas creche is still up. This is not due to laziness - all other vestiges of Christmas in my home were dispatched after "Twelfth Night" or Epiphany. I always leave my creche up for a time, usually till the Feast of the Purification, February 2, my personal closure to the Christmas season, because it has a message for me that needs to be held over from the rush of Christmas. This year, I think I'll leave it up until Ash Wednesday - it's early this year - or maybe even till Good Friday.

Perhaps it was the cruel carnage of September 11 and the scorching aftermath of the military campaign in Afghanistan, but this year I was much more aware of the profound connection between the joy of Christmas and the sorrow of Good Friday. The liturgy of Christmas allows us, even compels us, to look at this connection, unsavory though the prospect of doing that may be.

It struck me this year for the first time that Evening Prayer on Christmas Eve (from the breviary) includes the canticle from Philippians (2:5-11) in which not only the incarnation (birth) of Jesus is celebrated, but his passion and death as well. It seems out of place there. But then, as though to reinforce death's right to be celebrated as well as birth, on the very day after Christmas, the Church celebrates a blood feast - the martyrdom of St. Stephen, the Deacon, the very first person to die for his belief in Jesus Christ (Acts 6-7).

Then, just two days later, the awful massacre of the baby boys by King Herod is celebrated - as a major feast! And, the day after that, the Church celebrates the feast of St. Thomas a' Becket, Archbishop of Canterbury, who was assassinated shortly after Christmas of 1170 by the henchmen of Henry II. Since most Catholics don't pray the breviary or go to church on those days, it may come as a surprise to most of you that the church casts this bloody shadow of Good Friday on the serene and angelic light of Christmas.

It is this mingling of Christmas and Good Friday that inspired T S. Eliot's poem,*"Journey of the Magi"*. In this poem, one of the Magi recounts the difficulty of their journey, and their satisfaction upon finding the newborn king. But, disturbed, he then goes on to ask whether they had been brought that far for 'Birth' or 'Death'. Expecting only a birth, they had experienced a death. Not a physical dying, but a realization that, having met the newborn king, they were being called to their own rebirth, impelled to let go of 'ancient gods'. Now back in his familiar kingdom, he concludes, with these bittersweet words of perhaps reluctant longing: "I should be glad of another Death".

To some all this may seem a wet blanket thrown upon the warm hearth of Christmas. The dark reality of the passion - betrayal, whips, bloody crown of thorns, the gallows of the cross - have no business, we say, clouding over the joys of Christmas. To some extent this is so, and I would not, say, preach a sermon on the passion and death of Jesus on Christmas Day.

But, we cannot escape the road that runs straight from the stable in Bethlehem to the rock called Golgotha. The distance is but five miles as the crow flies, and it is even shorter in the Christian journey.

Everything about Jesus calls for an upending of what we call human wisdom. So, if a peasant baby as king threatens every conception we have of human wisdom, remember Herod's cruel crusade against baby boys who might be his rivals - it is inevitable that that king would triumph, not through military, political and economic means, but through ignominious execution.

We would rather be more 'upbeat' about Christianity. We prefer to think that we can somehow weld human values to Christ's values. This is true to some extent, of course, because Jesus was as fully human as he was divine. But in doing so, unfortunately, we often reduce Christ's values to a support system for what we want to believe.

Take for example, the practice that has arisen since September 11 of putting out signs that read, "In God We Trust", and other such expressions of confidence that God sees things our way. What I fear about the "In God We Trust" signs is the unspoken implication that if we trust God, i.e., go to church, pray more often, God will protect us from terrorism, that we can bring the big divine guns to bear on Al Quaeda. It is the most recent incarnation of the old chestnut: "God Wills It" (the cry of the Crusaders), or "God is on our side", a war cry that even Abraham Lincoln, who would have appreciated God's vote of confidence in his war against the Confederacy, felt compelled to reject. "In God We Trust", also found on our currency, is a wonderful expression of faith. But it means what it says: God is the fundamental source of our hope and our trust.

What it does **not** mean is that God supports our politics, our life style, our economy, or our military, just as God, despite their passionate appeals to holy war in his name, does not support Al Quaeda. God supports God, and calls upon us to trust God, not just when all else fails, but as we undertake the various fallible exercises of human wisdom required to manage the world according to the lights of Jesus Christ. As Abraham Lincoln is reported to have said:

> "The question is not whose side God is on,
> but are we on God's side?"

This connection between Christmas and the Cross brings out the realism of Christianity. It is realism that embraces the whole, not just a part of human nature. The incarnation of God in Jesus at Christmas shines light upon the nobility of humanity. God thinks enough of humans to share our being! The crucifixion of God in Jesus Christ however exposes the dark side of humanity. Men are willing to kill a prophet because he teaches a truth they do not wish to hear. The blood-feasts in the aftermath of Christmas serve this realism. Fortunately, it works both ways. Just as the shadow of the cross falls upon Christmas, so the light of the Magi's star shines over Good Friday.

Upon Which Rock?
The Church's One Foundation
Summer 2002

I am writing this in mid-April. As I do so, some thirty Christians, most of them Franciscans, men and women, are trapped in one of the most sacred places of the world - the Basilica of the Nativity in Bethlehem. Christians, they are trapped in their own church by non-Christians. Trapped because an armed group of Muslims has taken refuge inside the church, and a pursuing army unit of Jews has laid siege to it with tanks and sniper's rifles. This tragic situation has become for me a symbol of a larger crisis that confronts Christians, especially Catholics, in this country today.

Like those poor friars and nuns caught in the cross fire of Israeli howitzers and Palestinian rifles, their lives endangered even as they pray in the great church that marks the spot of their Savior's birth, the church we love seems often to have become a relic trapped between the 'devil' of fundamentalist rage and the 'deep blue sea' of an aggressive secularism.

At the same time as this dramatic event in Bethlehem, another event crowds our hearts this Easter season - the recrudescence of something we thought was behind us, the criminal sexual behavior of some of our priests. A priesthood, already depleted by age and half-full seminaries, already buffeted by the revelation of these scandals 10-15 years ago, has once again, for the same crimes, been hung out like unwashed underwear to the shame and embarrassment of Catholics everywhere, and let it be said, to the glee of many, including some cheap-shot late night comedians.

Events like this bring the doomsayers out of the woods to pronounce the demise of the Church. "How can a Church that denies the right of women to make a free choice about the fate of her pregnancy, that refuses to ordain women, that requires most of its priests to be celibate, opposes most forms of birth control, and rejects sexual activity outside of marriage possibly be relevant in a liberated society whose conventional wisdom relegates sexual activity, even of the most perverted kind, to just another expressive, even recreational activity?"

Are we, like those Franciscans in Bethlehem, prisoners of other forces, holed up in a beautiful old Church that the world has little respect for except as a museum piece from the past? Is it **'apocalypse now'** for the Catholic church? Is the world passing Catholics by?

Of course not.

We need only recall that this is the same Church that once had three Popes simultaneously vying for power; that once had Popes with mistresses in the papal palaces, and a Pope that lead his own troops into battle against other Catholic kings; that perpetrated the atrocities of the crusades and the inquisition, was decimated by the

Protestant Reformation, and has had to apologize for its conspiracy in destroying some indigenous cultures. Despite all this historic depravity, which dwarfs our current serious concern about kinky sex, this same Catholic Church is not only by far the largest Christian body, but the largest religion in the world and growing.

But this is not the time to trumpet our 'successes'. We have sinned. We have even less reason to brag for the simple reason that the successes of the Church are not ours, but God's. Oh, we have something to do with it. But, not a lot. There is a little ritual in the Mass, often overlooked and frequently not even carried out, when, at the time of the offertory, the celebrant tips a tiny drop of water from a glass cruet into the chalice full of wine. The droplet of water of course slips invisibly into the wine and is completely absorbed. The ritual is intended to remind us how much we contribute to the Eucharistic mystery. It is as little as that drop of water let fall into the cup of wine. It is mostly God's work. So it is with the endurance and 'success' of Christianity.

We do need humility at times like this. In the midst of this latest outbreak of media attention, an Evangelical Protestant friend of mine told me that he knew how I must feel. He reminded me that he and all other Evangelicals had been similarly shamed by the sexual and financial antics of televangelists some years back, especially Jim Bakker and Jimmy Swaggart. Remember how we smirked self-righteously over that one? No more.

Some have suggested that while these sexual scandals certainly do not sound the death knell of the priesthood, they might well mean the end of clericalism. They are right. Clericalism is an arrogance often associated with the priesthood that acts out the misbegotten belief that because they are priests or Bishops they are better than everyone else, that they need give no time to the criticisms of others, that they deserve as an elite class to be treated in an appropriately servile manner. Its funeral is long overdue.

What we need mostly at times like this is to remember something that lies at the basis of all biblical, Christian and Catholic faith. Trust in God. We who exercise leadership in the church are so well educated, so well trained, and, especially here in the USA, so professional, that it is very easy to succumb to the illusion that all we have to do is marshal all our skills and virtues and we will be able to save the Church (save: a word that Jesus and Paul used frequently to describe what God does!).

Moreover, to deal with the scandals arising from criminal sexual behavior of priests, we have joined forces with our brother and sister professionals the lawyers, the insurance people, the psychologists and psychiatrists. We are well advised to do so. But none of these are enough; none of these has the ultimate answer. Human skills, as philosophers love to say, are a necessary part of the solution, but they are not enough!

What is 'enough' is to constantly remind ourselves that when we fail in our efforts, we are not to lose hope. Trusting too much in ourselves as individuals, families, communities, the Church - is the surest path to losing hope. So, we are required to remember whose Church this is, whose promise it was to be with us until the end of time, and our faith that the Church was not founded on the 'rock' that was Peter, but on the 'Rock' that - as is so often attested to in the psalms and elsewhere - is God.

The Franciscans who are, as I write, hostages in their own church, can help us here. Franciscans all profess a vow of poverty. Poverty, whatever it may mean in terms of material goods, is ultimately a willingness to let go of excessive confidence in our own resources ... to stand naked before our own ineptness ... to let go of control of our lives, and to hand them over to God. I am sure that, wide-eyed as they may be with anxiety, these heroic men and women are also calling on this bedrock of their profession. So should we.

The Church of the Nativity, built by human hands, can be reduced to rubble. God's Church never will be.

Jonathan Foster, O.F.M.

We Are All Like Matthew
Spring 2003

As some of you already know, I recently hung in my office an elegantly framed print of Michelangelo Caravaggio's painting "The Call of St. Matthew". Like much baroque painting, this one tells a story, making explicit one not told, merely alluded to, in the Bible (Matthew 9:9). In Caravaggio's painting, Jesus, a lightly bearded man with a determined profile (and a halo above his head to make sure we don't mistake him!), has entered, accompanied by Peter, what appears to be a counting room full of tax collectors.

There are five of them, all brightly clad in the fashionable hose and blousy tunics favored by well-to-do Renaissance men. One - perhaps "security?"- even has a sword strapped to his thigh. Three of them are young and clean-shaven, two are mature, full bearded men. A shaft of light coming in from a window invisible in the painting, plays full onto the face of one of the latter. It is Matthew at the far right edge of the painting, even as Peter seems to be questioning the wisdom of such a choice (as well he might since most Jews hated the tax collectors as minions of Rome), Jesus is pointing an imperious finger right at Matthew, clearly summoning him.

Matthew's response catches the eye. A surprised, unbelieving look on his face, he points with his left hand towards himself as though to say, "You can't mean me?" His right hand however is busily engaged with the right hand of one of the younger tax collectors rifling the coins spread on the table as though to make sure that this brusque and outrageous summons by an itinerant preacher in peasant garb was not going to interfere with the watchful pursuit of his share of the takings. The painting was created between 1598 and 1601. The original hangs in the little Roman church, St. Louis of the French, and I first saw a print of it in my bedroom at St. Procopius Abbey where I was making a retreat.

What struck me about the painting, and I spent a considerable amount of time studying it and gazing on it, is a tension I experience constantly in my life, and that is, I believe, felt by everyone whom I see in my ministry - the experience of 'call' and 'response'. It is no coincidence that the hand Jesus extends towards Matthew is the same hand that his relative Michelangelo painted in his famous depiction of the creation of Adam in the Sistine Chapel. It is a hand that does not merely point. It commands. Indeed, it creates. But just as the call of Jesus is so overpowering, just so reluctant is the response of Matthew.

He tries to escape the call in two ways. First, as the left hand points towards himself, he seems to politely question whether Jesus has indeed gotten the right man. "After all," he might well be saying, "I'm a quisling, a Jew who works for the Romans. No self-respecting Jew likes me, and probably with good reason. What use would I be to someone like you, a very religious preacher who probably attends synagogue every Sabbath?" Second, even as he questions the call, his right hand is pressed firmly down on some coins that seem to be the object of contention between him and another of the younger men, who has his hands on them as well. These coins represent what he has spent his entire life doing - growing wealth, even as he endures the hatred of his countrymen. There is no small commitment here, and he isn't letting go of those coins easily.

I recognize all this. I have been hearing this call for over 50 years. This fierce uncompromising call to be a Catholic Christian, to be a Franciscan, to be a priest, to undertake the various ministries I have been invited to undertake throughout my life, indeed to found the ministry for which I now work, never moderates. In each of these calls I have found myself, like Caravaggio's Matthew, responding with hesitation and questions, skeptical, tentative. And I have always kept tightly gripped in my hand some coins that I hold back just for me.

I am comforted to think that even Matthew might have had the same reservations as I do. I take Caravaggio a bit further. Jesus looks very stern and uncompromising in this painting. My guess is that in the very next, unpainted, scene, Jesus lowers his head to Peter and smiles compassionately, if a bit wryly, "You're all alike, you know."

Culture Christians
Catholicism & Political Dissent
Summer 2003

Franz Jagerstatter was a young Bavarian farmer during the Nazi years in Germany, and like most young Germans, he was conscripted into the German army. Though uneducated, he was deeply Catholic and understood his faith better than most of his fellow Christians. He understood that what the ruling regime was up to was wrong. So, he refused to show up. He would not serve. Though threatened and finally arrested, and despite the fact that he was the father of a young family, he continued to refuse. In our country, he would have been granted conscientious objector status. Not in Nazi Germany. For his beliefs, he was executed. Just one more in an endless stream of Christians and Catholics who have been imprisoned, tortured, executed, or even assassinated for their opposition to the ruling authority.

No such outrage befell those who opposed the recent war Iraq. Nor could it in America. It's one of the reasons why we are the great country that we are. But, there is a lesson here for all Catholics and Christians, many of whom were vehemently opposed to the war, including almost all their leaders. Catholics all are aware of the passionate objections made by Pope John Paul II. Hundreds of demonstrations, many of them large, blossomed across the country. But once the war was joined, and especially after we triumphantly overwhelmed the Iraqis, those voices went quiet. Did the "victory" change people's minds? Hardly. But a subtle intimidation had settled over the land. To oppose the war suggested that your patriotism was suspect, and, even worse, that you weren't "supporting our troops". In one instance, some parish leaders in the Chicago area undertook efforts to fire a member of their staff who had not only opposed the war but engaged in civil disobedience to make his point.

Opposition to ruling regimes and states by Christians has a long history. Read, for example, Acts of the Apostles, Chapter 4. Peter and John have been arrested by the Sanhedrin, the legitimate legal authority in Jerusalem, and ordered not to speak or teach at all in the name of Jesus. Peter's reply is the purest silver of political Christianity: *"Whether it is right in the sight of God for us to obey you rather than God, you be the judges. It is impossible for us not to speak about what we have seen and heard."* Upon their release, that's what they continued to do.

Christians, when they have judged the state to be acting contrary to the Gospel, have been standing up to rulers ever since. Most martyrs have been killed by the state or what passed for ruling authority. Both Catholics and Protestant leaders in England, for example, were executed by the reigning monarch for taking positions contrary to the 'official' faith (viz., Queen Mary executed

Protestants; Queen Elizabeth executed Catholics). Fortunately, in most countries, opposition to the state is no longer a capital offense. "Peace Churches" such as the Church of the Brethren and the Mennonites are by law granted conscientious objector status. The Catholic Worker movement, founded by Dorothy Day, is also pacifist, and its status as such is guaranteed by the government. It is a little known fact that even during World War II there were here in the USA conscientious objectors, some of them Catholic.

But this political protection does not protect critics of the state from the scorn of citizens who enthusiastically support the government. Fifty years ago, one of the great theological minds of this century, H. Richard Niebuhr, in his book, *Christ and Culture*, identified five different models of how Christians relate to the culture they live in. One of them he identified as "culture Christians". These are people deeply rooted in their own political and economic culture - say, American - but still stoutly consider themselves Christians. What they do, says Niebuhr, is use Christianity to justify their political and economic beliefs, and, when their faith is critical of their politics and economics, put the culture first.

Back in the fourth century, St. Augustine, in the *The City of God*, steered us away from this uncritical mixing of faith and culture. He distinguished the "heavenly city", which is the body of the faithful guided by the Gospel, from "the earthly city" guided by human aspirations. Christians live in both cities, and must serve them both, but the "earthly city" must always be judged by the "heavenly one". American Christians therefore must serve both their faith and their country. But, when they believe that the country is at odds with the faith, then we must all join with Peter and John, and "speak about what we have seen and heard".

Reflections of a Bird-Watching Spiritual Director
A Dispatch from Petoskey, Michigan.
Fall 2003

I am very pleased with many things about my life, but today I count two that I am particularly pleased about: first, that I am a bird-watcher; and, second, that I am a native of Petoskey, Michigan, and get to spend some time every summer there with my sister and brother-in-law. Their home sits out in the country on a forested ridge above a wide valley through which snakes the Bear River on its way to the bay off Lake Michigan on which Petoskey sits.

One sunny day this past summer I spent several hours leisurely bicycling along the battered old River Road that parallels that stream, stopping to look for birds where side roads cross the stream. One of these crosses the river at a site known to locals as Wah-Me-Me. It was once the location of a sawmill in the days when lumber, not tourists, was Petoskey's main industry. You can still see remains of the old dam that formed a pond there. As I turned onto this side road, intent primarily on keeping my balance and watching for traffic, something high in a dead tree caught my eye. I braked quickly to a stop in the middle of the road, and put my binoculars to my eyes. What came into focus was a pileated woodpecker. Now these birds are not endangered, and I have seen a half dozen or so in my thirty years of birding, but they are sufficiently uncommon that each sighting is an exciting experience, and they are such spectacular birds - coal black, as large as a crow, brandishing a flaming red crest and an imperious call that can be heard from a great distance that even if they were as common as deer, every sighting would still be an adventure.

I visit this site every year about the same time, but this was the first time I had ever seen a pileated woodpecker there. Birding is like that. You can go to all the right spots at all the right times, but a sighting, especially of less common birds, is always a gift, and frequently, an 'accident' that happens while you are looking for something else. Bird-watchers know this. You go birding on the birds' terms, not your own. You enter this world as a guest. And so you can't thrash aggressively and noisily about and expect to see many birds. You can't be a threatening presence. You have to be quiet. Frequently, you just have to sit still and wait. No sudden movements. One of the most discouraging moments for any birder happens when you are moving quietly through one of Chicago's Forest Preserves and some pet owner charges down the trail yelling at a yapping dog.

I have been reading books on the spiritual life for over 40 years, but only once have I encountered a writer, an Orthodox Bishop named Anthony Bloom, who drew a connection between bird-watching and the spiritual life. The connection is so uncanny that you have to think that there aren't many spiritual directors who are also bird-watchers. "Earth's crammed with heaven", Elizabeth Barrett Browning once wrote, "and every bush afire with God." But, most of the time, most of us miss God because, like many birders, we look for him on our terms, not his.

Like a birder, who has perused all the very best field guides but only goes birding when he feels like it, we think we know precisely where God is to be found, what he will look like, and how he will reveal himself to us. Indeed, many spiritual writers have contributed to this arrogance by setting forth a variety of disciplines that seem, if used properly, to guarantee a divine encounter. Annie Dillard is not considered a great spiritual master, but I am very fond of an insight she once expressed about our 'search' for God: "The 'pearl of great price'", she wrote, "although it may be found, may not be sought." 'Seeking' suggests it is all up to us and our dogged determination; 'finding' however asserts that it is always a gift from God.

Entering God's world, like entering that of birds, is always on God's terms, not ours. Like birdwatching, some of the same disciplines are required. You have to be alert and attentive at all times. You have to give God time. You have to recognize that you're a guest in God's world. You must always expect to be surprised. At the same time, you must always be prepared to be disappointed, for you may do all the "right" things and nothing may happen, no revelation may occur. Just as in bird-watching. We enter the world of birds not as their makers, not as their owners, certainly not in control of them. So also do we enter God's world.

May you be blessed with Grace, and perhaps, if you watch carefully, with a pileated woodpecker as well.

Catholic Pride...An Oxymoron?
Winter 2003

Catholics in the US have taken some big hits in the past couple years. The most significant of these of course has been learning of the sexual abuse of children by some priests and the cover-up by some bishops. It has called forth shame and anger in most Catholics. But it has also flung a spotlight on an old enemy that still prowls in the darkness...bigotry against Catholics. When I was growing up, the tension between Catholics and Protestants in my hometown was said to be so strong that sporting events between the public and Catholic high schools were never scheduled. Or, at least I was told this was the reason. I was content to call them 'pot-lickers" when they called me a "cat-licker".

Although we might have thought in these days that bigotry had evaporated with the past, it apparently has not. Nor in its contemporary form can we lay it at the feet of the old Protestant nemesis. You still hear, in some fundamentalist circles, the old canards about Catholics being cannibals because they eat Jesus' body, or worship Mary and other saints. But, according to Philip Jenkins, most anti-Catholic bigotry comes from outside religion. Jenkins is Distinguished Professor of History and Religious Studies at Penn State, and is the author of *"The New Anti-Catholicism: The Last Acceptable Prejudice"*. Although he is a former Catholic (Episcopalian now), he grinds no axes in this straightforward and generally sympathetic account.

The principal sources of bigotry against Catholics today, according to Jenkins, are: political and cultural secularism, radical feminism, radical gay and lesbian activists, the news media (always eager for a prurient story), movies and television, and some historians of the Church's involvement in the Holocaust. In part, this bigotry arises from frustration with the Church's unrelenting stand on a whole range of gender, family and other moral issues. Because the church refuses to bend on issues that other Americans have developed a consensus on - birth control, abortion, sexual promiscuity, married and female clergy - she has become fair game for wholesale mocking misrepresentation (not unlike medieval bearbaiting), that, as Andrew Greeley has also pointed out, would not be tolerated were it leveled against blacks, Jews, even Muslims. The sex abuse crisis has simply added an incendiary element to this smoldering grassfire.

But something else is new about this exercise of bigotry. Some of it is coming from Catholics. In the past, Catholics had their disagreements, but, out of concern for the Church's reputation, these were not publicly laundered, and we joined arms when the enemy stood at the gate. But, today Catholic critics of their own church have joined their secular colleagues in bashing that church, especially its clergy, bishops and the Vatican.

This, according to Jenkins, has emboldened the media to trot out the old stereotypes of the Church: authoritarian, oppressor of free speech, chauvinist, squeamish about sex, and generally out of touch with the modem world. And there is of course no way to argue with these positions, because they have hardened into conventional wisdom, expressed, as Jenkins puts it, in the unassailable claim that, "Everybody knows *that*."

Catholics should willingly face the truth about themselves. When the news is bad, we should, rather than deny it or cover it up, acknowledge it and do something about it. But when the news is good we should be proud, even brag about it. I wonder about this. We seem rather to be embarrassed about being Catholic. We seem too willing to join in the piling up on our fellow Catholics, especially the beleaguered clergy. We seem only too willing to admit that we are preoccupied with sex (as though Americans in general were not!). We join too quickly in the mocking laughter at the quaint, habited nuns. We apologize to a tut-tutting world for our unmarried clergy - nuns, priest, bishops - suggesting that if we could just get them legally and sacramentally into bed, we'd have a healthy church. We read a best-selling thriller like *The DaVinci Code* which vigorously attacks Catholic institutions such as the papacy and Opus Dei, and rather than be offended, treat it solemnly as if it were some credible judgment of Catholicism on a par with a papal pronouncement.

We are told these days by our leaders that Catholics must be more evangelical about their faith, try to spread it, as our Protestant brethren do. I agree. But right now I'd settle for some simple, even indignant pride, about being Catholic.

Jonathan Foster, O.F.M.

You Gave Me Wonder
Some Reflections on a Popular Novel
Spring 2004

Perhaps the biggest star of the publishing world this past year was mediocre thriller called *The DaVinci Code*. At last report, over four and half million hardback copies had been sold. While the first 150 pages are a real page-turner, the rest of the book collapses into long explanatory speeches and increasingly bizarre twists of events that finally exhaust the credibility of even those most willing to suspend disbelief. As an avid consumer of mystery novels, I would advise you, on that score alone, to go elsewhere. So, what explains the popularity of this book? It is the plot, of course.

The plot revolves around the true "holy grail", which, it turns out, is not the chalice from which Jesus drank at the Last Supper, but is the interred body of the biblical Mary Magdalene, Jesus' lover and wife. The plot implicates the Vatican and a Catholic organization, Opus Dei (real), in hiding that body and keeping that secret. That Jesus had a wife, and that the "whore of Babylon" along with its contemporary gigolo, Opus Dei, colluded in burying this embarrassing truth, is a surefire attraction for any storyteller.

What bothers me is not that Brown wrote the book. Fiction writers have been mining the Bible and the history of religions for years looking for stirring tales, historical or not. What bothers me is that people read it and take it seriously. Catholics protest that they haven't heard about such things before, and demand that we give an explanation. At least two Catholic parishes in the Chicago area have staged large gatherings, featuring prominent local theologians and biblical experts, to solemnly address the issues raised by this thriller. (For those who are interested, a scholarly and devastating critique of the book's outrageous use of history appeared in the publication, *Crisis,* September 2003 and available at *www.crisismagazine.com*) I am sure the publishers and Mr. Brown are delighted with all this sophisticated attention. Another book, featuring the "theology of 'the Simpsons'" was published this past year and, while I haven't read it, it strikes me that there might well be more reason to pay attention to that than to *The DaVinci Code.*

Having said all this, let me fall captive to my own reservations and draw some conclusions, not from the book, but from the phenomenon it has created.

Wittingly or unwittingly, *The DaVinci Code* has tapped something here. Perhaps it is the simple curiosity to learn something hidden. Perhaps it is simply the thrill that comes from watching special effects or following an exciting story. Or, perhaps it is voyeurism that yearns to peer in upon something secret and intimate. Whichever of these, or all of these, express a desire in all of us for something to take us beyond the experience of daily life. We long for the mysterious, the transcendent, the supernatural. "The world is too much with us" wrote Wordsworth. G.M. Hopkins mourned that "all is seared with trade; bleared, smeared with toil; and wears man's smudge and shares man's smell." What we're looking for, I think, is an experience called *wonder*.

The Jewish philosopher, Abraham Heschel, recalled at the end of his career: "I did not ask for success; I asked for wonder. And You gave it to me." For Heschel, wonder is the fundamental experience recorded in the Bible. The Bible, Heschel notes, speaks frequently of "the fear of the Lord". But this fear of the Lord is not dread. It is first of all a sense of awe, reverence, and wonder for the God who made the world and who saves his people. Herschel goes so far as to assert that unless we have this sense of wonder, this "fear of the Lord", it is impossible to have real faith. As the great writers of the Bible contemplated the world they lived in and the history that had been theirs, they were compelled to stand there with their mouths open and fall to worship a God so grand. Biblical faith is indeed about wonder.

It is the call to such wonder that I think such phenomena as *The DaVinci Code* appeal. But such a book does not satisfy our need for wonder. It merely offers wonder shrunk to curiosity. Curiosity can tell us much about human beings and our world. Only wonder can lead us to a sense of what God is and does.

The Great Handshake
Dealing with Factions within the Catholic Church
Summer 2004

I began writing this column June 29, on the Feast of Saints Peter and Paul. Until a few years ago I had always wondered why these two founding pillars of the church did not each have his own feast, but were commemorated together. In the summer of 1998, I got an insight as to why. I was taking a course on St. Paul that summer, and the biblical scholar who taught it drew attention to the considerable tension between two great saints. Ironically, it was this tension that, rather than isolating them to their own feasts, threw them together. This is how it happened.

The early church was hardly a place of harmony. Within a very few years after Jesus left this earth two dominant factions had arisen. The first considered that Christianity was little more than a reform of Judaism, and so insisted that if you were not a Jew, you had to become one before you adopted Christianity. That meant circumcision and the observance of some dietary 'kosher' laws. The second believed that Jesus intended a far more radical rupture with the past, that the 'Law' and its requirements were cancelled by the new covenant. The first viewpoint was represented, though not consistently, by Peter. The second viewpoint was emphatically the viewpoint of Paul.

The clash between these two parties came to a head at a general meeting of all the early Christian leaders in Jerusalem, just 15-20 years after the departure of Jesus (Acts 15; Galatians 2). After a vigorous, and quite likely an angry debate, the Apostle James proposed a compromise. A handful of the old laws were to be retained, but circumcision was not required. Clearly Christianity was seen to be something quite new.

At the conclusion of this meeting, Paul tells us that James, Peter and John "gave me and Barnabas (Paul's colleague) their right hand in partnership." An older translation of this verse, which I prefer, says that they gave each other "the handclasp of fellowship". I am much taken by this image of the "handclasp". Three "fishermen" closing their rough workingmen's hands over those of Paul, the "tentmaker". You can almost hear the dry rustle of callused palms as they pledged unity and cooperation. The church might well have cheered.

But the treaty didn't hold. Shortly thereafter, Paul heard that Peter was waffling on the agreement and was compelled to confront him personally for his failure to live up to the agreement. And so it went. According to my Scripture professor that summer, Peter and Paul and the factions they represented were in constant tension until, and even after, the death of the two great leaders.

And so it has gone throughout history. One part of the church, protective of its traditions, is loath to let go of them. Another part, impatient with the past, is eager in the name of freedom to move on. One part conservative and traditional, another part liberal and forward looking. One part Peter, another part Paul. One part the Vatican, another, say, the American Catholic Church. One part Opus Dei, another part, The Catholic Theological Union in Chicago.

But, neither has a corner on truth and good judgment, and both depend on each other. Without the Vatican, institutions like CTU would shrivel up and die. For they would, eschewing their roots, spring up to represent nothing but themselves. At the very least they would lack a visible target for the spears of change they are constantly brandishing. But, without CTU and its pioneering and cutting edge, the Vatican, as it has threatened to do more than once in its history, would shrink into irrelevance. For its blood would grow old and stale, congealing around some comfortable, if irrelevant, piece of history or culture.

So, Peter and Paul are locked together for good. They belong together, but they do not fit perfectly. This means that they are constantly shifting and struggling to get a more comfortable fit, and are constantly learning that what is comfortable for the one is not necessarily so for the other. That, of course, produces even more tension.

The trick is not to get rid of this tension. *The trick is to welcome and rejoice in it.* The followers of Paul should not be discouraged by the victories here and there of the followers of Peter. Nor should the followers of Peter be alarmed by the sometimes precipitous misadventures of the Pauline camp. The Church will not be poisoned to death by iniquitous liberals, nor will it be strangled to death by despotic conservatives. They are required to keep their eye on each other, even cry caution from time to time; but they are both blessed by God, because they are both doing what they are supposed to do - indeed the only thing that they can do - maintaining a balance of tradition and change in a kingdom whose real work is done neither by Peter nor by Paul, but by Jesus Christ.

So, this is why we celebrate the two saints together. They could not survive apart. Nor can the church. Peter and Paul shook hands on that. So can we.

Christmas Column: Why I Like the Magi
Winter 2004

I am writing this on the last day of October, just three days after ordering my Christmas cards for this year. Among them are a box of cards that express a Christmas theme that has in recent years had considerable attraction for me. This is the story of the 'Magi', the 'Wise Men', the 'Three Kings', those stately gentlemen sitting upright on camels, working their way out of the East, guided as were most people in those days before maps and Mapquest by a particularly bright star or comet, convinced that there must be Someone Special at the end of their journey.

There is a reason why I have come to appreciate their role in the Christmas tale. It is not because of the gifts they brought - they were terribly impractical gifts anyway - and the custom we have adopted from them of piling Christmas presents on each other. (A lovely modem retelling of the gift giving aspect of this event is O. Henry's famous short story, *Gift of the Magi*.) Nor is it out of admiration for the long and difficult journey they made to find the newborn king, movingly recreated in the poetry of T S. Eliot the *Journey of the Magi*, and W H. Auden *For the Time Being*. Christmas after all is not about what we do, but about what God does. And this is why the story of the Magi is so important to me.

The significance of the Magi for me goes back to my seminary days before the liturgical changes subsequent to Vatican II. Epiphany, the official liturgical celebration of the Magi was part of a three feast triptych then that also included the Baptism of Jesus and the Wedding Feast of Cana. *These three feasts - all in January were presented as celebrations of various aspects of God's revelation of himself to his people.* The Feast of Epiphany celebrated the revelation about Jesus to foreigners and non-Jews, an element that would be central to the universal character of Jesus' ministry. On the Feast of the Baptism of Jesus, God is presented speaking thunderously from a cloud, formally endorsing, as it were, Jesus as his son. The miraculous conversion of water into wine at Cana is called by John's Gospel the first of the 'signs' Jesus would perform, signs revealing his divine nature.

So, the story of the Magi is not about gift-giving at all. Nor is it about our journey, our laborious efforts to find God. It is instead, as is all of Christmas, about God's gift of himself to us, about God's journey if you will to reach us, to visit us. It reveals something about God that beforehand had only been hinted at, that God's love for his creatures exceeds his expectations that they behave properly. But it also says something entirely new about God that had not occurred to anyone before and which, admittedly, we don't quite get still today: that God became one of us, that God shared our nature, our joys, our desires, our hopes, our excitement, our passions, our needs, our pain, our frustration, our disappointment, even our anger. Humanity and the place humanity lives, the earth, are sacred because it is there that God has 'pitched his tent' (the literal meaning of John's "the Word became flesh and dwelt among us"). This is why the liturgy and many of the songs of Christmas stress a love for nature and a desire for peace. Christmas is a call to respect the world that God not only made but has shared by living there.

This is why so much of our celebration of Christmas misses the point. Our parties, our lavish gift giving, our prodigious feasts - increasingly consumed in restaurants - our Christmas trips to vacation venues like Florida and Vail, justified by "Oh, we'll still go to Church" are celebrations of us, of family, of community - not of God. Even such Christmas good deeds as working in soup kitchens and shelters for the homeless are not as important on that day as honoring the God among us. Christmas is about God, not us. This is what the Magi saw. In T.S. Eliot's poetic recreation of the journey of the Magi, he has one of them say upon his return home:

> "This birth was hard and bitter agony for us,
> like Death, our death.
> We returned to our places, these kingdoms,
> but no longer at ease here in the old dispensation,
> with an alien people clutching their gods.
> I should be glad of another death."

When was the last time Christmas had such a sobering message for us?

You probably won't get a 'Magi' card from me this Christmas, but let me now wish you the same revelation God gave them, to see that God is really with us.

The God of Tsunamis
Spring 2005

In the wake of the terrible carnage wrought by the tsunami in the Indian Ocean, my mind turned beseechingly towards God. I have studied all the answers to the question of 'Why natural disasters?', but when one of this magnitude happens, I turn to God again, painfully wondering. As I did so, an image entered my consciousness. It was that of a larger than life statue that stands in Chicago's Graceland Cemetery over the grave of a prominent Chicago hotelier. The statue, the work of sculptor Lorado Taft, is that of a figure swathed in black from head to toe, head bowed in sorrow and horror. This was my image of the God of the Tsunami - standing in grief among the ruins left by his violent earth and rampaging ocean. Whether God was to blame or whether He was doing anything about the disaster was not the issue for me. Only God, horrified.

This isn't much of an explanation. But the thousands of years of contemplating God and natural disasters haven't done much better. It's easier to understand disasters perpetrated by humans - like Rwanda, the

Holocaust, the Gulags, and the unholy wars in Iraq and Palestine. We can blame ourselves. But what can you say when there is no one to blame but God?

Having said that, there are two things that your can say.

The first was said to Job. Job had suffered a mix of human and natural disasters that took everything from him, including his children and his health. In agony he wondered why. His friends suggested that it was all his just punishment for a secret, horrible sin. Job knew they were wrong, so he turned away from them and complained to God. In response, a somewhat testy sounding God reminds beaten down Job that there are going to be some things that he will never understand simply because he isn't God. This may seem a heartless answer, but it does caution us against assuming that human wisdom in anyway approximates the wisdom of God. Too often we have an unthinking image of God as a wise sovereign who would never knowingly let His people suffer - God as Perfect Man but still human. We forget the words of God found in Isaiah (55:8-9):

"For my thoughts are not your thoughts, / nor are your ways my ways. / As high as the heavens are above the earth / so high are my ways above your ways / and my thoughts above your thoughts."

The second word spoken to Christians about suffering is that of the cross. It is God's Son, the Trinitarian God who made the entire universe, including tectonic plates prone to earthquakes, who hung upon that cross. We can perhaps imagine a million 'better' ways that God might have chosen in order to redeem His people. But the fact is that God chose what He chose - the course of pain, humiliation, and death. There is something marvelously simple and transparent about this. God chose the one experience all of us can recognize and relate to, an experience we have all had, or will have - suffering. Christianity is a great democracy of loss, and God is not indifferent to it. If God does not prevent suffering, we are strengthened to know that, when we walk through a dark valley, God, who has walked it before, still walks with us.

All this is, I am sure, of little or no comfort to those millions who have lost family and livelihood, but perhaps it is of some help to those of us who have suffered nothing more than anxiety over the meaning of it all.

Jonathan Foster, O.F.M.

The Shepherd and the Rock: A Letter to Pope Benedict XVI
Summer 2005

Dear Holy Father,

I have been told that you have made your personal e-mail address available to the whole world. I was pleased to hear this, and it has emboldened me, a Catholic priest who has already pledged his prayers and support to you, to offer you some advice as well.

Benedict. I don't know what went through your mind as you chose that name, but I'd like to tell you what went through mine when I heard your choice.

First, it recalled to me the last Pope to carry that name, Benedict XV, who tried valiantly and vainly to stop the savage carnage of mud and blood carried out in Europe from 1914 to 1918. You have inherited another 'world war', the terrorist struggle between Islamic radicals and the West. Your predecessor's pleas to the United States to stay out of Iraq were not only not listened to, but even dismissed by many as religious naïveté, just as were Benedict XV's.

Conservative American Christians, who were frustrated by John Paul II's calls for nonintervention, are now apparently in the ascendancy in American society and the American church. They, who might otherwise be admirers of yours, will be anxious for you to line up in support of America's 'crusade' for democracy. Don't be dissuaded by them. We American Christians often have a hard time reconciling our church's teachings with our social and political convictions. We need you to help us stand apart from those convictions, even if it appears to be foolish and naive (1Cor 1) to the rest of the world.

Another and perhaps more significant reason why the name Benedict resonates with me is that for centuries during the dark ages, Benedictine monasteries and Benedictine monks with their careful rhythm of work and prayer, their scriptoria, their attention to scripture - 'lectio divina' - and their vow of stability, proved the anchor that kept Europe - and the Catholic church - from sliding into barbaric chaos. Today, in an age furiously dominated not by barbarians, but by technological change, we could use more monasteries and monks, and a Church that provides the same foundation stones they represented. This suggests to me a priority for you in the years God will give to you - deeper spiritual formation of Catholics. An interest in spirituality, in this country at least, has become so prominent that it is almost faddish. Despite some shallowness, there are some real instincts at work here that need to be nourished. The ultimate 'rock' of Christianity is not just adherence to the teachings of Jesus, but discipleship, following the Shepherd where he leads us. You could not do better than be the kind of shepherd that takes us to richer spiritual pasture.

We are told, Holy Father, that you are a friend of stray cats. As a Franciscan, I find that this softens my heart, as I am sure it will soften the hearts of all. How do you feel about theologians? Especially those that, like some of those cats you used to feed, stray a little too close to the boundaries or even wander out of the yard? May I suggest that you go a little easy on them? As you know, among the more liberal Catholic theologians your election was not received with enthusiasm. They, like all peoples on the margins, are always challenging to the Church, but I believe they want to forward the Christian enterprise as much as you do. They recognize, however, that they have to do it from a different perspective. They recognize that the 'teachers in Israel' must not only preserve the tradition, but, like the householder in Jesus' parable, explore its implications, poking around in his storeroom, bringing out both the old and the new (Matt 13:52). Just as much as you must be Peter, the principle of unity, they must be Paul, the principle of diversity.

Finally, let me speak from the heart of a priest of 45 years. The years following Vatican II have been difficult for those of us who have been its ordained ministers. We have seen a massive exodus of fellow priests, many of them our friends. We have seen the schools we attended close, or stand near empty as few take up the challenge we accepted. We have experienced the desperate horror of seeing so many of our brethren suspended, even jailed for predatory criminal behavior. We have been pulled down off the pedestal we were elevated to with ordination, and while this has by and large been good for both priests and laity, it has been a difficult transition for many. We are getting old and working too hard. Perhaps hardest - for me - is looking back and seeing so few who follow behind us, and seeing that those who do are not very young. Without the young, no institution has any hope. We desperately need more priests, younger priests. You're getting advice from a lot of different sources on this matter, and some of them we know you're simply not going to pay any attention to. But there is one thing you can do. You can let married men become priests, or, as the case may be, return to the priesthood. Of course, you are already doing this. I don't know how many former Protestant pastors, Anglican priests and Eastern Rite priests - many of them married - are working as Catholic priests in the USA. One of the largest parishes in my diocese now has a pastor who goes home every night to his wife and children. You have concerns about doctrine in this matter of ordaining priests. This is one area, however, that does not involve doctrine, only discipline. You could change that overnight. True, these priests would not be the twenty-somethings we need eventually to attract, but they would be steps in the right direction of thinking more creatively about candidates to the priesthood. If you do this, there would be loud sighs of relief not only from people like me, but from the Catholic laity generally. They, like all of us, worry more about where the next Eucharist will come from than they do about whether the celebrants of those Eucharists are married or not.

I have much more to say - 45 years of priesthood in the post Vatican II years will do that for you. But, this is enough.

Respectfully,
Jonathan Foster, OFM, Mayslake Ministries

Jonathan Foster, O.F.M.

A Big Year for Apples
Fall 2005

I have just returned from vacation with my family in Northern Michigan, where I have spent every Labor Day for some twenty years now. In my sister's backyard there is an apple tree of uncertain parentage whose branches this year were bent almost to the ground by an abundance of small red apples. As I bicycled and drove around the country roads where I grew up, I saw many wild apple trees along the roadside - planted by some unknown Johnny Appleseed - that groaned equally under the burden of their crop. I am told that this is not unusual about apples - two or three years of little or no yield, then a mighty bounty of them. I recalled one year at Mayslake, where we had a small orchard of tasty apples, that there was such a huge crop that the weight of the apples broke the branches that bore them.

One evening on my vacation, when my sister and I were out driving around the countryside, we came upon an orchard that stands on township grounds. She quickly parked, dug out a bag, gleaned the windfalls, shook down some branches and collected enough apples to make two pies and some applesauce. Next year, and the year after, in all probability, we will, like Jesus and the barren fig tree, seek in vain for apples from these same old trees.

There are two attitudes we can take toward such abundance. The first is to take it for granted. When we get lots of apples every year, when the weather is perfect for growing corn, when the stock market and the economy spill welcome fruit into our laps, or, because we live in America, whose land and history teem with abundance (think of our gluttonous national holiday of Thanksgiving!), it is very easy to get used to our abundance. Then we come to expect it, to even feel that we are entitled to it. Worst of all we come to trust it.

Think of the parable Jesus told about the rich man and his barns. He had such a big harvest that he had to level the old ones and throw up new ones, allowing himself to sink into a fat contentment over all he had. Much good it did him, for he died that night! (Luke 12:16-21). Before the Hebrew people entered the promised land, Moses warned them about this. He told them that it is such a rich land that once they are settled in it they are going to forget that they don't own it - God does. That they didn't get it because they are such good, hardworking people - God gave it to them. So they are never to take it for granted. (Deuteronomy 8 and 9). With all our blessings and wealth and opportunities, Americans are most prone to this temptation.

The second attitude is simply to be grateful. The word 'grateful' comes ultimately from the Latin word 'gratia', which describes the act of giving freely whether the beneficiary deserves the gift or not. It is the heart of who God is. Although, in the wake of the catastrophe of

Katrina, I do not know why some of us experience abundance and some experience scarcity, I do know this - that, as I enjoy the fruits I have, I need to recognize that I have no claim on them, and that I had better be grateful to God for what is given to me.

The apples we picked at the township site made a delicious pie (I'm eating the last of it for dinner tonight). We will remember them fondly next year, but will not whine if the trees again stand empty.

All I Want for Christmas is a Few More Priests
Winter 2005

I felt let down by the recent synod of Bishops held in Rome. Devoted to the Blessed Sacrament and the Eucharist, it of course had to deal with the only people who can 'do' Eucharist - ordained priests. Before the synod, a number of daring Bishops had proposed that the church consider ordaining 'viri probati' ('men of proven character') to the priesthood. These would be older men, mostly middle aged, recognized in their communities for their virtue and wisdom. They would be given adequate training, but far less than the normal track of seminarians. They might be married or single. They might even be priests who had left the formal priesthood years ago, but are willing to serve. They would serve only in their own local communities, neighborhoods, small towns, missionary outposts, and their primary function would be to celebrate the Eucharist. As you might surmise, most of the bishops proposing this were from areas desperately short of priests. It seemed a sensible solution to a growing problem, not only in mission lands, but in our great cities as well. Indeed the Episcopalians here in the US have been doing this for many years on the Indian reservations of the West and in Alaska.

However, the vast majority of the Bishops at the Synod felt that this was a matter of such little importance that *it was not even included on the agenda.* So, all we got out of the synod was a further appeal for prayers for vocations and more intense recruiting - both of which we have been doing for so many years now with such few results that one must wonder if God is not answering our prayer for vocations by putting these 'viri probati' right in our faces.

I recall a reflection that came to me some years ago as I stood on the shores of Lake Michigan in northern Michigan. I visit a remote part of that lakeshore every year and every year for the past 10-15 have noted the steady drop in the water levels of the lake. On this particular occasion, this steady withdrawal of the lake from the stony beaches made me think of the 'priest shortage'. Like the lake growing shallower every year, every year the number of priests in this country shrinks some more. I tried to see the positive side of this by noting and welcoming the new plants and flowers growing up in the lake bottom abandoned by the retreating waters. They suggested to me the emergence of a whole generation of new ministers in the church, mostly lay, and, this I assured myself, was hopeful.

But more powerful was the feeling of discouragement over the continued depletion of the ranks of those, who, like me, had committed their lives to this indispensable and irreplaceable ministry. Not only are we getting weary as we continue to work well beyond even a reasonably delayed retirement age, but I wondered if the people are not becoming less and less confident of a Church that cannot attract youth to its leadership ranks. Does anyone out there have any idea of what it is like to have spent your life on a mission you thought was so important, but which now very few are interested in?

It also struck me then that not only are aging men required to do all the priestly work of this large and growing Church, but that they would also be expected to have the idealism that youth typically bring to ministry. As well as wisdom, I wondered, do people also expect enthusiasm and boundless energy from us? I wanted to trust that, as the waters of the lake will eventually return, so will God in God's good time renew the priesthood.

More recently I have begun to wonder if God has not already spoken, but that the higher clergy are not listening. So, how is the official church helping us out? By sending us more and more priests from places where priests are apparently plentiful, and, like interchangeable spare parts, can be shipped anywhere in the world. Typically, however, these good men do not know or appreciate our culture, and do not often speak our language very well. As England did during our Revolutionary War, it's like hiring mercenaries to fight your wars for you.

Beyond this, the American Church is not considered worth taking special efforts and risks to help solve its own problems. Just send in the ringers. The 'viri probati' proposal would at least be a step away from that. If these men are little different from most of us in age, at least, as we await younger graduates from our seminaries, we will know there is someone competent on the bench.

Why did the synodal bishops not even grant this proposal the dignity of consideration? I do not presume to know. Perhaps one of the reasons is that Rome, where the synod was held, may be occupied at any given time by as many as *15,000 priests* - students, tourists, diplomats, curial employees, men on sabbatical, etc. In Rome, priests may be *looking for work* while in the part of the church I serve, *work is looking* for priests. More likely, the reluctance to take up this matter is simply a romantic attachment to a clericalism long discredited which cannot imagine anyone other than an unmarried male, no matter how old, presiding over our Eucharists.

Some of you may recall that I submitted the same proposal to Pope Benedict last summer, via his published e-mail address. I did not even get an acknowledgement. I suspect that will be pretty much the fate of any similar proposals. This just adds to the sadness. It is one thing to be denied help. It is quite another to act as though your appeal for help is not even worthy of a second look.

The Synod failed to recognize a great opportunity to give not just me, but the whole church, a great Christmas present!

In the Playground of the Lord
The Spiritual Life
Spring 2006

    I used to play golf years ago. I quit because I couldn't enjoy it, and the reason I couldn't enjoy it was that I wasn't any good at it. (I once entered a tournament and won a prize - for the highest score reported!) My folks on the other hand started playing golf later in life. Their favorite golf course was an old farm north of town which offered 'pasture golf', a series of roughly maintained fairways and holes, the latter consisting of coffee cans buried in the ground. They really 'played' golf, because they clearly played not for any purpose such as shaving their handicap or winning a tournament, but simply for the pleasure of it. This spring, Mayslake Ministries will be offering its second golf outing. The first, last summer, participated in by about 60 golfers, was characterized as pure fun, pure play, and we hope the same will be the case this year.

    Play is something that happens in other places as well, even in the Bible. The most striking mention of play occurs in Proverbs (8:30-31), where 'Wisdom' ('Sophia', apparently an Old Testament precursor of the "Word" of John 1) describes herself (yes, it's a she!) as playing before the Lord as he set about building creation. *"Then I was beside him as his craftsman, / and I was his delight day by day, / playing before him all the while, / playing on the surface of his earth."* The image is of a carefree child doing what kids do - playing, even "helping" - under the watchful eye of Dad who is doing some carpentry work nearby.

Other instances in the Bible where play is mentioned: the description of hippopotamuses "playing" with other animals (Job 40:20); Zechariah's characterization of the messianic age as one in which boys and girls play in the streets (8:5); David "playing with bears and lions" (Sirach 47:3). And of course the most touching reference to play in the whole bible - the messianic scene, often heard at Christmas, where a child is described as playing without fear at the den of the dangerous cobra (Isaiah 11:8).

I have considered, ever since college days, that play "plays" a significant role in the Christian life. At that time, we had a philosophy teacher who made the entirely credible point that the very extravagance of the multi-galaxied universe, and even the lavish prodigality of life on our own tiny planet, has to point to a God who created for the sheer delight of it, that creation was a form of divine "child's play".

If even God plays, what about us? Indeed, scripture often refers to human worship as a form of play: the playing of musical instruments, the thronging of processions, the shouts of praise, the feverish dancing, and, yes, unfortunately, even the creation of molten images, and sexual profligacy, as at Sinai. People get carried away with the excitement of God, and they just, well, **play.**

The image of play helps us understand the significance of the spiritual life. Play, especially children's play, is not productive. It has no goal, no bottom line, few rules (which always change) and is often discontinued when another more interesting form of play appears. It is the sheer creative expression of the player. So is much of the spiritual life, which may be viewed in somewhat the same way as the description of "Wisdom" mentioned above in Proverbs. God is at work, creating and maintaining the universe, and has placed us - as he did Adam and Eve - within his sight, and given us a few boundaries or rules outside of which we are not to stray. But the boundaries are wide and the playground attractive. So, God urges us to enjoy his creation, its pleasures, its delights, to be always mindful of where it all comes from, that he is never far away, and that the whole purpose of the arrangement is for him to share his life with us, and we with him. God is the Ringmaster of the Circus and there is, in this vision, little room for bluenosed Puritanism. Thus, to playfully enjoy God's creation - and to be aware as we do, that it is God's creation - is the sum of much of the spiritual life.

Take prayer in particular. Prayer can take many shapes and forms. We usually think of certain sets of words and certain hymns. But it can include posture - kneeling, standing, genuflecting, bowing; prostration, raising one's arms and hands, walking in procession, waving palms. It can include many ways of singing, from Gregorian chant to Rock and, I am told, now even Rap. "Who sings, prays twice", as St. Augustine wrote. It can be poetry, but not just the dull, sentimental doggerel that is so often presented to us as religious poetry and hymns. It can include art - real Christians are not iconoclasts, or icon-abhorring Muslims. It can include dance. It can include gardening. It can include standing on the deck to watch the sun rise. It is a walk on the beach or among the trees. It can include the sexual play of spouses.

In all of these, as in all true play, the point is *not* to make some point, or achieve some end. The point is to simply enjoy and thereby give honor to God. We don't have to consciously offer every beautiful sunset up by murmuring sweet nothings to God. But, we have to enjoy it, we have to play, and then sometimes remember that the one who made it so was the First Playground Superintendent.

Good Words for an Old Bishop, Retiring
Summer 2006

Just a couple weeks from the day of this writing (June 14), a familiar face in the Chicago-land church will fade from the headlines, passing on the episcopal torch to a younger man from the South. I am speaking of Bishop Joseph Imesch, Ordinary of the Diocese of Joliet for the past 27 years.

Bishop Imesch moves into a well deserved retirement - a working one, I understand - but he does so under some grey clouds of resentment (on the part of more than a few) for the way he handled the sex abuse issue in this diocese. I am in no position to pass judgment on the legal, procedural and political issues involved in this scarring scandal, but I firmly believe that what he did or did not do was not occasioned by a conspiratorial desire to cover the behinds of ecclesiastical 'good old boys', but that whatever missteps he took were aggravated by a lack of skill in public relations. He has been called arrogant, but such a description is farthest from my experience of him.

I remember the first time I met Bishop Imesch, around 1979 or '80, shortly after he became our Bishop. I was in the narthex of Holy Ghost Church in Wood Dale, where I was weekend supply, wearing my habit, when I saw this priest walk in off the parking lot, without retinue, wearing simple clerical attire and carrying a small black bag. I walked over to him to introduce myself. He put out his hand and said, "Hi, I'm Joe Imesch." I had never heard a bishop introduce himself that casually, and to this day, it remains for me a snapshot of the kind of down home simplicity of the man. I hear the word 'arrogant' applied to him regularly these days, and I have never experienced that in him. Frank, yes, but never arrogant with that 'hubris' the scriptures so roundly condemn.

Shortly thereafter, I became director of Mayslake Retreat House in Oak Brook, the font and forerunner of this ministry. Sometime during those years Bishop Imesch was appointed to be Chair of the group of bishops and theologians who drafted the ill-fated Pastoral letter on women in the church. They met in various places to do their work, but for one extended period of perhaps a week they met at our retreat house, Mayslake. What had been apprehension about demands this episcopal entourage might make on us never materialized. They were one of the easiest groups, among many, to host and to accommodate. And we all enjoyed seeing several bishops running around in wash pants and sweatshirts. (One of them, Bishop Levada, now occupies the lofty position held by Joseph Ratzinger before he became Pope Benedict XVI). Arrogance is the last word I would have applied to them, least of all to their leader.

Bishop Imesch's very appointment to head up this task force also belies the current accusations of arrogance. Male, clerical and episcopal arrogance has always been - and still is - a source of pain to many American Catholic women. It is to Joe Imesch's credit that he sought to reduce that pain through his work on the pastoral. I recall that other than the three or four requisite bishops, the rest of his task force was composed of women scholars and leaders. Before ever a word was put to page, consultations with thousands of Catholic women throughout the United States were held. Sadly, the Pastoral was too much for the rest of the American bishops. In one of its early drafts, it even dared to propose the entry of women into the all male hierarchy, howbeit at its lowest level, that of the diaconate. Sadly, for whatever reasons, the bishops considered the document too radical, and it was, despite an enormous amount of work, finally shelved. I wonder who was the arrogant party in this decision? It certainly wasn't Bishop Imesch.

When we started this ministry in 1991, the first thing we did was approach the Bishops of the two dioceses in which we did our most work - Chicago and Joliet. We were barely a flyspeck on the ecclesiastical radar screen at that time. We had little money, no home, no official affiliation such as the Franciscans to support us, and we were mostly lay people bravely presenting ourselves as a lay-run ministry. Despite the improbability of our venture, Bishop Imesch graciously received us, and welcomed us into the diocese, a welcome that has lasted for fifteen years. He did however insist that we do not ask him for money!

It is of interest that this very month when Bishop Imesch retires, another Chicago celebrity is leaving under a similar cloud. This is Maestro Daniel Barenboim, Music Director and Principal Conductor of the Chicago Symphony Orchestra. Everybody acknowledges his superior musicianship. But, because he spoke with some lack of tact about the Chicago public's taste in music, and because he refrained from mixing socially among Chicago's movers and shakers, many are not sorry to see him go. He didn't even seem to be that fond of Chicago. His focus was on music. So also Bishop Imesch's focus has been on ministry, though clearly he seems to be very fond of Joliet. Both men are proof that you can be very good at what you do without being very good at explaining what you do to the public.

I was present at one of Barenboim's farewell concerts, and it was touching to see the standing ovation and shouts of 'Bravo' that kept him coming back for four well deserved bows. I would hope that the Catholics of this diocese can offer Bishop Imesch similar salvos of appreciation.

"What Was it Like?" - A Pilgrimage to Russia
Fall/Winter 2006

As some of you know, I was fortunate last summer to spend two weeks with the Franciscans in Russia, mostly in Saint Petersburg. When I got back, the question people asked me was always the same, "Russia! What was it like?" That's a very small question for a very large country with a very large history. And so, I always tell this story.

There is a Catholic church in Saint Petersburg named St. Catherine's (as much after the tsarina who built it, as St. Catherine of Alexandria, its patroness). An elegant cathedral sized structure, it was built in the eighteenth century by the Russian Orthodox tsar to accommodate the hordes of Catholics he had imported from the West to design, decorate and build this most beautiful of all Russian cities. Designed to hold 2000 people, it was serving some 30,000 Roman Catholics living in Saint Petersburg on the eve of the Bolshevik revolution of 1917.

After the Bolshevik revolution had succeeded by the early 1920s, and after the pastor of St. Catherine's had been imprisoned, tortured and executed, the church fell on hard times. During the Stalin era however, in 1938, the church's doors were thrown open to the proletariat, who were invited in to trash it. Which they did, leaving it in ruins, good for nothing for the next fifty years except for such as a motorcycle warehouse and a museum on atheism. However, during the orgy of vandalism, a young Russian Catholic girl, Sophia Stepulkowska, also entered the church and managed to get the large wooden crucifix down from behind the altar. The rest of the vandals ignored her, perhaps because they just thought she was grabbing her share of the loot, and she managed to get the crucifix back to her home and safekeeping. It was kept in hiding thereafter in another small church.

In 1991 the Soviet Union collapsed. The more open regime of Boris Yeltsin moved to restore religious properties unjustly stolen by the government. And so the ugly wreckage of St. Catherine's was handed back to the Catholics of Saint Petersburg in 1992. The restoration began immediately, but still today, almost fifteen years later, it is only half completed. But the crucifix is back! From its hiding place, it was installed once more in the church. But, not in its traditional place behind and above the altar. Part of the right hand wall of the church was left unrestored, leaving a gaping wound of exposed masonry and building stones above a pile of rubble. It is on this ugly scar that the crucifix now hangs, a shrine not only to the passion of Jesus Christ, but to the fierce determination of the Russian people to survive.

Few peoples have suffered as the Russians have. For centuries they writhed under the heel of the tsars and their wives. Saint Petersburg is a beautiful city, but very quickly you learn that it is so because of the levees placed upon peasant serfs by the unfeeling and powerful aristocrats. If a tsar wanted to build a beautiful palace or church, he simply whistled for every available serf to come running. They would work like slaves and live in squalor till the magnificent building was finished. He would also lay a tax on everybody to cover costs, and if a given serf couldn't pay, his son was drafted instead. This went on for centuries so it is not surprising that Communism found a home among these beleaguered and oppressed peoples. One of the few bright notes in the period of the tsars was, with the cooperation of winter, their crushing defeat of Napoleon in the early years of the nineteenth century.

But, the Communists were no improvement. From the time their Bolshevik founders overthrew the government in the great rebellion of 1917 till the end of the Soviet Union in our times, it is estimated that 18,000,000 people passed through the infamous work camps we know as Gulags, countless millions of whom died there. All the while the Communists were turning the country into a vast collective, extinguishing all private initiative, suppressing freedom of thought and expression, and developing itself into a vast, frightening, military power, grotesquely swollen on nuclear steroids, reckless and indifferent to the needs of its people.

As if this were not enough, from 1942 - 1945 the German army swarmed all over Russia, killing millions more and destroying much of Russia's great architectural and artistic heritage. Saint Petersburg was particularly hard hit, having been besieged for two and a half years in which the population was deprived of all but the bare minimum of food, shelter, and heat, while there were daily bombardments by aircraft and long-range artillery. Over a million Russian civilians died in that siege and they are buried in a huge common cemetery in Saint Petersburg. Most died of starvation.

While the tsars were religious (Orthodox), the communists were aggressively atheistic, making every effort to stamp out religious belief, the "opium of the people", as their mentor, Karl Marx taught. Nowhere else in the history of the world has there been such a systematic attempt to wipe out religion. But even two generations (70 years) of this have failed.

This is the dominant image of the Russian people that I take home from my brief sojourn in their midst. They are survivors - political, economic, military and above all religious survivors. My friend, Fr. Jim Edmiston, OFM, and I tried to get into the old Alexander Nevsky Monastery on the feast of St. John the Baptist (July 7 in their calendar) but we had to stand in line because of the numbers waiting to enter, and once we were in, had to keep moving to avoid being swept away by the crowd of worshippers.

The scene would have broken Karl Marx' heart.

Sunset in Key West
Spring 2007

There are cultures and religions that worship the sun. We think immediately of Egypt and the Sun-God, Ra, who sailed across the sky in a splendid barge during daylight and spent the dark nights fighting evil. This is not surprising in hot and sunny Egypt, but other less-favored climes turned to sun worship as well since it was clearly the source of both life (little can grow without its warmth) and death (by its punishing heat).

On the other hand, I recently participated in an experience of the sun that was far more akin to entertainment than worship. I was visiting friends in the Florida Keys this past month, and we spent most of one day in Key West, the westernmost of the Keys and the southernmost town in the continental USA. A custom has grown up there of gathering on the beach near Mallory Square to watch the sun set across the Gulf of Mexico to the West. The evening we were there was classic. It had been a pleasant sunny day, warm but not hot, and the sun was making its departure in a cloudless sky.

But the sun wasn't the only attraction for the hundreds, perhaps thousands, of people who had made their way down to the beach from Old Town Key West. There were also street performers, jugglers, tight rope walkers, impersonators, dog handlers and a veritable flea market of booths selling cheap trinkets and souvenirs. We watched a guy juggling a chainsaw, and another one who had trained his dog to urinate on the crowd (actually water from a hidden spray bottle). Most of the attention was focused on these more mundane entertainments, but as the sun sank lower in the West, people turned to watch across the water.

Near us a pack of alpha males began a throaty cheer, urging the sun on as though it were a favorite but slow-moving turtle in a race. And when the sun finally settled out of sight and a pink dye spread across the sky, many in the audience applauded. Good show! Then we turned our back and trudged through the park, back to more terrestrial attractions in the Old Town.

What came to mind as I watched was a book I had been reading by Carl Sagan, the eminent astronomer, *The Varieties of Scientific Experience: A Personal View of the Search for God*. Though he was not much of a theologian, Sagan was a splendid astronomer and possessed a great gift for imparting to others his wonder and enthusiasm for our universe. The book contains many incredible color plates drawn from the photographic archives of the Hubble Space Telescope. But Sagan's stars are far more wondrous than the pictures of them. There are so many of them, so huge, so hot, so far away and so seemingly indifferent to the little dot of blue we call the earth that after looking at the night stars for a while, we begin to glaze over - or is it a little fear? - and seek surcease by going indoors to watch television.

Although most of what was going on in Mallory Park the evening I was there was innocent fun, I couldn't help but think of hubris, a Greek and biblical word for a pride, arrogance, or insolence that does not know its place and treats the great and wonderful with a dismissive trivialization, even contempt. Or, even ignores it. It is like talking on a cell phone and eating candy bars during a live performance of the Chicago Symphony Orchestra. How bold we are to treat the sun as a kind of entertainment, giving it a polite hand when it does its thing by disappearing, but ignoring it otherwise, taking it for granted as a nice lamp, but cursing it when it does not provide us with good weather for fishing and sunbathing.

We could do with more awe and wonder, for the sun, yes, and for the whole planetary, stellar and galactic array. And we could do with a little more humility about our place in the cosmos. We know from photos taken from outer space that we are a pretty planet, but we are so infinitesimal that even if there is intelligent life elsewhere in the universe you wonder if they would even know we are here.

The Bible has a word for this sense of wonder. It is called "fear of the Lord", a phrase richly pregnant with meaning. For it reflects not only the understandable dread we experience when we look too long at the stars, but it captures also the awe that expands our soul when we perceive our littleness in the presence of these great shining behemoths that so gracefully circle about our night skies. This 'fear of the Lord' we are told frequently in the Bible is the 'beginning of wisdom'. Indeed, the modern Jewish philosopher/theologian, Abraham Joshua Heschel, has said that without a sense of wonder there is no faith. Unless you can wonder, unless you can let yourself go and swim in awe, you will not be a believer. I think he's right.

I do not wish to look down a long puritanical nose at the Key West antics. This nightly homage to the sun is fun time in a fun place, and it does show a bit more respect for the sun than we usually give it. But I wanted to recall that the sun, however functional and entertaining, is in its deepest heart a sign of Someone Else who, as the poet Gerard Manley Hopkins wrote: "over the bent / World broods with warm breast and with ah! bright wings".

The Death of Sacred Space
Lamenting its loss.
Winter 2007

Two events this past year have saddened the ministry we pursue in Mayslake Ministries. The first was the announcement last winter that our professional association, Retreats International (representing several hundred retreat houses in Canada and the U.S.) after eighty-some years, was going out of business. The reason is not yet clear, but certainly it has much to do with lack of financial resources.

The second is the announcement last summer that one of the bellwether retreat houses in the Chicago area, the Cenacle in Warrenville, is also - next summer - closing its doors for good. This is particularly sad news since the Cenacle Sisters were the first - way back in the early 20's - to open a retreat house in Chicago. The Warrenville Cenacle, now nearly 70 years old, is actually the second Cenacle Retreat House in Chicago to close, the other being a large facility lodged in the old Walgreen mansion in Chicago's Beverly neighborhood. It closed in the middle eighties. A third Cenacle house, on Fullerton

Avenue in Chicago's north side, and the site of the original Cenacle, is still open, but it is run by a lay staff, and is primarily a conferencing facility. Among the most disappointed clients of the Warrenville site are Protestants, who are discovering the richness of the retreat experience, solitude, sacred space and spiritual direction. There are almost no Protestant retreat facilities in the Chicago area (I know of only a small house in Elburn), so Protestants in the western suburbs have in recent years made extensive use of the Cenacle, and have developed a genuine affection for this lovely and welcoming place. The Cenacle at Warrenville is the fourth major retreat house to close in the Chicago area since 1981. The others are Mayslake (our place of origin), Villa Redeemer in Glenview, and the Cenacle in Beverly. At least five smaller retreat houses have also closed. While two new houses have opened in Frankfort and Mundelein, and the Resurrectionists in Woodstock added 50 new rooms to their facility, these have barely begun to make up for the space lost in other houses. So, at least nine retreat houses in the Chicago area have closed, and only two - both smaller - have opened.

What's going on here? The most obvious explanation of course is that it is a matter of money. Most retreat houses are, and have always been, staffed by religious and priests, members of the sponsoring congregation or diocese. These dedicated people neither required nor expected salaries. They lived on room and board and pin money. The steep, and in the case of women, precipitous decline of religious in this country has deeply affected the ability of the sponsoring communities to provide such staff. Competent laity therefore must be hired, and they rightfully expect reasonable remuneration.

Reasonable as such salaries are they still painfully stretch the retreat house budget. Moreover, unlike earlier days, the retreat house cannot expect to be subsidized by its parent community when their books don't balance or when the roof needs to be replaced. (Indeed, some religious orders saw the retreat house as a cash cow for the community! In the case of Mayslake, it wasn't just a regular check that the Province wanted but the very valuable land in Oak Brook that the retreat house sat on). Religious orders and dioceses that run retreat houses are therefore stretched to the breaking point by the lack of money. It's no wonder they go under. Likewise is it any wonder that, even as we observe a sharp uptick of interest in spirituality in general, attendance at retreats has declined nationwide? Have Americans perceived that with the collapse of Retreats International and the closing of places like the Warrenville Cenacle that the time of the retreat house - like high school seminaries - has passed?

So, those of us who do this ministry have to look at increasing our income to stay in business. One of the little known and embarrassing secrets of retreat houses is the very "unbusinesslike" way in which they use their buildings. For a modern hotel or motel to make ends meet, they must have an average in excess of 60% occupancy every day of the year. Retreat houses, because they are weekend intensive, have a typical occupancy rate in the 20-30% range! This was acceptable in the days of subsidies and unpaid staff, but no longer. Hence, many retreat houses are turning to other more lucrative guests to use their facility - businesses and not-for-profits for meetings and workshops, even weddings and family reunions. They are becoming conference centers.

And as they do so, something is lost. Sacred Space. Sacred space is important because it allows us to step out of our quotidian world of subdivisions, shopping malls, traffic jams, offices and children's activities and experience a larger one. Sacred space helps us to realize, because it is still part of our world, how sweet that ordinary world is. Sacred space is also the reason why we spend so much money, time and imagination in building and maintaining churches and cathedrals. It is the reason why we are so proud of and fiercely protective here in Chicago of such naturally sacred spaces as our lakefront, our Forest Preserves, and such jewels as the Morton Arboretum and the Botanic Gardens. It is of course, ultimately, the reason why we have retreat houses. Retreat houses provide us with quiet buildings, peaceful chapels, natural grounds, ponds, and sometimes, as at Warrenville, a river that runs through it.

They sever our ties with TV, radios, internet access, newspapers and all those other straps and bands that fasten us so unrelentingly to our regular world. They don't demand as one prestigious golf club does on the West Coast that we check our cell phones at the door, but perhaps they should. For we go there as a weary lover who misses God and intends simply to spend some time with him.

How do we preserve these critical oases of the spirit? As I reflect on these sad events, I am reminded that the original movers and shakers of the retreat movement were not clergy or religious but lay Catholics. The first retreats in America, in the first decade of the twentieth century, were organized by Catholic laymen. The priests gave the retreats, but the laity put up the buildings and recruited the retreatants. It was arguably the most successful spirituality movement in US church history. It is perhaps the time for us to turn again to the laity to counteract this downward trend. Dioceses and religious orders, buffeted by the cost of scandal and the steep decline of personnel, clearly lack the people, the financial resources and perhaps the passion to invest themselves once again in sacred space. The laity however has the financial resources, the business acumen, and, it is more and more likely, the ministerial expertise, one that will not be satisfied with just being hewers of wood and carriers of water.

Is the retreat house shoe on the lay foot? As the clamor for sacred space began a century ago with the laity, so now its rescue is very likely also in their hands.

Jonathan Foster, O.F.M.

Editor's note: In the Spring 2008 issue of the Quarterly Newsletter of Mayslake Ministries, Jonathan published some of his poetry for readers. Quoting from this newsletter, "Please read, interpret, mull over, ponder ... or just enjoy!"

The Spider's Web
Spring 2008

A spider stalking whatever prey might pass that way
spins a web across the path.
Last night he caught a falling leaf
that hung, a work of art, on shimmering strands.
Each day he catches me. I crash right through
and have to brush the sticky stuff away.
He rushes out to see what he has caught,
he stops, chagrined, then shakes his head,
and wearily starts to build the web again.

Might God not take a lesson here?
Might he not spin much stronger webs?

October 10, 2005

About the Author

Fr. Jonathan Foster, O.F.M., a member of the Franciscan Friars of the Sacred Heart Province, has worked in the Chicago area since 1962 as an educator, retreat house director, retreat master and spiritual director.

He is the founder of Mayslake Ministries, a retreat and spiritual formation ministry in Downers Grove, IL. He has been extensively involved in the ministry of spiritual formation at St. Margaret Mary Parish in Naperville, IL where he has been spiritual director of the men's "Christ Renews His Parish" retreat program since 1995.

A native of Petoskey, MI, he derives inspiration for his writing from nature, the Bible, liturgy and observations from daily life.

Made in the USA
Middletown, DE
26 November 2015